MERCY

FOR

ANIMALS

MERCY
FOR
ANALS

ANIMALS

||||||||||||

ONE MAN'S QUEST TO
INSPIRE COMPASSION AND IMPROVE
THE LIVES OF FARM ANIMALS

NATHAN RUNKLE

with Gene Stone

AVERY
an imprint of Penguin Random House
New York

AVERY

an imprint of Penguin Random House LLC
375 Hudson Street
New York, New York 10014

Most Avery books are available at special quantity discounts for bulk purchase
for sales promotions, premiums, fund-raising, and educational needs. Special books
or book excerpts also can be created to fit specific needs. For details,
write SpecialMarkets@penguinrandomhouse.com.

Library of Congress Cataloging-in-Publication Data

Names: Runkle, Nathan, author. | Stone, Gene, 1951- author.
Title: Mercy for animals : one mans quest to inspire compassion, and improve
the lives of farm animals / Nathan Runkle with Gene Stone.
Description: New York : Avery, an imprint of Penguin Random House, [2017] |
Includes bibliographical references.
Identifiers: LCCN 2017018268 | ISBN 9780399574054 (hardcover) |
ISBN 9780399574078 (ebook)
Subjects: LCSH: Animal rights. | Human-animal relationships.
Classification: LCC HV4708.R86 2017 | DDC 179/.3—dc23
LC record available at https://lccn.loc.gov/2017018268
p.   cm.

Printed in the United States of America
1   3   5   7   9   10   8   6   4   2

BOOK DESIGN BY MEIGHAN CAVANAUGH

To protect the privacy of some individuals, I've changed a few names and
identifying details. Additionally, while many conversations have been transcribed
verbatim from video footage, I've re-created others from memory to the best
of my ability, or from the reporting of undercover investigators.

Cover: Nathan Runkle with Magnolia, a rescued cow who now lives
at Animal Place in Grass Valley, California photograph by Travis Chantar.
Other animal photos appearing in this book were taken by Sylvia Elzafon.

For Joyce

CONTENTS

III.

A KINDER TOMORROW

MERCY

FOR

ANIMALS

PROLOGUE

TIME: 1:24 a.m.

DATE: August 28, 2001

LOCATION: Buckeye Egg Farm, Croton, Ohio

POPULATION: 300

'm seventeen years old, hiding in the tall grass, clutching my backpack. My adrenaline is pumping, my heart pounding so fiercely it feels as though it might burst out of my chest.

My three partners—Amie, Jim, and Mandie—lie beside me. We are dressed in black from head to toe, spelunking lights strapped to our foreheads.

The glare of headlights sweeps over our heads as several huge, grain-filled trucks roll slowly past us, stopping just fifteen feet away. The drivers step out. They are here to fill the massive grain bins that supply feed to the more than one million animals who fill the long, windowless sheds beside us.

We continue to lie still.

What we're doing is illegal. We know that. If caught, we could be thrown in jail. But the rewards are worth the risks.

Then Mandie's cell phone rings.

"Hello?" she whispers. "I can't talk right now." She hangs up.

I roll my eyes in disbelief. I don't know whether to laugh or flee. Luckily, the truck drivers hadn't heard the ringtone. The enormous industrial fans that ventilate the egg-laying sheds—which span the length of two football fields—provide excellent sound cover.

After ten minutes, the trucks still haven't left. I decide it's time to move.

"Let's go," I whisper.

Crouching as low as possible, we run to the opposite end of the nearest shed, to a closed door. I try the knob. The door opens.

As we step inside, the overwhelming stench of ammonia immediately hits our noses and stings our throats. I shut the door, and we switch on our spelunking lights, illuminating the building's dark interior. Ahead lie mountains of manure. The shed, like all the others on this farm, is crammed with egg-laying chickens. Overhead, the hens are crowded inside cages, each the size of a file-cabinet drawer, and each cage confining seven to ten adult birds. In these conditions, the birds are unable to fully spread their wings—let alone walk, perch, roost, dust bathe, or experience the most basic freedom of movement.

The wire cage floors are slanted, meaning the birds can never stand upright and that the eggs they lay will immediately roll away from them. The eggs then land on a fabric conveyer belt that gently hauls them away to an adjacent building, where they will be carefully

cleaned to remove blood and feces and then placed in happily deco-
rated cartons proudly declaring "Farm Fresh Eggs."

That charming image is a far cry from the reality that lies before
us. The endless rows of cages are stacked like stairs, allowing the
birds' feces to fall into the manure pit in which we now stand.

"How are we going to get up there?" Mandie asks.

"We need to squeeze through that space between the floor and the
cages," I answer, pointing up.

Amie, the smallest of the group, goes first. We huddle around her
as she places a manure-coated foot into our cupped hands. We push,
she pulls. She makes it.

Next up is Jim, followed by Mandie and then me.

When the four of us reach the shed's second floor, we find a sea of
avian eyes staring at us, filled with curiosity and distress.

Next, we don rubber boot covers, surgical gloves, and masks to
protect us from the dust and debris floating through the hot air. We
then remove our black jackets, revealing T-shirts reading MERCY FOR
ANIMALS. The sentiment is the official name—and the mission—of
the organization I'd founded just a year and a half earlier.

We have come here for two reasons. First and foremost, we intend
to investigate and document conditions inside one of the country's
largest egg-producing factory farms. Second, we plan to rescue animals who are dying from injury or neglect.

We fan out into two groups and get to work.

Amie and I form one team. Rats scurry around us as we tiptoe
along the rows of cages, inspecting their occupants. Most of the hens
are nearly naked from feather loss. Many are covered in their cage

mates' excrement. Some appear to have eye and sinus infections, broken bones, and bloody injuries.

I stop, unzip my bag, and remove a handheld video camera. I turn it on, check the tape, and switch on the light. We are ready to film.

Amie stands beside me and narrates as we slowly walk down the long aisles, carefully pointing the rolling camera into each cage. The birds, cowering together, look quizzically at us.

Amie spots a hen trapped between the egg-collection belt and the long feeding tray that extends under the row of cages. Her frail body is lodged in place, her wings pinned to her sides. Her cage mates have trampled her backside, rubbing away her feathers and leaving her delicate skin bruised and covered in cuts. But she is alive.

As my camera rolls, Amie explains what we are seeing.

"We are at Buckeye Egg Farm in Croton, Ohio. We've discovered a hen trapped underneath the feeding tray. I'm now going to try to get her out."

Amie reaches down and tries to gently push the hen's body backward to dislodge her. That doesn't work. She then tries to pull her in toward the cage. Still nothing. Amie next lifts the feeding tray. That works. The hen is now free.

Amie picks her up, slowly pulling the rest of her body from the cage. She holds the hen in her arms, quietly petting the animal's head as she examines her condition before placing her back with the others.

Leaving the injured hen behind breaks our hearts, but there is much more work to do. Over the next two hours, we find many more hens stuck in cage wire, most of whom we aren't able to reach in time. We also find the rotting remains of dead hens who have been left to decompose in their cages. Their cage mates stand on their lifeless bodies, laying eggs for human consumption. We film it all.

It's now nearly four a.m. We pack up our gear, put on our jackets, and quietly head for the exits, dousing our headlamps. It's time to leave before the workers arrive. But we will be back.

SECTION I

||||||||||||

A RAT, A PIGLET, AND ME

1.

Down on the Farm

TIME: 7:52 a.m.

DATE: April 13, 1984

LOCATION: A couch in a farmhouse just outside the village of Saint Paris, Ohio

POPULATION: 2,051

I suppose it only makes sense that I would someday found an international animal-rights organization, given that I was delivered by a veterinarian.

My mother, Joyce, had been planning a home birth, but on the early spring morning she woke up with excruciating contractions, the midwife wasn't around. As Mom panted and pushed her way through labor, it became clear that, ready or not, I was about to make my appearance. My dad, Mark, determined problem solver that he is, immediately took the shoelaces out of Mom's new tennis shoes and sterilized a pair of scissors, ready to ligate and cut my umbilical cord. He later found out that Mom already had a sterile kit at the ready.

When the midwife finally arrived, my father decided to step aside and let her finish the work. Instead, he began filming the birth. A far better veterinarian than he was a director, Dad stood in front of the camera during most of the action. The greenish-hued recording contains many excellent shots of his back.

The small, hundred-year-old farmhouse where I was born was like many others in west-central Ohio: two stories tall, with a wraparound porch and wooden clapboards covered in chipping, eggshell-colored paint surrounded by massive oak trees. The farm and its white barns still stand today. So do my relatives—within a twenty-mile radius, you can find more than thirty Runkles.

My family had already been living in the area for many generations, farming corn, soybeans, wheat, and hay. Our history as farmers dates back to sometime in the 1820s, shortly after Ohio became a state. The descendants of German and Irish immigrants, we arrived in covered wagons. Joseph Parke, my paternal great-great-great-great-grandfather, kept a handwritten diary chronicling his journey from New Jersey to Ohio with his wife, Hannah, and their children. The journal details the often-treacherous travel (anywhere from fifteen to thirty miles a day), typical expenses (33 cents to $1.70 a day), and the wildlife they encountered. Dangers abounded. One evening, Joseph wrote: "Here our little boy got a corn grain up his nose but received no injury." It's because of Joseph that I know the exact date my father's ancestors arrived after crossing the Ohio River from Pennsylvania: Monday, May 22, 1820.

Joseph and his family ultimately settled in Troy, Ohio, and raised farm animals. He eventually sold the farm and retired soon after, but the story of farming in our family continued across the next two centuries. The Runkle farm in Sidney, Ohio, where my dad grew up, has been in his family for at least five generations. My dad's mother's family, the Cochlins, were also farmers, who worked land in nearby Wapakoneta that they had owned for more than a century.

Grandma Donna is the family historian. Her ability to recall childhood memories in eerily clear detail is remarkable. She tells tales of feeding the chickens and milking the cows, and then playing with the pigs and watching them eat "slop."

While my grandma grew up eating meat, she had a connection with the animals her family raised. The animals on the Cochlin farm had names. They were allowed to roam, run, play, and just be animals. When the end came, it came quickly. They were killed right there on the farm in the fastest way anyone knew: with a shot to the head by a good marksman. Few people could do the job right, so it was a very marketable skill. Similarly, chickens were killed by placing them on a solid chopping block and quickly decapitating them with a razor-sharp corn cutter.

When my grandma was growing up in the early 1900s, she and her family took care of sick animals by cradling them in their arms and bottle-feeding them. Sometimes a mother sheep would birth more lambs than she could nurse, or one lamb would be too small to reach her mother's milk. My grandma's family would take these lambs into the house and stay up all night to care for them. Unlike today's factory-farmed cows who are milked relentlessly and live for only a few short years, my grandma's cows were milked gently by hand and lived well for many years. They were given names like Molly and Nell.

The pigs were never confined indoors in tiny cages. They were allowed to roam along with the cattle, and piglets followed their mothers wherever they went. The pigs were given names, too. As my grandma recalls, "They loved to be rubbed and petted."

When my grandmother was a sophomore in high school, she met the love of her life, my grandfather Don. Introduced by friends at a high school basketball game, they were soon engaged. After they married, Grandma moved to the Sidney hog farm, where my paternal grandfather's family had been living for many decades.

My grandparents, too, showed respect for the animals they raised. Although the pigs were all bred for slaughter, the family took good care of them until that very last day. For example, soon after Grandma Donna arrived, my great-grandfather Emmett decided to remodel the farm. Emmett, who'd worked full-time on the farm since leaving sixth grade, said that no matter what other farmers might be doing, *he* would never use farrowing crates—tiny metal stalls in which the pigs couldn't even turn around. "They're too hard on the sows," my grandma recalls him saying. Emmett took great pride in his sows. He wanted them to live good lives before they died. Eighty years ago, the concept of industrialized animal agriculture was just beginning to emerge, and my great-grandfather didn't like it.

Nowadays, factory farms account for almost all farm animals raised and slaughtered in the United States. These industrial facilities in which animals are treated as mere cogs in a machine are nothing like my grandma's farm. The roots of this industrial, factory-farm system can be traced to World War I, when the federal government was guaranteeing generous prices for crops and animal products to support the war effort. Whatever farmers could produce, the government would buy. In response, farmers borrowed heavily by mortgaging their farms, bought more land and animals, and produced as much food as possible. These farms prospered for a short while, but when the war ended, so did the government's price guarantees. The price of corn dropped by nearly 80 percent, and beef prices dropped by 50 percent. Then, just as farmers were clawing their way back, the stock market crashed. The price of food dropped so low that many farms were abandoned and snatched up by the banks. The old model of food production was quickly insufficient. Producers had to make food plentiful and affordable, and they had to do it with a smaller workforce. This led to fewer but much larger mechanized farms. Much, much larger. Despite producing more food today, the agriculture industry's share of the workforce has shrunk 80 percent over the past sixty years.

It's a change my dad saw unfold. He was born and grew up on the same farm and attended the same grade school as his mother. Whereas she had traveled to class via horse and buggy, he got to ride a bus. The Runkle farm had milk cows, pigs, and chickens, as well as numerous cats and dogs. All summer throughout his school years, Dad worked on the farm with his father and grandfather. Back then, family farms like ours were small—about 80 to 160 acres—with two or three tractors, each generating less than 50 horsepower. Today most such farms comprise closer to 2,000 to 5,000 acres and are tended by a phalanx of 200- to 300-horsepower tractors. Land back then was worth about $100 to $200 an acre. Now it goes for $8,000 an acre or more. Consolidation was already under way when my dad was growing up, however. Every few weeks, he and Grandpa used to go to the farm auctions, where farmers who were going under sold their land and equipment at a discount.

Dad's favorite part of farm life was the animals. As soon as he was old enough to walk, he'd hurry over to the stables to spend as much time as he could with the ponies. When he was only about six, he brought a sick lamb into the house and cared for him day and night for weeks. When he was ten, he had an Arabian mare, Ginger. She was so tall that to get on her back, he had to climb up her front leg.

Dad understood and loved animals, and they loved him right back. It was no surprise to anyone that he decided to become a veterinarian. After two years of college, he applied to and was accepted at the Ohio State University School of Veterinary Medicine.

My mom, Joyce June Summers, grew up a hundred miles northwest of my dad, in Shelby, Ohio. She, too, adored animals and found solace in their gentle, loyal company. Her first pet was a dog, Spot, but as she grew, so did her family of animals. There was Tiny the cat, Joy the goat, Cleo the ferret, Tippy the raccoon, and Deba the skunk. Mom's pride and joy, however, was Star the horse, a lean fellow with dark red hair punctuated by a white, star-shaped patch of hair at the center of his forehead. I owe my life to Star. Without him, my mom probably would not have met my dad.

While Dad was in vet school, he started a horseback-riding program for summer camps and placed an ad in the school newspaper for an instructor. One of the applicants was Joyce, an elementary school teacher who had previously taught riding at a Girl Scout camp. He hired her.

After a couple of years in the job, she wanted to do what Dad did—

haul horses to camp and help to manage the program. Dad told her that if she bought a truck, she could do just that. So she purchased a 1979 Chevy three-quarter-ton pickup, Dad got her a trailer, and they started working together. They fell in love, married, and moved Mom onto our family farm.

With these two as parents, my fate was sealed.

If you were to look at photographs of me as a kid, you might think I was actually raised by animals. Sure, there are a few pictures of me with my parents, but there are plenty more of me beside a cat, dog, frog, or horse. From the moment I was allowed outdoors by myself, I sought out every creature I could find—looking under rocks for crawdads, searching small ponds for minnows, combing the fields for toads to chase. If a baby bird fell out of a nest, I'd bring her home in a box and nurse her back to health with an eyedropper. If feral cats were wandering about, I'd befriend them, rescue them, and find someone to adopt them. Sometimes my older sister, Lana, and I would hear mewing in the barns and discover a litter of feral kittens buried deep in the hay. We would dig them out and get them adopted as well. Of course, we kept some of them, such as Benjamin, a gray-and-white tabby who was part of our family for fifteen years.

But the most significant relationship I had with an animal was with a sweet rat named Caesar.

Caesar was born in a small shed beside a big red barn and a bright yellow house next door to ours. My parents rented the house to a couple named Gene and Sylvia—hardworking, outgoing folks who bred rats, mice, guinea pigs, and beautiful white rabbits for sale to local research labs and universities. I remember wire cages stacked on top of one another, the smell of ammonia, and dead animals lying in the corners of cages, their live companions huddling next to them. Looking back, I'm appalled by what I now understand was happening across the cornfields from our family farm. All of these creatures were destined for the same short, grim life of being fed chemicals, drowned, shocked, or starved in the name of "science."

One afternoon in 1990, when I was six years old, I went over to Gene and Sylvia's with my mom to collect the monthly rent check. Sylvia knew of my deep love for animals, so she decided to show me one of the smaller sheds where the rats were being raised. Reaching into one of the cages, she grabbed a rat by his tail, hoisting him into the air. I watched as his little legs stretched out in panic as he tried desperately to grasp for something to hold on to. Sylvia lowered him into my waiting arms and told me he was a Siamese rat. His markings were exactly the same as those of the widely loved Siamese cat. His coat was a pure, glistening white, and the fur around his nose a soft gray. His emotive eyes were big and black. He looked regal, so I named him Caesar.

"Do you want to take him home?" Sylvia asked.

I was ecstatic. "Mom, can I *please*?"

"He's a big responsibility," she said. "You'll have to take very good care of him."

"Yes, I know, Mom. Of course I will."

Caesar found a loving home with my family. Plucked from his cage and granted amnesty, he was one of the lucky ones. I later learned that the going price for one of Sylvia's rats was a mere dollar.

For the next two and a half years, Caesar was my constant companion, sitting on my shoulder as I walked around the house, the star of my photo shoots as I learned to work a camera. He knew his name and came running whenever I called it. He was smart and gentle. We had a true bond.

I was so proud of him. When friends would come to visit, I'd take them to my room to meet Caesar. But most would shriek in disgust, "Ewww, a *rat*!" Otherwise calm and rational adults would become frightened children at the mere sight of Caesar. They'd quickly turn a cold shoulder. Gasp. Avert their gaze.

I couldn't understand. They didn't know Caesar as I did. They were judging him for *what* he was, not *who* he was. I was coming to understand that, when it comes to the desire for freedom, companionship, and respect, all animals are alike. The different treatments and fates we impose on our fellow creatures aren't about them but about us.

In June 1993, Steven Spielberg's *Jurassic Park* had just hit theaters. My fondness for dinosaurs was second only to my love for modern-day animals, so I convinced my parents to drive me to nearby Piqua to see the film on the big screen. The movie ignited my imagination, but it was also scary. I ran upstairs to my bedroom when I got home and looked for Caesar.

I found him lying motionless on his side in his cage. When I picked him up, his body was cold and stiff. My best friend was dead. I was heartbroken.

Caesar received a proper burial under a mulberry tree. A makeshift grave marker read CAESAR RUNKLE RAT, 1990–1993.

Not all my early interactions with animals were so positive. The same year I met Caesar, my cousin and uncle asked me to go on my first hunting trip in the woods behind my grandma's house. (In our family, if farming came first, hunting was a close second.) I didn't have a gun. Still, I agreed to come along. They assumed I was joining them because I wanted to become a hunter. But I really just wanted a chance to see more animals.

Things didn't go as planned. First, I didn't want to keep quiet. My uncle had to keep shushing me. Perhaps my fidgety childhood energy was to blame, or I secretly hoped to warn the animals of the danger ahead. Then, suddenly, my uncle spotted a rabbit, firing quickly before she could escape. *BOOM! BOOM!* The sound of the rifle startled me, leaving me momentarily speechless and deafened. We approached his prey, only to find that the poor rabbit wasn't dead. Lying on her back on the forest floor, she stared up at us, trembling in fear and pain, a look of sheer terror in her wide eyes.

I will never forget that moment: three bullies hovering over this little brown rabbit who was just trying to lead her life in the woods. Even at six years old I felt an enormous sense of injustice. Worse, my uncle then picked up the rabbit and twisted her neck, making me feel sick as I watched him pull her head completely off.

That was my first, and last, hunting trip.

Such incidents made it clear that I always had it in my heart to be an advocate. I connected with animals. I understood them. I loved them. I was also a loud, outgoing, and inquisitive kid. I would talk to anyone and always stood up for whatever I felt was right. I was driven, determined, and willing to take risks, with an abundance of energy. Friends nicknamed me Taz, after the Warner Bros. cartoon character, the incredibly speedy Tasmanian Devil.

But activism wasn't a standard career choice in my conservative corner of Ohio. Then again, I wasn't concerned with fitting in with other kids. I had always felt different. For one thing, I didn't seem to perceive the world as other kids did. To learn anything, I had to use my senses and my body: see, hear, and do. Tasks such as reading, writing, and spelling were exceptionally difficult for me.

I'd been slow to talk as a child, and with these challenges at school, my mom feared I had a learning disability. By the time I was six I'd already seen several psychologists—consultations that continued for years, and eventually involved a half-dozen experts. The tests they gave me included putting together complicated puzzles, reciting lists of names, spelling words, and identifying patterns. They even gave me brain scans. I wasn't sure why I was there or what they were testing for, but I nervously went along.

The test results baffled doctors across the state. My IQ was in the so-called superior category, yet I showed serious weaknesses in "linguistic processing" and "short-term auditory memory," along with "confusion in laterality and directionality" and "mild attention deficit." I seemed to be "intellectually gifted" and "learning disabled" all at once.

Then Dr. Marlene Bireley, an experienced child psychologist at Wright State University, cracked my code. Dr. Bireley, who conducted numerous evaluations on me before making a diagnosis, had a term for kids like me: "Crossover Children." She was so taken with the extremes in my various brain functions that she asked if she could include my story in a book she was writing on the topic.

No doubt it was my unusual brain that made me an outsider in the world. And perhaps it was that outsider view that allowed me to develop such a close bond with animals—who couldn't speak or write at all.

Finally, the day came when I found a way to channel my passion and my unique perspective into action. I was eleven years old. It was a typical Ohio winter evening: cold, dark, and snowy. Our family was sitting in the kitchen watching the local six o'clock news out of the big city—Dayton. Near the end of the broadcast, a short piece came on about a small group of local animal-rights activists who were protesting the sale of fur coats at Dayton Mall. Bundled in scarves and winter jackets, they were willing to stand outside in the frigid air to speak up for animals. The segment featured graphic footage of a drowning beaver caught in an underwater trap, a mink dying in a leg-hold device, and a dog just like mine with her mangled leg trapped in one. My heart broke as I stared at the images, cringing at the pain and fear radiating from the animals' eyes as they struggled to survive. But I also felt excited. "Animal-rights activist." There was a name for people who felt as I did! I wasn't alone. And these people weren't just talking about saving animals. They were taking action.

Now that I knew there was such a thing as an animal-rights activist, I was determined to become one. I immediately decided to learn as much as possible. This was in the days of dial-up Internet, before instant connections, so I was limited mostly to library research. It wasn't until four months later that I saw a real opportunity to educate myself, when I found out about an Earth Day fair at that same mall in Dayton. Giving in to my endless pleas, my mother agreed to take me.

Once at the event, I scanned the booths. They focused on various environmental causes, from recycling to tree planting, but the one that hooked me was run by the local animal-protection organization. I took some of their literature about factory farming, vivisection, and fur, and then spent the entire trip home reading. This was the first time I had ever heard about veal crates—cruel stalls in which animals were chained, crammed so tightly they couldn't turn around or extend their limbs. By the time we arrived home, I'd made up my mind. I was now a vegetarian.

My mom was mildly amused. Always supportive of my choices (and surprisingly progressive for a rural Ohioan), she agreed to accommodate my dietary switch. Years later I found out she was actually proud of me.

She also watched lovingly as her hyperactive son dove passionately into the subject of vegetarianism and animal rights. As often as possible, I went to the local library, hunted down books on the topic (there weren't many back then), and studied their jackets to find addresses where I could write for more information. I ended up contacting dozens of places such as PETA (People for the Ethical Treatment of Animals) and HSUS (The Humane Society of the United States), asking for everything they could send me.

Soon our mailbox was overflowing with cards, letters, and pamphlets. I ended up with an enormous collection of materials, which I'd pore over religiously. I wanted to learn everything. I wanted to make a difference. I believed that I could, even if I didn't yet know how. I had to try, and why not right away?

I began by talking with kids in school about the subject, even asking my teachers if I could give presentations. They agreed—reluctantly, I suspect, but perhaps they appreciated my initiative. My first presentation on animal rights ranged from the injustices of fur and vivisection to the cruelty of factory farming. Later, when I was in the fifth grade, I rented a projector and gave a slide show on animal testing by cosmetics companies. (HSUS had sent me an entire deck of slides about the topic.) I talked about the Draze eye test, in which researchers place burning chemicals in animals' eyes to test for irritation, and the LD50 (lethal dose 50 percent) test, in which researchers feed chemicals to a group of animals until half of them die. I recalled my pet rat Caesar: If I hadn't rescued him, this would have been his likely fate.

The images I showed my classmates were graphic. When I think back, I am amazed my teachers let me carry on with my crusade.

Another time, I sent a petition to then president Bill Clinton, asking him to support animal rights. I not only asked my classmates to sign it but also their parents, families, neighbors—everyone I knew. Months later, the White House sent me a form letter on endangered species, probably the only template the administration had concerning animals.

Eventually I'd form an animal club at school with six classmates, making bird feeders and talking about how to help animals. I even got a few of them to go vegetarian. Their parents reluctantly went along.

Besides helping animals, my life's passion at this point was competitive figure skating—something I expected to become my life's work. I had started skating when I was eight and within a few years was winning a great many local and state competitions. At one point I was selected as one of four boys and four girls competing for the United States in an under-twelve contest in Milan, Italy. The other skaters included future Olympic gold medalists Evan Lysacek and Sarah Hughes.

But as I morphed from a short kid to a tall teenager in what seemed like a flash, my skating faltered. I was miserable. It was 1997, and I had started attending a public junior high school in rural Ohio, where I didn't know a single person. This was not a good experience for a skinny, vegetarian, soon-to-be-former figure skater. I was bullied, harassed, and unhappy. My parents decided it might be best if I were homeschooled—and so they took over my education.

As skating diminished in my life, my greater passion was coming into focus. My new, more flexible school schedule allowed me to devote more effort to animal rights. In 1997, I was able to convince my parents to drive me to Washington, DC, for an animal-rights conference, and ended up joining dozens of other activists at sidewalk protests against Miller's Furs, animal testing at the National Institutes of Health, McDonald's, and a circus using elephants. We stood outside in the cold, black tape over our mouths to symbolize the animals' silent suffering. The protests felt empowering but were not terribly successful. As people drove by, some honked in support while others spit at us or threw chicken bones.

The rest of the weekend was taken up by the conference itself, which enthralled and inspired me. I had never met so many people who thought the way I did—I had no idea that so many such people existed. Once back home in rural Ohio, however, I quickly felt isolated. One moment I'd been in animal-rights heaven, the next, surrounded by hog and dairy farms.

As I learned more and more about the dairy industry, I realized that by eating eggs and milk I was supporting cruelty to animals. But I couldn't quite give them up. I kept thinking I'd wait until I had my own house and was responsible for my own food. Being a vegetarian already seemed like such a strain on my good-natured family. I didn't want to see how much farther I could push them.

Then, in May 1999, when I was fifteen years old, I had a terrible nightmare. I dreamed I was a dairy cow. This wasn't surprising, given that I had seen so many videos of what these poor creatures endured, as well as having spent so much time with the animals themselves. In the dream, I saw the world through the cow's own eyes and felt the sensations of her body. I found myself confined to a tiny isolated stall, chained by the neck, unable to turn around, and hooked up to a milking machine. My newly born calf had just been yanked away from me. I felt nothing but panic, desolation, and helplessness.

When I woke up the next morning, I had made up my mind. I was now vegan.

Are We Meant to Eat Meat?

Meat eaters often defend their diet by pointing to our canine teeth—why else would we have them? But a few canine teeth do not mean humans are carnivores. Many herbivores have far more ferocious canines than ours yet never touch meat. Hippos, for example, have some of the fiercest choppers in nature, but they don't feast on other animals. They prefer grass. Gorillas also have sharp fangs, but their diet is composed of fruit, leaves, seeds, and insects.

Dr. Milton Mills, associate director of preventive medicine with the Physicians Committee for Responsible Medicine, points out that carnivores have very large mouths in relation to their heads and extremely powerful jaws for ripping flesh. Their teeth are sharp, pointed, and spaced far apart so they remain free of debris. Carnivores' saliva lacks digestive enzymes, and their enormous stomachs take up

60 to 70 percent of their digestive system. This allows animals to gorge themselves on prey and digest it slowly over time, since food might not be available for many days.

Humans have none of these traits. As Dr. Mills writes, "The human gastrointestinal tract features the anatomical modifications consistent with an herbivorous diet." Our facial muscles are designed for methodical chewing, not attacking. Our teeth are crowded together and designed for crushing and grinding plants, not tearing flesh. Our saliva contains salivary amylase, an enzyme responsible for digesting starches. And our stomachs only take up about 25 percent of our digestive system, meaning we can only eat small amounts at a time. Unlike carnivores, we can't get by on one meal per week. "In conclusion," Mills writes, "we see that human beings have the gastrointestinal tract structure of a 'committed' herbivore."

2.

Mercy For Animals Begins

A few days later, I heard about an event that changed the course of my life. My local high school was offering an agricultural class for upperclassmen that included a dissection. The teacher, Mr. Jenkins, was a local farmer who had raised more than eleven thousand pigs. On the morning of May 6, 1999, Mr. Jenkins walked into one of his barns, grabbed a half-dozen piglets, and attempted to kill them. But things didn't go according to plan. When Mr. Jenkins arrived at school, one of the piglets was still alive— standing on top of the others piglets inside a plastic bucket. She was crying out—terrified as only a small, defenseless animal can be.

After spotting the piglet, a senior student in the class, who worked part-time on the Jenkins farm, proceeded to grab the baby animal by her hind legs and, in full view of the other students, slam her head-first into the concrete floor. Twice.

The piglet still didn't die. Instead, she lay writhing in pain, blood pouring out of her mouth, still breathing. When this was brought to Jenkins's attention, he responded, "It's just a pig. I don't care what you do with it."

Another, more compassionate student then grabbed the piglet—still alive but now suffering from a fractured skull—quickly left the class, and ran down the hall to the classroom of Molly Fearing. Molly, a first-year teacher, was a fellow vegetarian and animal lover. Heart breaking, Molly cradled the piglet in her arms, ran to her car, and drove fifteen miles to the nearest animal hospital. The little piglet was still alive when they arrived, but the veterinarian had to euthanize her—she was just too badly injured to survive the repeated assaults. The hospital offered to dispose of the piglet's remains, but Molly wanted to give the animal a proper burial on her farm, which she did.

Molly was so horrified by the incident that she took photos of the dead piglet to document the poor animal's bruising and suffering, and then went to the sheriff to file an animal-cruelty complaint. Soon official charges were filed against Jenkins for "improperly destroying a domestic animal"—in other words, he should never have brought a live pig to school for dissection. The student who abused the piglet was not charged, however.

My hometown of Saint Paris quickly divided into two camps. The local newspaper was deluged with letters both defending and condemning Jenkins. While many students were deeply upset by what they had witnessed, local pig farmers didn't understand the fuss—this was hog farm country, after all. Scores of animals were killed every day.

On the first day of Jenkins's trial, farmers showed up at the courtroom in droves, packing the benches to rally around their neighbor. They needn't have bothered. The judge dismissed the charges, decreeing that, according to Ohio law, something can't be considered cruelty to animals if it's "standard agricultural practice." And slamming piglets headfirst into the ground is, in fact, "standard agricultural practice."

The moment I heard about the decision I became infuriated. I couldn't stand the hypocrisy: The government had handed over the power to decide what was right and wrong—cruel or humane—to the very industries that were profiting from these terrible misdeeds. If someone had slammed a puppy into the ground in front of a class of teenagers, he'd be in jail. But a piglet? There were laws allowing people to do that.

I knew the term "standard agricultural practice" as a result of years of studying animal protection on my own. In any form of farming, there are certain ways that things have always been done. In the pork industry, farmers often kill piglets by slamming them into the ground, and on poultry farms they cut the beaks off baby birds using hot blades. These practices aren't just traditions. They are published in official industry trade manuals and agricultural textbooks, and are taught to workers on factory farms. To save money and protect profit, the industry tends to practice the cheapest way of killing an animal—even if it's cruel, even if it doesn't always work on the first try.

The cruelty didn't stop at piglet slamming and chicken de-beaking, I discovered. The more I learned about standard farm practices, the more upset I became. Just down the road from my house, steers were being castrated and cows' horns were being sawed off without anesthesia. How could the farmers do it?

"Standard agricultural practices."

I was also upset that Molly had been forced to resign from her teaching job. At the time, in this part of the country, it was a greater offense to stand up to another teacher for animal cruelty than to slam animals headfirst into the ground. The school's superintendent had told her that she would never teach again. And, in fact, Molly never did find another teaching position. Instead, she started hanging doors on cars at the nearby Honda plant.

I knew then and there that I needed to do something to advocate for farm animals who had no voice or rights. So I sought out Molly a few weeks after the piglet case was dismissed. After much discussion, we decided to form an organization: Mercy For Animals. I came up with the name one October evening while Molly and I were driving back from an event in Columbus. It summed up our mission in three short words. Farm animals were completely helpless. We humans held all the power. And we could use that power either to abuse and exploit them, or to help and protect them. We could choose mercy.

Right from the start there were challenges. Molly was an ex–public school teacher and I was a fifteen-year-old homeschooled student. We had no money. But we had something invaluable: a passionate desire to right wrongs.

In MFA's first few months, our main goal was simply to make local residents aware of the issues. Unfortunately, few people listened or cared. We pressed on. We decided to begin holding meetings at the local library in Champaign County. Posting simple flyers in banks, grocery stores, and gas stations around town, we hoped that a few people would notice and show up.

We held our first MFA meeting in February 2000. The only other people to come besides Molly and me were a woman named Susan Dunne; her husband, Marcus; and their newborn daughter. Susan was an eccentric character who drove a large white van covered with dozens of animal-rights bumper stickers. She was blunt and forward with her opinions, for better or worse, but she was also loyal and dedicated. Remarkably, Susan is still a member of MFA.

Slowly, a few other people—all adults—began to show up at meetings. Already, I was leading a group composed mostly of people three to four times my age. I didn't think much of it. I was too driven and focused. I never wanted my youth to be an issue; I just wanted to be seen as an effective activist.

After about a year, we started to have an impact. We still had no money in the bank but plenty of passion in our hearts, so most of our work consisted of placing posters in libraries, writing letters to the editors of local papers, and organizing a few protests.

That summer we decided to demonstrate at the McDonald's in Urbana, Ohio, doing our part in a wider international animal-protection campaign. During the longest trial in the United Kingdom's history, dubbed the "McLibel Trial," McDonald's had recently been found "culpably responsible" for cruelty to animals. Following the verdict, American animal advocates like us used the publicity to launch a campaign to convince McDonald's to improve their treatment of egg-laying hens. The demands were modest: provide the hens with a few more inches of cage space (72 square inches, up from 52), stop starving them (to prompt the birds into laying more eggs—a common practice), and audit suppliers' slaughterhouses to ensure that no animals were conscious when skinned.

A handful of us showed up for the protest during what turned out to be a torrential downpour. We lined up outside the McDonald's, all decked out in our ponchos and umbrellas as the ink ran down our tattered signs. We got a few honks of support. Mostly we got ignored. And very wet.

We needed a new strategy. Then, nature intervened.

At the time, Ohio was the nation's largest egg-producing state. The title was due largely to the presence of one company, Buckeye Egg Farm, which confined more than a third of the state's thirty million hens. Buckeye Egg Farm's history was already riddled with scandals and legal violations. Founded by a man named Anton Pohlmann, known as the Chicken Baron in his native Germany, the company began causing major problems soon after opening its first site in Croton, Ohio, in 1983. First came a manure spill into Otter Fork Creek that killed more than 150,000 fish and contaminated groundwater. Then, over the next decade, Pohlmann expanded operations, causing more groundwater contamination in addition to soil erosion and other environmental damage to rural communities around Ohio.

In 1995, Pohlmann was hauled into court due to a widespread salmonella outbreak at one of his egg factory farms in Germany. When the judge ordered him to exterminate the infected flock, Pohlmann instead simply shut off the food, water, and air-conditioning in the sheds housing these chickens, leaving thousands of caged birds to die slowly from starvation, dehydration, and heat exhaustion. The following year, German officials charged Pohlmann with cruelty to animals after he was caught feeding his birds an illegal, highly lethal disinfectant. He was barred from ever again owning animals or operating a farm in Germany.

Despite his conviction in Europe, Pohlmann continued to grow his operations in Ohio, causing complaints ranging from fly and beetle infestations to labor violations that included employing children and undocumented immigrants. In 1999, manure lagoons at Buckeye Egg Farm ruptured, causing a fifteen-mile fish kill in Raccoon Creek. The Ohio Environmental Protection Agency mandated a cleanup. But Pohlmann did not comply, resulting in the state's filing a twenty-seven-count lawsuit against Buckeye for violations of environmental laws and threating to seize Pohlmann's assets.

These abuses were mild compared with the terror that hit the farm in September 2000. A major tornado roared through the town, destroying trees, taking out power lines, and decimating Buckeye Egg Farm. The tornado ripped the roofs and sides off a dozen metal sheds, each confining more than 150,000 hens crowded into row upon row of stacked cages. In all, more than a million animals were left trapped in mangled wire and without food, water, or protection from sun, rain, and dropping temperatures.

The news broke the following day. By mid-morning, I'd received a call. It was Ritchie Laymon, a longtime animal advocate from Columbus who served as one of my mentors and was in many ways the mother of the animal-protection movement in Ohio. (Ritchie had organized the fur protest I'd seen on my local news years earlier, propelling me on my path of animal activism.)

"They are allowing hens to be rescued," she told me, "but we have to hurry. No one knows how long this will last." Ritchie, who was smart, forward-thinking, and funny, had been battling Buckeye Egg

Farm since Pohlmann first set up shop in the state. This was a rare and promising opportunity.

I immediately called Molly and we headed off to U-Haul to rent an extended van, removing the seats to make room for our precious cargo: injured chickens. We then drove to the factory farm in Croton. The sheds, which normally appeared to be unassuming warehouses, were now open to the elements, revealing the full horror that had long been taking place inside their walls. Rows of small cages stacked four high lay collapsed on top of one another, running the length of two football fields.

Molly and I pulled into the entrance, where we were met by Cayce Mell, founder of OohMahNee Farm Sanctuary, an organization that rescued and provided shelter for farm animals in need.

"Are you here to help rescue?" she asked us.

We nodded.

"Great! We've negotiated the release of some of the hens in exchange for good press for the company. What you're going to see is very disturbing. But we need to stay focused to get the animals out of here."

She motioned Molly and me forward. As we pulled down the driveway alongside the enormous factory-farm sheds, the appalling situation came into focus: rows of dilapidated cages stretched as far as my eye could see. Trapped inside were tens of thousands of animals, their bodies already battered from spending their lives confined in tiny wire boxes with many other birds. Some were already dead. Those that had survived were suffering from broken bones and crushed body parts. Eggs were piling up inside the cages, unable to roll onto the now-destroyed egg-collection belt. Thousands of hens had been crushed to death inside the cages, their faces pressed up against the wires, mouths opened in distress, their final moments of agony frozen in time.

During the tornado, the cages had been slammed to the ground, landing in the mountains of manure that collected below in the shed's waste pits. Many hens had drowned in the manure. Others had escaped their torn cages and were limping around. A group of surviving hens huddled together in the corner of what remained of one of the sheds, trying to stay warm in the chilly fall air.

Feathers, dirt, and dust filled the air. The smell of ammonia and rotting eggs permeated the space. Flies were beginning to swarm.

There were countless stories of suffering around me, but the image seared in my memory is of one battered hen who had managed to escape her cage and was standing alone outside, shivering, terrified in the midst of the debris. She was wet and cold, her eyes half closed. If there was a hell on earth, she had found it.

We pulled the van up to a designated area and opened the back doors. Workers from the factory farm were climbing around the rubble, gathering handfuls of hens. They carried them by their legs, upside down, six in a hand, to the van, then lowered them onto the waiting straw. Molly waited patiently, trying to strike up small talk with the farm management.

"We can take more," Molly said, motioning for the workers to put more hens in the van.

Grabbing my video camera, I slipped away to document the nightmare that lay before us. By the time I made it back from filming, the van was full. One hundred fifty-three hens were now safe and about to get far, far away from this mess. Destination: the OohMahNee Farm Animal Sanctuary in Hunker, Pennsylvania.

Today was the first time the hens had ever been outside of a cage. The birds walked around in the back of the van, pecking at the straw we'd lain out and exploring their environment. As the van began to move, the hens began to settle. We played classical music to calm them down, and before long, they were all asleep.

Meanwhile, the windows were steaming up from all the body heat—and the stench of 153 animals just pulled from a manure-soaked factory farm was almost unbearable. But we had no time to spare. In our laps, Molly and I both held hens who were near death and in need of additional warmth, attention, and protection. In Molly's slept a hen with a broken leg; in mine, one who was clearly ill.

Arriving at the eighty-six-acre sanctuary just past dark, we pulled onto the gravel driveway and made our way down to the old red barn where other volunteers were waiting. We backed up as close to the barn as possible and jumped out.

"We have to get them out of there fast, or they'll start piling on top of each other," said Jason, Cayce's husband and cofounder of the sanctuary.

In just a few frantic minutes the van was empty, every hen now in the barn.

Despite the horrors we had witnessed that day, it ended joyfully for these lucky few birds. For the first time in their lives, the hens were able to act like who they were born to be. Watching them take their first steps of freedom was heartwarming and heartbreaking at the same time. They would cautiously put one foot in front of the other, toes spread wide to maintain balance. They were wobbly, not yet confident, slowly stretching their wings as if awakening from the slumber that was their past life. Their curiosity shined through as they explored the straw, the shiny watering trough, the orange plastic mesh. They had gone from knowing only a wire box to the freedom of a life in nature.

The hens began to build nests. Within the first hour, many of them were making themselves at home, preparing to lay their eggs. Others found elevated areas on which to perch. Both were basic, and highly important, chicken behaviors—things they had never been able to experience before.

It was now ten p.m. We had to return to Buckeye. More hens needed help.

For the next four weeks we worked with advocates from around the Midwest to rescue more hens. It was exhausting—physically, mentally, and emotionally. We knew we had to hurry and keep moving; lives were at stake. In the end the project became the largest farmed-animal rescue in US history, with more than five thousand hens saved. While the tornado proved lifesaving for those animals, sadly most of the one million hens had died anyway from starvation, gassing, being crushed by bulldozers, or suffocating after being thrown alive into huge trash bins.

Eventually Buckeye Farm stopped allowing rescues, saying that the situation "had become physically and emotionally dangerous to humans."

The last animal to leave was rescued by Ritchie, who found a hen whose wing had become entangled beneath cage debris. Ritchie named the little creature Chick Corea, after the jazz pianist, and brought her to live with her, her husband, and their rescued dogs and cats in their suburban Columbus home. For years, Chick Corea was a beloved member of the Laymon household, always running alongside the dogs to greet guests at the door. At one point, she climbed onto the family's answering machine, accidentally deleting the outgoing message and replacing it with one of her own, complete with *bawks* and *squawks*. She became quite the famous fowl, appearing in newspaper photos around the country and serving as ambassador for all the hens who'd perished during the disaster.

One dramatic rescue mission was now over, but Buckeye Egg Farm remained in our sights.

3.

Growing Up and Coming Out

Mercy For Animals was now heading in a positive direction. However, several years earlier, my family life had started to deteriorate. One afternoon in 1996, when I was eleven years old, my parents arrived home after a doctor's visit. My dad had accompanied my mom to the appointment after a mammogram had found a suspicious lump.

"We got some bad news at the doctor's today," he said in his typical straightforward style. "Your mother has breast cancer."

"But it's not necessarily a death sentence," my mom added, her voice concerned but still strong. "There are many treatment options."

I don't remember much more about that conversation—it's as if I've blocked it from my memory—except that my sister burst into tears. I was sad, and scared, but I didn't fully grasp what I was being told. At that age, how could I? I thought my mom was invincible, that we'd all just move forward and soon this would be behind us. Meanwhile, as Mom pursued treatment, my parents remained calm, although Dad's voice cracked a bit sometimes.

However hopeful we were that Mom would survive, over the next six years her health worsened. She went through chemo, lost all her hair, and then gained weight from taking a multitude of drugs including steroids. She was in and out of the hospital. My parents didn't talk about it much—or if they did, their conversations took place when I wasn't around. They wanted me to believe she would be fine. I wanted to believe it, too.

But as the disease progressed, it became more and more obvious that Mom was dying. At the time, I was growing from a boy into a young man. On one hand, I had already begun separating from her: bracing, protecting, and distancing myself. This was the only way I knew to soften the blow I could see coming straight toward my sensitive heart. On the other hand, Mom and I remained very close. She was always so truly and deeply supportive of my life's choices, especially animal advocacy and building MFA. When I'd announced that I would no longer eat meat, Mom had immediately bought several new cookbooks. Suddenly, our household was vegetarian. When I'd wanted to be driven hundreds of miles to events, Mom found a way for that to happen. When, at sixteen, I received a youth activist award at an animal-rights conference in Washington, DC, Mom accompanied me.

Yet she was also worried. She saw MFA not as a career but as a hobby. One evening, when I was creating protest posters rather than doing my homework, my mom said, "Nathan, you can't protest your entire life." I needed to find something more practical to do, she added. She was concerned that she wouldn't be around to help me find it.

Mom struggled to survive as long as she could, but by 2000 her health had deteriorated to the point where no one could pretend she was going to live, herself included. My mother loved Montana, where one of her best friends from college had settled, so my parents decided to build a house there and moved that same year.

I spent the next Christmas with them. Soon after I returned to Ohio (where I was living alone), Dad called to say Mom's health had taken a bad turn—she didn't have much longer. I flew back to Montana. When I walked into the house, my mom came to the door to greet me. As we hugged, I could feel deep, pure joy and love radiating from her.

I spent the next week with her, watching her fade away. During a lucid moment Mom asked me which of her belongings I might like to keep. In the true selfless spirit that defined my mom, she was reading a book for people with terminal illness and had reached the chapter on how to plan for your own passing.

"Your wedding band," I said. "Nothing else."

She nodded, treasuring this one last, clearheaded moment between mother and son.

A few days later she died.

I slid the wedding band off her hand moments after she passed. Her hands were still soft and warm. The ring became my emotional cushion. It made me feel as if she were close by.

After Mom's death, a priest showed up at the house to talk to me.

Although he was well-meaning, when he asked me if I would pray with him, I declined. I felt uncomfortable with the priest because of the church's stance on homosexuality.

By this point I was well aware that I was gay. I can actually remember the exact moment I realized I liked men. I was eight years old—the same age at which I'd discovered skating. A movie called *The Princess Bride* was on TV. I don't remember the plot, but I do remember that the pirate in the film was handsome and that I had a crush on him.

I'm not one of those gay men who falls in the middle of the Kinsey scale. There was never any confusion in my mind as to whether I preferred girls or boys. All my school crushes were on the latter, particularly on a boy in my after-school gymnastics class named Jacob, an athletic kid with shaggy brown hair. After class Jacob and I would spend time together in his bedroom. He had an outdoor tent set up on the floor where we would sit naked, exploring each other's bodies with our hands. There was no kissing, but I knew I liked the feeling of touching him.

Still, the word "gay" hadn't yet entered my mind. As with most of the gay men I've met, there was a long period of time when I knew how I felt but didn't want to accept it. I wanted it to be a phase, something that would go away. I wanted to be "normal." To have a family, a happily-ever-after.

Kids have amazing gaydar, though. My neighbors, the kids in junior high, the hockey players on the rink—all of them called me a faggot and threatened to beat me up throughout my school years. Once, when I was twelve, I was at a high school football game with my sister and our neighbor Alan. Alan's family and mine were close. But this day he pointed at me and called me a fag in front of his friends. I didn't understand. Up until then he had been like a brother.

That was just the beginning. He said it often, and always with such hatred and conviction. It was soul crushing. Why, I wondered, did people to whom I have done nothing wrong hate me so much? I didn't let them see me cry, but at night the tears flowed.

I had never told Mom about my orientation. I was a scared boy who didn't feel safe being openly gay. After all, I didn't have a peer-support system, and I was afraid what my family and neighbors might think. But I had wanted to tell her so desperately. When she was on her deathbed, I tried. Yet I couldn't say the words aloud. Sometimes the pressure of time provides a rare opportunity to start one of your life's most important conversations, because you know regret will follow you forever if you don't do it now. But I was too young to fully understand that.

One night, just before she died, I was sitting next to Mom on her bed. She was barely conscious. I took my index finger and spelled I-A-M-G-A-Y on her palm, over and over. I fought to hold back tears. My heart was breaking. My mom always had the most beautiful hands. Even after the cancer treatments ravaged her body, her hands remained lovely. And here I was, writing on them words I could never say to her face.

I'd always felt it was harder to be gay than it was to be an animal activist. I could handle any verbal blows thrown my way if someone spoke negatively about animals. That wasn't personal. But from a young age, I found it much harder to stand up for myself—especially when I was constantly being told, by both society and those I loved, that part of my core identity was shameful. I was terrified that if I came out, my family's love would disappear. My grandma was always a loving and thoughtful person. But even she would make terribly homophobic comments: Homosexuals were bad people, sinners against God. AIDS was God's cure for homosexuality.

So I never did formally come out to my family. They found out in a roundabout way. By 2002, I was living in Columbus and seeing my first boyfriend, Damien, a twenty-three-year-old African American. Damien was tall, strong, confident, and protective. That year, we decided to have a New Year's Eve party. Along with many of our gay friends, I invited my sister, Lana; her husband; and some of their friends.

At one point during the festivities, Damien and I were holding hands. Lana spotted us and politely asked, "Nathan, is this your boyfriend?" I nodded.

She pulled me into my bedroom and blurted, "I have been waiting so long for you to tell me this!" She then asked if Dad knew. I said I hadn't told him but just assumed that it was obvious to everyone. Lana volunteered to make it official.

Despite my fear, I was pretty sure Dad would have no problem with the announcement. I was right. A few days later, he took Damien and me to brunch, where we all talked and laughed. Several years later, Dad entered the fray to defend me when I came out indirectly to my extended family by refuting a bigoted chain e-mail sent by my cousin. I pressed "reply all" and told everyone that people who hate gays hate me, and that it was time for them to embrace a more inclusive set of morals. Dad's support at this time, when my conservative family and the rest of the country didn't understand or accept gay people, meant everything to me.

(My grandmother came around as well. She is now my strongest advocate. But it took many pointed conversations with her for this evolution to take place. Watching her change instilled a deep optimism in me that the possibility of change resides within us all.)

But back in the early 2000s, as I was becoming a fearless advocate for animals, I was still a master of avoiding my own life. I'd learned how to defuse any situation. I learned to run, to hide, to cower, to deflect. I'm not proud of it. Still, it kept me alive and unharmed. Until, that is, I was in my mid-twenties when, during the predawn hours in downtown Dayton, Ohio, I was brutally attacked by a complete stranger, simply for being a gay man. During the assault, he threw me to the ground, shattered my nose, fractured my skull, and left my face extensively bruised and bloodied. After two facial surgeries and many weeks in and out of bed, the physical injuries of my attack faded. The memories never will.

The assailant was never charged because he was never found.

It has been said that becoming a victim of violence can shake your trust in humanity. For me, the opposite happened. In the days and months following, I experienced nothing but kindness: flowers, tearful phone messages, and deeply moving cards from kindhearted individuals from across the world, many who I had connected with over the years as an animal activist, piled up at my bedside. People shared stories of their own violent attacks, loving thoughts from their families, drawings from their children. Perhaps most endearing, I learned that a group of activists in Philadelphia had named two recently rescued goats in my honor—one, "Nathan," and the other, arguably less fortunate, "Runkle."

I appreciated the support, because I was in a lot of pain. And something else happened: The pain of others became less of an abstract concept to me, and more palpable. Pain, whether experienced by a man, woman, child, dog, or pig, is head-pounding, teeth-grinding, please-make-it-stop real. In the aftermath of my attack, I found myself connecting on an even deeper level with physically and emotionally abused animals.

MFA never meant more to me than it did now. By mid-2001, we were searching for more strategic and powerful ways to draw attention to the plight of farm animals. Fortunately, a new idea was hatching.

4.

Rebel with a Cause

In the summer of 2001, I and hundreds of energized animal-rights activists from around the world were bustling about the Hilton Hotel in Alexandria, Virginia, just outside Washington, DC. Hanging from the walls of the lobby and other public spaces were black-and-white photocopied posters announcing the premier of the documentary *Hope for the Hopeless*: *An Investigation and Rescue at a Battery Egg Facility.*

At noon I made my way down to the hotel's screening room. It was standing room only, and the excitement was palpable. As the lights dimmed, the eighteen-minute film began. Produced by the burgeoning DC-based animal-rights organization Compassion Over Killing, *Hope for the Hopeless* chronicled the late-night investigation and rescue missions of a group of activists at an egg factory farm in Maryland. The images were compelling: camera lights illuminating dark rows of cages, egg-laying hens packed in so tightly they couldn't move. Many of the birds had bloody wounds, infections, and broken bones. Others had already died and were left to rot on the cage floors. But there was hope. Young, courageous activists stood next to those cages, their faces in clear view, their eyes filled with compassion. They weren't there only to observe. They were there to intervene.

By the end of the film, I doubt there was a dry eye in the packed theater. Even in a roomful of battle-tested animal activists who had seen it all, a renewed sense of possibility was brewing. This was the debut of a new and exciting tactic for the American animal-rights movement. It was called Open Rescue.

Created in Australia two decades earlier by a pioneering animal advocate named Patty Mark, Open Rescue was based on a simple, nonviolent philosophy: providing aid to injured animals on factory farms and documenting cruelty, all while openly sharing one's identity and accepting the potential consequences of one's actions. Open Rescues were illegal, as they involved entering factory farms at night without permission. But their purpose wasn't property damage or destruction. It was simply to help and to gather evidence.

By the 1990s, the tactic was gaining momentum in America, championed by a young activist named Freeman Wicklund and his team at Compassionate Action for Animals in Minnesota, and later by Compassion Over Killing. Having seen firsthand the horrors of Ohio's egg industry, I was inspired to begin Open Rescue work myself. I didn't know how, or with whom, but I knew that it was going to happen.

When I returned from the conferences, I called Amie, Mandie, and Jim, with whom I had worked during the Buckeye Egg Farm tornado rescue. We organized a meeting at Strange Brew, an eclectic vegan restaurant housed in a former butcher shop tucked away on a side street in the small town of Springfield, Ohio.

"It's been a year since the tornado," I told them. "People have stopped talking about the plight of the animals on Ohio's egg farms. I think it's time we change that."

"What are you thinking?" Mandie asked.

"I want to do an Open Rescue," I said, and then explained how the tactic worked. As I did, I could feel the energy and excitement at the table growing.

"I'm in," said Amie.

"Me, too," added Mandie.

"Let's do this," said Jim.

Then we discussed targets. We decided that we would investigate not one but two egg farms. We already knew conditions were bad at the infamous Buckeye Egg Farm. But we also wanted to see what life was like for hens at the second-largest farm in the state: Daylay.

We spent the next month studying a makeshift manual, produced by Wicklund, on how to conduct an Open Rescue. It was far more complicated and involved than we had imagined, but we were determined to see it through. There was so much to consider: biosecurity (preventing the spread of germs), rescue supplies, video equipment, surveillance, field training, handling and finding homes for animals, publicizing our findings, and arrest and court proceedings.

To show our openness and desire to first work within the bounds of the law, we sent certified letters to both factory farms requesting a tour.

We waited patiently as our deadline approached. The day came and went. No reply. It was time to take action.

So just before one a.m. on August 18, the four of us met at Amie's house in Dublin, Ohio, just outside Columbus. Our first task was ensuring biosecurity: Because birds on factory farms are under constant stress, forced to live in overcrowded, germ-ridden sheds, it was important to protect both them and ourselves from disease. Following protocols outlined in the manual, we all showered down with antibacterial soap. Then we disinfected our clothes, boots, bags, and equipment and put on protective outerwear, rubber shoe covers, and rubber gloves. We checked our bags, ensuring we had extra gloves, breathing masks, cameras, measuring tapes, and water. The water wasn't for us. It was for animals we might find in need of aid.

When it was time, we piled into an SUV and began the hour-long drive to the sleepy town of LaRue, Ohio, population 729. LaRue was home to another of Buckeye Egg Farm's massive facilities. All the way there we listened to Moby's *Play* album, feeling unified as freedom fighters about to risk arrest and incarceration in the name of animal rights. Making our way onto the dark, backcountry roads, we turned off the music and quieted down.

"There it is," Jim said, pointing to a cluster of sixteen long, windowless, muted-green metal sheds with white roofs and industrial fans along their edges. We drove past them and down the quiet road until we found a large tree to park behind. Hearts pumping, adrenaline rushing, we gathered our bags and pulled the elastic bands of our spelunking lights over our heads. It was now almost two a.m.

We used a row of trees bordering the sheds as cover from any potential cars or sleepless neighbors. The clanking sound of metal fans filled the air, the bright lights at the foot of the sheds shining vividly on the pavement. We didn't know if we would run into security cameras or an alarm system.

I walked up to one of the white doors at the end of a shed and turned the knob. It opened, and we walked inside. Total darkness. One by one, we switched on our headlamps and took it all in. The smell was overwhelming. So were the sights. We stood in the manure pit—seven-foot-tall mountains of chicken feces stretching as far as our lights would let us see. Chickens who had escaped their cages were huddled in the corners, covered with manure. We put on our breathing masks.

The sheds consisted of two levels, the second floor confining more than 150,000 hens in cages stacked four high. Soon we were standing in what felt like an alternate reality. Cages, packed with suffering animals, surrounded us—a living nightmare brought to life courtesy of the egg industry.

As was true of more than 95 percent of the nearly 300 million egg-producing hens in the United States, the birds before us were imprisoned in crowded battery cages, long rows of wire cages holding an average of eight birds per unit. Factory farming is a business, focused on the bottom line. Egg producers have learned that if they cram more hens into a single cage, they may see less productivity per bird (because they aren't happy or healthy), but they can also expect more productivity per cage overall.

Cages are expensive. Chickens are cheap.

As we continued to walk down the narrow aisles between the

cages, we discovered dozens of hens who had become trapped and immobilized when their bodies became lodged underneath the feeding trays or when their wings became entangled in the cage wire. Once trapped like this, it is nearly impossible for a hen to free herself. With no access to food or water, trapped birds are at great risk of dying slowly from starvation or dehydration.

One trapped hen, however, was about to get a new lease on life.

When Amie first saw (the soon-to-be-named) Cecilia, she was lying at the front of her cage as seven other hens trampled her dilapidated body. She was sick and weak, small despite being an adult hen. Amie carefully picked up the small creature, and Cecilia did not resist. This was probably the first time in her life since she'd been de-beaked and crammed into the cage as a chick that she had left it or known a kind touch from a human. She didn't seem afraid. Perhaps she was too exhausted. Her legs were hanging limp. I filmed Amie as she sat Cecilia on the floor of the aisle. We wanted to see if she could stand or walk. She couldn't. Her legs collapsed beneath her.

Unable to reach the water tube at the back of her cage from where she had been lying, she was severely dehydrated. When Amie offered Cecilia some water, she immediately began to drink. But she still couldn't walk and was in obvious need of veterinary care.

It was nearly four a.m., time to leave. With farmworkers starting early, we knew we were pushing it by staying so late. We met in the manure pit and left quietly, Cecilia in tow.

The next morning, we reviewed the footage we had captured. It wasn't good. Our equipment was inadequate, and our team lacked proper video skills. We needed to up our game, and fast.

"I know a guy we might be able to borrow equipment from," said Amie.

I knew who she was talking about. I'd met Derek Coons a few months earlier at a local animal-rights meeting. A handsome tech-nerd with shaggy brown hair, Derek had grown up just a dozen miles away from me, in Piqua, Ohio. He was also a devoted animal advocate who had stopped eating meat after watching lobsters being boiled alive at his first job as a cook at the local Red Lobster restaurant. The sights and sounds of the struggling lobsters scratching their claws against the side of the pots as they tried to escape had made a traumatic impression.

Derek now hosted a show on the Columbus public-access channel that featured graphic footage of slaughterhouses and factory farms from undercover investigations. Amie reached out to him to ask about using his camera next time. But Derek had other plans: He wanted to join us. The four of us quickly decided his skills would be helpful. Our Open Rescue team had now grown to five.

Two weeks later we again met at Amie's, showered down, loaded up our supplies, and drove to the Daylay compound. Again, we parked the car behind a tree and approached the shed door. And again, the door was unlocked. As we stepped into the manure pit, closed the door, and turned on our lights, we immediately noticed something. A hen, still alive, half submerged in wet manure.

Derek turned on his camera and light as Amie made her way over to the hen. She knelt down next to the frightened bird and began to narrate.

"We're at Daylay Egg Farm in Raymond, Ohio, and we are on the bottom floor of the building where the manure pits are. All the cages are directly above us. One of the hens has fallen out of a cage, there are other dead hens around, but she is still alive." Amie was visibly shaken. "She is trapped in the manure. There are flies everywhere. The manure is wet, so her body is stuck and she can't get out. We are going to try to get her out right now."

Amie carefully reached her gloved hands into the wet manure. "Oh, her whole body is just sunk into there," Amie said, her voice shaking as she fought to hold back tears. "The flies and bugs from the manure are all over her skin."

Mandie, Jim, and I stood behind Derek as he filmed. The hen's dark eyes stared back at us with a look mingling trust and fear. Her breath was shallow. We wanted to get her out of there as fast as possible. We wanted her to know that there was something better. Surely no creature should have to exist knowing nothing but pain and suffering.

But it was too late. We couldn't save her. The hen took her last, weak breaths in Amie's arms.

We all worked to compose ourselves. There was still much work to be done. We made our way to the second floor and began documenting the abuse. At this farm, conditions were even more shocking than at Buckeye. The cages in each shed were stacked seven tiers high, a sliding ladder attached to them to allow workers to reach the hens in the top cages. More than 250,000 birds were packed in the shed we were now inspecting. And here, even more hens were confined to a single cage. The suffering was palpable, and overwhelming.

Illness and injuries were rampant. In an attempt to minimize costs and maximize profit, even the sickest of hens were denied veterinary care in factory farms like this one. Some of the most pervasive illnesses were terrible eye and sinus infections. These ailments were caused by the filth saturating the air—the high concentrations of ammonia had triggered inflammation in the chickens' bodies, leading to difficulty in resisting infection, which was only compounded by the enormous amount of dust and debris they were forced to breathe. Sick animals were left to die.

BUZZZZZ. BUZZZZZ.

It was 4:15 a.m. The vibrating alarm I had set on my watch was going off. We quickly packed up our things and got out without a hitch. We now had a team, and a rhythm.

We returned to Buckeye Egg Farm and Daylay Egg farm three more times between late August and mid-September 2001. Cameras rolling, we documented many hours' worth of appalling conditions, rescuing a total of thirty-four animals along the way.

All thirty-four of the hens were diagnosed with the bacterial disease caused by *Pasteurella* and were treated for ten days with penicillin. Eleven hens underwent surgery. Two blind hens had to have their eyes drained. Two others were found to have acute vitamin deficiencies and received injections. Others succumbed to their ailments.

The surviving hens were moved to local animal sanctuaries, where they recovered beautifully, their wounds healing and their white feathers returning. "The girls," as they came to be known, were given a new life in which they were able to walk around freely, dust bathe, perch, and socialize with their new friends. They were the lucky few.

We had the evidence. Now it was time to turn our attention toward telling, and showing, the public what we had seen.

On October 18, 2001, Mandie, Jim, Derek, Amie, and I put on our nicest clothes and headed to the Ohio Statehouse in Columbus for a press conference we had organized. We didn't know what to expect. Would anyone show up? Would they care? Would police be waiting to arrest us? We were prepared for anything.

We made our way to the statehouse atrium, where a barrage of TV news cameras were lined up in front of the speaker's podium. Newspaper reporters, tape recorders in hand, filled the seats. Our press release had worked—we finally had a platform to tell the stories of the animals we'd rescued and of those we had had to leave behind. These animals now had a voice.

The press response was encouraging: Our work made headlines around the state. Radio stations broadcast reports that were heard from small towns to big cities. The investigative unit of Ohio's largest television news station prepared an in-depth exposé based on our findings. For weeks they aired commercials featuring footage we had taken during our late-night missions. They also ran full-page ads in Ohio's largest newspaper, the *Columbus Dispatch*, promoting "The Video the Egg Industry Doesn't Want You to See."

People were finally seeing the hidden costs of cheap eggs. We felt empowered, but we wanted more. We wanted the farms to be held responsible for what they had done to Cecilia and the other hens. We wanted them to be charged with criminal animal cruelty.

On the same day as our press conference, I'd sent letters to law enforcement in the counties where Buckeye and Daylay were based, outlining the myriad abuses that, MFA maintained, violated the state's anticruelty laws. As proof, I enclosed video footage along with statements we'd gathered from veterinarians and animal welfare experts, urging prosecution.

But the winds soon shifted. One late October evening my cell phone rang. A detective was on the other end, informing us that a criminal investigation had been opened... but not into conditions at Buckeye or Daylay. The Licking County Sherriff's Department was gathering evidence to prosecute MFA for our actions. We were the potentially guilty ones now.

It was time to seek legal counsel. We met with Paul Leonard, a seasoned attorney who was also a former mayor of Dayton. He had a soft spot for animals and had agreed to talk to us free of charge.

The news wasn't good, however. Paul told us that rescuing animals from a factory farm could be considered burglary (as the chickens were the farm's "property"). And trespassing through unlocked doors could be considered "breaking and entering." We could each be facing up to thirty years in prison for these crimes.

"You broke the law," Paul said. "I'm not sure what the best legal defense would be. We can claim the 'Good Samaritan Defense,' but that's always a gamble."

The law he was referencing was a little-known statute that says a citizen is justified in breaking a law if the actions are taken to help save the life of someone in imminent, mortal danger. The defense was rarely used, even less so when the victim was an animal, let alone a chicken.

We'd known there were risks. But then weeks and months passed without charges being filed against us. Eventually the detectives stopped calling. I can only speculate why: The egg farms realized that dragging us into court would only renew scrutiny of their mistreatment of animals. The trial, and resulting media attention, wouldn't be worth it.

. . .

At the same time as I was leading Mercy For Animals, I had
been growing up—or at least trying to. Physically, I had shot up
from an undersized boy to a nearly six-foot-tall teenager. Emotionally, I was struggling to understand who I was and where I was going.
When I was young, I'd been fully aware that I was different from
other kids. I never fit in at school. This was one reason I was homeschooled and why I never considered going to college. With my heart
set on helping the only real friends I had—animals—I felt as though
those four years of study could be better spent in the real world mas-
tering the ropes of activism. MFA felt like my child. I knew it needed
constant attention to grow and mature. If I abandoned it for college,
it might well wither and die. Besides, there was no such thing as a
bachelor of science in animal advocacy.

It was time to hone my craft and build my organization; to do that,
I decided I should apprentice myself to the largest and most famous
animal-rights organization in the world: People for the Ethical Treatment of Animals, or PETA. Established in 1980, PETA was cofounded
and run by the British American animal-protection advocate Ingrid
Newkirk.

For three years, starting at age fifteen, I split my time between
nurturing MFA and working directly with PETA. I traveled around
the country with senior staffers to help them coordinate and lead
scores of always eye-catching (and often controversial) demonstrations. For example, in the summer of 2000, one of my mentors, PETA

vice president Bruce Friedrich, asked me to go to the Southern Baptist Convention in New Orleans. The mission: Dress up as Jesus and hold a sign reading BLESSED ARE THE MERCIFUL—GO VEGETARIAN… all day, every day of the three-day convention. The atmosphere was hot, humid, and hostile. The Baptists kept approaching us and reading us quotations from the Bible—proving, they said, the spiritual virtues of eating animals. It was exhausting and frustrating, and I didn't make a very convincing Jesus.

After the second day, I told Bruce I'd had enough. So he put me in a chicken costume. Going from Jesus to a chicken was a good move. The costume was hot, but I preferred heatstroke to hearing all these people tell me that Jesus wanted them to eat meat.

Not far from us a group of gay activists was practicing civil disobedience. One by one, they would walk peacefully up to the entrance of the convention center, try to go in, and be refused entry. They were then arrested, one after another. I started crying inside my chicken costume. I was so moved by these people, all willing to stand up for, and be arrested for, gay rights. Standing up for *me*, at a time when I wouldn't stand up for myself.

Inspired by what I learned at PETA, I began organizing and leading more colorful protests of my own. In the freezing Ohio winter, I led "I'd Rather Go Naked Than Wear Fur" protests. As the campaign slogan implies, the demonstrations center on a stunt: stripping naked in public to protest fur sales. The idea is you'd rather wear nothing at all than support an industry that profits off gassing, trapping, clubbing, and skinning innocent animals alive for their pelts. I was too young to strip down myself: The law forbade it. So I convinced others (including my brother-in-law, a buff all-American football player) to shed *their* clothes and stand out in the snow in their underwear. Covered only by a vinyl banner bearing the campaign slogan, my partners in activism stood there for hours with their lips turning blue and their bodies nearly going into shock. The outrageous stunts (performed all over the country, not just by my little crew) proved successful, generating national headlines. We were putting the issue of animal cruelty in the fur industry on the public radar right as the holiday shopping season was about to begin.

Another time, during a 2001 campaign to pressure Burger King into adopting minimal animal-welfare standards, I was dispatched to a local elementary school along with Caroline, a sixty-five-year-old volunteer stuffed into a brown cow costume. The mission: distribute bloody "Murder King" crowns to kids as a media stunt. The crowns featured images of bloody, dead animals impaled on the crowns' golden spikes. The stunt lasted only minutes but did the trick. Parents, teachers, and the principal weren't happy, but the press loved it. They swarmed Caroline and me as the kids grabbed the crowns. That night, every local TV station carried the story. They also aired graphic undercover footage: cows hung upside down at slaughterhouses, chickens crammed in cages, and pigs locked in stalls at Burger King suppliers. A few weeks later, Burger King agreed to make changes.

Then there were the naked tiger women. I was traveling the country with PETA, standing anywhere from the front lawn of the White House to downtown intersections in cities from Memphis to Los Angeles. We were shadowing the Ringling Bros. and Barnum & Bailey

Circus, showing up a week before they did in each city. The goal: to get people thinking about the miserable lives endured by tigers, elephants, and other animals held captive by circuses. These animals were not only forced to perform unnatural acts but also "trained" to do so using violence and intimidation, their spirits broken by beatings and deprivation.

My job was as makeup artist: painting naked women up as tigers. First I'd brush on a solid coat of orange paint, followed by the all-important black stripes. A black nose and whiskers topped off the look. I traveled with the painted tigers to each protest location, helped them disrobe, and then lowered a small, makeshift wire cage over them. I'd hold up a banner behind them reading WILD ANIMALS DON'T BELONG IN CAGES. BOYCOTT THE CIRCUS. Once again, the protests captured the media's attention (as well as the interest of creepy men hoping to catch a glimpse of naked women). Every now and then, the authorities would arrest one of the naked tigers for indecent exposure, leaving me to speak with the press, deal with the cops, and bail the tiger out of jail. (More than a decade later—after facing hundreds of protests and declining attendance—Ringling permanently closed down, after 146 years.)

As I said, these tactics were controversial. That was the point: to grab the attention of the media and public just long enough to get people to consider the plight of animals on factory farms or in circuses. We didn't care what people thought of us. We cared that they thought about the animals they were eating, wearing, or exploiting for entertainment. And it worked.

So while other teenagers were stuck in classrooms studying textbooks and taking notes during lectures, I was already out in the world, having dived headfirst into working for social change. I was learning complicated adult lessons in activism, campaign strategy, public relations, mass media, and corporate relations. And I was able to travel around the country, even if that sometimes meant seeing it through the eyeholes of an animal costume.

Inspired by what I learned at PETA, I began planning my own stunts. Every year the Ohio Pork Congress holds a weekend-long event at the Dayton Convention Center. The congress features demonstrations and exhibits on the latest technology in factory-style farming: gestation crates, farrowing crates, antibiotics, and so on. Then there's a dinner banquet capped by the crowning of a Pork Queen.

MFA used to stage annual protests at the congress. We'd hold a candlelight vigil outside the convention center, not only as a tribute to the pigs but also to create a powerful visual for the local news media. If we were lucky, the papers and TV stations would show up, film us for a few minutes, take comments, and then report on the plight of pigs on factory farms.

In February 2002, we decided to up the stakes. In a time before social media and YouTube, the only way to be seen and heard by the masses was through the mainstream media. I'd learned from PETA and our Open Rescues that to generate even fleeting coverage, we had to take dramatic steps. That meant putting our reputation, dignity, and even freedom on the line. To expose the cruelty endured by animals to an audience larger than the congress attendees, and to capture the same type of thirty-second news clip that had opened my heart to animal rights, I planned to take steps that would place me back in the crosshairs of the law.

The plan was to infiltrate the banquet hall and disrupt the dinner (as well as the crowning of the Pork Queen). Amie and I were the key players. I would be in charge of the video camera, while Amie was to star in the disruption.

Before the dinner started, Amie boldly walked onstage and announced, "I would like to propose a toast..." The room immediately went silent. Glasses were raised. Anticipation filled the air. Amie continued, "to the over one hundred million pigs your violent, bloody industry kills every year for nothing more than a palate preference."

Amie then unfurled a banner picturing a sow locked in a filthy crate, captioned CHOOSE COMPASSION OVER KILLING. PLEASE, GO VEGAN. By this time, the audience had become enraged.

Amie didn't stop.

"Pork producers, you have a lot to be ashamed of," she yelled. "What you do to pigs before they become dinner is offensive. They never take a breath of fresh air until they're on the back of a truck headed for slaughter. After living in a putrid-smelling hell, they are finally hung upside down and their throats slit, often while they are fully conscious."

Meanwhile, I filmed the entire scene, including the part where two massive security guards came onstage and began dragging Amie off into the wings as she struggled to keep talking.

The plan had been to pass the videotape of the fracas to the national news media and gain valuable press coverage. But just as I was about to leave quietly, tape in hand, someone in the audience spotted me and my camera.

"Get him!" he yelled. "He's with her!"

Amie was no longer the target; I was. I sprinted toward the exit, followed by scores of pork producers who quickly stood up, pushing chairs together in the crowded banquet hall, trying desperately to prevent me from escaping. Finally, three of them tackled me to the ground. I couldn't move: I was smothered by a thousand pounds' worth of pork producers. Someone then ripped the video camera from my hand.

Amie was able to escape the convention center, but I was arrested. While being detained, I asked for my camera back. An hour later one of the pork people returned it, along with a tape. It wasn't mine. It didn't even fit in my camera. No one ever saw the real tape again.

Because I was two months shy of eighteen at the time, I ended up being taken into juvenile detention.

My mom had died a month before. My dad was still in Montana. So Grandma was the only guardian around, and the other MFA activists called to notify her. Frightened by the news, she agreed to come get me. She had to drive for an hour, and by the time she arrived at the detention center, it was clear she had been crying most of the way. She was terrified that I had gone the route of a criminal.

Before leaving to take me home, she asked the police officer, "As a grandparent, what can I do to redirect him?"

The officer replied, "If protecting animals is his passion, you shouldn't interfere."

After we left the building, I gave my grandma a proper introduction to my (much older) activist family. Linda, another activist and a mother herself, told my grandma that she would be proud if I were her son. At that moment my grandma understood—this was my calling.

So, apparently, did the judge in my case, who turned out to be a vegetarian. My "sentence" was to write a letter of apology to the Ohio Pork Producers Council. I replied that the only apology I was prepared to offer was to the animals I was unable to protect from this violent industry. The judge, who appreciated the sincere beliefs behind my misbehavior, then compelled me to write a two-page essay on the First Amendment right to peaceful protest under the Constitution. I used the assignment as an opportunity to discuss the historical importance of civil disobedience, citing the examples of Dr. Martin Luther King Jr., Rosa Parks, and Mahatma Gandhi.

I also received a fine of $25. I paid it and went on with my activism.

Our next big action came in December 2002. A year had passed since our last Open Rescue, and we were ready to step back inside an egg factory farm.

The reason: After taking a beating in the press over its animal cruelty, the egg industry had responded by developing an "Animal Care Certified" program, complete with a special label featuring a jaunty check mark. Packages marked with that label contain eggs from hens who had supposedly been raised "humanely." The concept sounded great to consumers, but a little research revealed it did virtually nothing to help animals and was a public-relations gimmick. The program required participating producers to remove just one hen from each overcrowded cage—a far cry from the definition of proper "animal care" envisioned by most shoppers.

Derek and I knew this scam had to be exposed. We decided to enter and collect footage at Ohio's third-largest egg producer, Weaver Brothers, which was now stamping the certification logo on every carton of eggs they produced.

Since our last major action, Mandie and Jim had moved north, and Amie was now focused on raising her family. So this time it would be just Derek and me.

On the night of the planned action, we showered down, disinfected our equipment, packed our bags, and headed toward Versailles, Ohio. Fifteen miles west of where Derek was raised, Versailles is a small, conservative town on the Indiana border. With fewer than twenty-six hundred residents, the community takes great pride in its chicken industry, hosting an annual Poultry Days Festival each June. The festival includes a carnival, a parade, the crowning of a Ms. Chick and Little Miss Chick, and the production of more than twenty-five thousand slow-roasted chicken dinners.

Needless to say, vegan animal liberators weren't welcome.

We drove my black RAV4 along the windy, backcountry roads until we spotted the Weaver Brothers factory farm. Then we parked the car in a small wooded area off the side of the road, grabbed our bags, and walked to the back of one of the sheds where chickens were housed. It was now just past one a.m. I cautiously turned the handle on a door. It opened.

Derek and I make our way up to the level where the hens were housed. Conditions seemed even worse than what we had seen at Buckeye and Daylay. The birds were covered in excrement and were packed so tightly in the old, worn-out cages that many were standing on top of each other. As we walked toward the front of the shed, we noticed a shopping cart. Inside was a mound of dead birds, dripping blood pooling on the ground in front of it.

As Derek's camera rolled, I noticed a small, dust-covered trapdoor in the floor. I pulled it open and shone my flashlight inside. This was no secret escape route. It was a cold, dark resting place for thousands of victims of the egg industry. Trash bins, packed to their brims with insect-infested bodies, filled the dugout. The floor was crawling with bugs and thoroughly littered with dirt, feathers, and the decomposing bodies of dead hens.

I noticed movement in one of the trash bins. A live hen was trapped inside. I would have easily mistaken this hen for a lifeless corpse had she not lifted her tiny head from atop the pile and blinked at me curiously.

I wasn't going to let her die.

The blast of the ventilation fans became louder and the temperature cooler as I lowered myself into the dugout. It was becoming increasingly difficult to hold back tears. I maneuvered my way between the cans, preparing to lift the hen to safety.

I spoke into the camera as Derek filmed, standing behind an old oil drum that had been converted into a trash bin. "We are in this dugout area where there are trash cans with dead hens in them. And when we opened the door we noticed this hen, who is still alive, on top of all the dead ones."

I reached my hands into the cold, rusted-steel bin and gently began to stroke her remaining feathers.

"She barely has any energy," I narrated. "She can hardly move. So we are going to lift her out of this trash can and get her some help."

As I reached under her body and lifted her from the can, I spoke softly to assure her everything would be okay. This hen was obviously underweight. She did not struggle. She didn't have the strength. Protected in my arms, she would soon be headed home with me.

Later, safe at last in the comfort of her temporary haven at my parents' place, the hen allowed us to clip her dirty, overgrown nails before we gave her a warm bath to remove the hardened feces that had become caked on her feathers, under her wings, and on her belly. Perhaps for the first time in her life, she touched the ground and was able to fully stretch her wings and move freely. She did little walking, though, for she was visibly fragile, weak, and exhausted.

Though she had made it out of Weaver Brothers alive, her survival was not assured. I carefully offered her a small amount of water through a narrow syringe. She lifted her weary, shaky head as she drank dropperful after dropperful. The next day I fed her a vitamin drink. Her energy increased, and her personality began to show. In just those few short hours, her trust in me had grown. Her health more stable, she was ready to make the trip to the veterinarian for treatment.

Dr. Peterson, better known as Dr. P., was waiting for us when we arrived at Troy Animal Hospital. I brought the green cat carrier holding the hen into the examining room and gently set it on the sterile, stainless-steel table. Dr. P. opened the carrier door and lifted the hen onto the table.

"Poor thing," said Dr. P., her eyes tearing up before she began the examination and blood tests.

After an extensive evaluation, the hen was diagnosed with eye and sinus infections as well as extensive bruising and abrasions on her wings and feet. Dr. P. confirmed that the hen was emaciated, weak, and suffering from severe muscle trauma. A fecal examination revealed the parasite coccidia. The hen then received fluid injections to help rehydrate her underweight body and give her much-needed strength. For five days, she was nurtured in a warm isolation ward and treated with medication.

We named the hen Hope, after our dream that one day there will be no more egg factories, no more battery cages, and no more animal exploitation. Hope went to live at Sunrise Sanctuary in Marysville, Ohio, run by Mindy Mallet. Mindy is a joyful woman, full of sincerity and love, and Hope flourished under her care. She soon developed friendships with the other animals and came running whenever her name was called. She was happy and free.

We still needed to collect more evidence of abuse before we could blow the lid off the egg industry's "Animal Care Certified" scam. And that meant we had to go back to Weaver Brothers.

Derek and I followed our routine preparations, drove back to Versailles, and parked my black RAV4 next to the same tree. We walked along the tree line, darted across the now-cleared cornfield, and again entered through the manure pits and made our way up toward the cages.

For the next two hours, we gathered more footage of the sickening cruelty to which the hens were subjected, now under the "Animal Care Certified" label. By 3:45 a.m., we were ready to leave. We lowered ourselves into the manure pit. We thought we were safe and breathed sighs of relief.

Then, a flash! The lights inside the shed snapped on. We heard talking and footsteps overhead. Had we been caught? Quietly, nervously, holding our breath, we opened the manure pit door and slipped outside.

Derek and I ran in a half crouch back across the field toward my car. But up ahead we saw not one but four vehicles. My car was surrounded by a police squad car and two others, headlights blasting. We stopped short.

Wearing our Mercy For Animals T-shirts and spelunking lights, covered in chicken manure, and sporting backpacks containing video footage from inside the sheds, Derek and I were in deep trouble, facing immediate arrest and possibly years in prison. Worse yet, it would all be for nothing—the evidence of animal abuse we had just taken would surely be destroyed.

We had to get away from the factory farm, fast. So we ran, knees bent, backs bent forward to make ourselves as small as possible, across the open cornfield toward a small woods behind the sheds.

At the edge of the woods there was a steep drop-off. We jumped down. Derek peeked his head over the edge long enough to see that there were now men with flashlights searching the farm premises.

"What are we going to do?" I whispered.

"I don't know, but I have to work in the morning," Derek answered.

Derek worked a day job at a technology company. He took his role there very seriously.

"It's going to be hard to work from jail," I said. "We have to get the hell out of here."

We made our way to the other side of the woods and out the back, then toward a road in the distance. We walked for miles before entering what would be considered the main street of a small town: a few brick buildings, a bank, and a gas station where we found a pay phone (our cell phone batteries had died).

Derek called his mom, Debbie, who lived in nearby Piqua. "Hi, Mom, sorry to wake you," he said. "Nathan and I need a favor. Can you come pick us up in Versailles, right now? I'll explain when you get here. Just hurry."

Debbie is a sweet woman. But being asked to come pick up her lawbreaking son in the middle of the night, along with the teenager who encouraged him in a life of well-meaning crime, wasn't her idea of a cheery wake-up call.

We retreated out of sight and kept an eye on the gas station from a distance. Twenty minutes later, Debbie arrived. We jumped into her car, covered in a mixture of chicken manure, dirt, and cobwebs, and slammed the doors closed.

We had escaped. But as I showered in Debbie's bathroom, the gravity of the situation began to sink in. What about my car? All the authorities needed to do was run my license plates. I had already made a name for myself as an animal activist—not to mention that two weeks earlier, MFA had sent letters to Weaver Brothers, asking for a tour.

If I returned to get the car, I would certainly be arrested on the spot.

Next it was my turn to make an uncomfortable phone call, this one to my dad, who was still living in Montana.

"Hi, Dad," I said. "Derek and I were doing an investigation at an egg farm again and we kinda ran into an issue."

"Okay," said my always calm and supportive father.

"I need someone to go pick up my car. I can't do it," I said.

My dad then called my uncle—the one who had exposed me to the world of hunting as a kid, who was a card-carrying member of the National Rifle Association and couldn't disagree with me more on the issue of animal rights. Reluctantly, he agreed. Since he wasn't involved in the break-in, he figured there wasn't anything the police could do.

Later that afternoon he showed up with the RAV4, thoroughly upset.

"Thank you for getting the car," I said.

"Don't ever ask me to do that again," my uncle replied. "As soon as I pulled up to get it, a cop car showed up. He asked if I'd ever heard of PETA, then took a copy of my driver's license and questioned me." But they'd let him go.

I forced a smile, thanked him again, and hoped that was the end of it.

The next afternoon my cell phone rang. "Private" number. I didn't answer, letting the call go to voice mail. I nervously checked the message later that afternoon.

"Mr. Runkle, this is Detective Rogers at the United States Department of Homeland Security," the angry female voice said. "You need to call me back right away."

I didn't.

Then a local detective started calling. Again, I ignored the calls.

Derek and I, nervous about the fate that lay ahead of us, began preparing to release the video we shot of conditions at Weaver Brothers egg farm. We compiled the footage, built a Web site, and planned our press conference.

The story broke in a major Ohio newspaper, the *Toledo Blade*, with the headline "Henhouse Tapes Point to Cruelty." The article included images taken inside the factory farm alongside a picture of the "Animal Care Certified" logo. Other stories about the sad fate of Ohio's egg-laying hens once again made headlines across the state. Our struggles were paying off.

Soon after, the Better Business Bureau ruled that the ACC logo was misleading to consumers. Not long after that, the Federal Trade Commission decided the same thing. The label was discontinued, and the egg industry walked away defeated.

We'd triumphed, but, just the same, it would be years before we ventured back inside an egg factory farm.

By 2003, Mercy For Animals was taking on a life of its own. While we still had no paid staff, our reputation and support base were growing throughout Ohio. We now had regional chapters in more than a half-dozen cities. At this stage, I had not yet formulated a long-term vision or plan for MFA beyond aiming to outdo ourselves each year—becoming larger, smarter, and more effective. It was simply a matter of putting one foot in front of the other.

At the time, MFA's work wasn't limited to protecting farm animals. We also protested the fur industry, circuses, and rodeos. Ohio's rodeo industry was brutal: bulls, steers, and horses were routinely jabbed with electrical prods, smeared with caustic ointments, and girdled with tightly cinched belts that squashed their groins and genitals to make these naturally docile creatures exhibit wild behavior. Broken ribs, massive bruising, and internal bleeding were common among these animals. Then, once their "entertainment" value had been thoroughly used up, they were sold to slaughterhouses.

For months, I attended rodeos to gather evidence of cruelty, talking my way into the back of the arena and using a hidden camera to document workers beating bulls with long metal pipes and shocking calves with electric cattle prods. We released the footage to the media, calling for legislation to ban rodeos and for major corporate sponsors to end their partnerships with these events. Neither happened. The industry was too powerful, and our protests didn't inspire enough people to act.

I was beginning to feel as though we were spinning our wheels. To put it another way, between topics and tactics, we were spread too thin. We needed to sharpen our focus. It came down to a simple calculation: How could we do the most good? Reduce the most suffering? Spare the most lives?

After much deliberation, Mercy For Animals decided to focus exclusively on farm animal protection issues. No more rodeo, circus, or fur industry campaigns. Our reasoning was simple: Every year in the United States alone, nearly nine billion land animals are raised and killed for food. (If you add the number of fish killed, the figure jumps manyfold.) These farm animals feel pain, loneliness, sadness, and terror in exactly the same way as any other creature: a pig the same as a dog, a chicken the same as a cat, a cow the same as an elephant. They all value their lives and their freedom and deserve to be protected from exploitation or abuse. While our society places arbitrary price tags on the lives of certain animals (like purebred dogs or exotic birds), some valued at thousands of dollars and others at only pennies, our ethical concern for them should be the same. We realized that the only meaningful difference between farm animals and companion animals was our perception of them—and these varying perceptions left farm animals vulnerable to unspeakable cruelty, in astronomical numbers.

This shift was an important step for MFA, but we knew it was going to be a difficult sell. It was easy to convince people that dogs and cats matter. But farm animals? Far more difficult. Yet these poor creatures had the fewest protections from abuse. Many people who think of themselves as animal lovers will donate generously to local humane societies but consider farmed-animal advocacy too fringe, too radical, or simply too impractical. But that's where our efforts were needed most. We refined our mission statement to "preventing cruelty to farm animals and promoting compassionate food choices and policies."

Finned Friends

The Earth is a blue planet; more than 70 percent of its surface is covered by water. Below that surface, just out of our sight, is an incredible world inhabited by beautiful,

(continued)

intelligent creatures. Life began in these oceans, and over the eons has evolved into more than thirty thousand species of fish—more than all mammals, birds, reptiles, and amphibians combined. Yet few people give much consideration to who and what these animals really are,

Animal ethnologist Jonathan Balcombe is different. In his book, *What a Fish Knows*, Jonathan sheds light on the fascinating world of fish. He describes how fish conduct elaborate courtship rituals, how they develop lifelong bonds with shoal-mates, as well as their ability to plan, hunt cooperatively, use tools, curry favor, deceive one another, and punish wrongdoers.

Despite these remarkable traits, humans have been catching and killing fish throughout our history. No one knows exactly how many fish die each year because catches are measured in combined weight, not individuals, but many estimates place the number in the trillions. Many are killed in the ocean by massive trawler nets, which indiscriminately catch and kill any living creature in their paths. This means that along with the fish targeted for capture, whales, dolphins, turtles, and sharks are also killed, and often in gruesome ways: crushed to death in nets as they are pulled up from the ocean depths, or, if they survive the nets, they are hacked apart or frozen while still alive on ships. Still millions of other fish are raised in factory-farm conditions: crowded into filthy tanks by the thousands. They endure stress, injury, parasites, and violent handling.

Fish deserve to be more than food. They deserve our compassion.

Now fully committed to helping animals within our food system, MFA stepped up our game by using the media in a series of new, creative, and hard-hitting campaigns. As we grew, we developed and released pro-vegetarian commercials on networks including MTV, BET, and Animal Planet, as well as placing print ads on buses.

These projects—which allowed us to reach thousands or millions of people for just a few pennies each—helped elevate the awareness of MFA and our work to the mainstream. The commercials were simple and produced on the office computer in our spare bedroom in the apartment Derek and I were now sharing. They consisted of slow-motion images of animals on factory farms locked in tiny cages looking helplessly into the camera. Violin music played while simple text appeared on the screen. "Behind closed doors," it said, "animals are suffering." Viewers were urged, "Please help them. Please go vegetarian." The commercial ended by promoting our free vegetarian starter kit. Requests flooded in as the ads were launched—first in Ohio, then Illinois, then nationally. Supporters came out of the woodwork to make donations to fund the ads—which we secured at a rate special for nonprofit organizations and negotiated for some of the ads to run for free as public service announcements during nighttime hours.

We released short documentaries on the findings of our egg farm investigations and continued our grassroots outreach efforts on campuses and at festivals and concerts. But we always knew that eventually we would need to get back inside the factory farms we were opposing to prove that the abuse we had documented was still taking place. It was just a matter of when and where.

In the fall of 2004, Buckeye Egg Farm was back in the news but not because of MFA. A year earlier, state officials had ordered Buckeye to cease production of eggs. After years of neighbors' complaints, court contempt rulings, and lawsuits over the stench, fly infestations, and manure spills at the farm, Buckeye was finally closing its doors.

But the saga wasn't over. While the farm was being sold, it was expected to resume production after investments were made in upgraded facilities such as new cages, fans, and manure disposal protocols. The new farm, pleasantly named Ohio Fresh Eggs, was soon being billed as the egg industry's golden child. Once more, we decided to investigate. Once more, we found horrible conditions despite claims to the contrary. Once more, we were almost caught, yet managed to escape at the last moment. And, once more, we released our footage to the news media, which ran stories across the state about the late-night adventures of the "Hen House Raiders" and the plight of the tiny victims we sought to help.

But it was becoming clear that Open Rescues were becoming too dangerous. By 2004, activists in Upstate New York and Northern California were being formally charged with criminal trespass, breaking and entering, and burglary for their Open Rescue work. Some were even tried and convicted and had to spend months in prison. Although we still firmly believed in the philosophy of Open Rescue, it was a tactic whose time had come and gone. MFA could do more good for animals outside of a jail cell than in one.

We needed a new approach.

Then came Pete.

Pete first got in touch with me in 2004 after hearing about our Open Rescue work on Ohio Public Radio. He had called to say how impressed he was with our missions and to offer his services as an investigator. He also mentioned that he had already gone undercover at more than four hundred puppy mills around the country. (These mills are like factory farms for dogs, who are later sold as pets.)

I was deeply suspicious. Pete seemed too perfect. Perhaps he was an FBI agent trying to infiltrate us. Plenty of other activist organizations had been permeated by government authorities posing as sympathizers to their cause. Given MFA's history, we had to be sure that everyone who worked for us was truly on our side. So I asked Pete for more information. He was responsive, but I never got back to him. I just didn't trust him.

Then, two years later, I received a phone call from Ritchie Laymon. She told me that she had run into someone from an organization called Companion Animal Protection Society (CAPS) who had told her that CAPS had recently hired an investigator looking to do undercover work at Petland stores in the area. (Petland is a chain of pet-supply stores said to sell animals purchased from puppy mills.) Because this was a long-term assignment, CAPS needed to find him an inexpensive place to stay. Would I be willing to house him?

I agreed. My place was already a common stopover for activists.

A few days later, I heard a sturdy knock on the front door. I took a deep breath and opened it. Before me stood a short, handsome, muscular man in his mid-twenties wearing a camo jacket and a baseball hat. Behind him, I spotted a big white pickup truck with a dirt bike strapped in the back. It was Pete.

Until now, the only guys I knew who looked like Pete were narrow-minded, meat-eating hunters who wanted to beat me up. Indeed, in many ways Pete and I were complete opposites. He was straight and short. I was tall and gay. He liked Slipknot death metal. I liked dance music. He liked dirt biking. I liked yoga. What had I gotten myself into?

As it happened, Pete and I became close friends and allies. Our commitment to helping animals bonded us on a deep level. In the evenings, Pete and I engaged in long, philosophical conversations about our lives and goals. Pete confessed that the reason he wanted to help CAPS was that he felt he related better to animals than he did to people. The shortest guy in school, like me he had been bullied when younger and couldn't stand the idea of anyone harming a helpless creature. Inside Pete's rough exterior was a truly soft heart—especially for dogs. I've never met anyone whom animals took to as much as they did Pete.

Pete was so determined to help dogs that he was willing to put his life aside to become an undercover investigator—something that took serious mental and emotional sacrifice. Thus far, he'd been very successful, including becoming the subject of a 2006 HBO documentary called *Dealing Dogs*, about Class B dealers, or people who collect or steal companion animals and then sell them to medical research labs.

A few months after wrapping up the Petland case, Pete took a one-off assignment with a farm-animal-protection organization. The case was prompted by a whistle-blower at an Ohio pig farm who alleged the farm owners were killing injured pigs execution-style, wrapping chains around their necks and hanging them from tractors. Pete packed his bags, headed north, and landed a job at the pig farm to gain access to its inner workings.

That was Pete's first factory-farm investigation. He was horrified by what he saw. On the weekends, Pete would come back to my apartment, where we'd review the damning hidden-camera footage he'd collected. This evidence led to a criminal case that would later become the focus of *Death on a Factory Farm*, another HBO documentary.

I was impressed by Pete and decided to try to convince him to join us at MFA. I explained that he could have a much bigger impact, and reduce far more suffering, if he focused on farm animal cases exclusively. When it came to misery, I said, a pig was no different than a dog. But when it came to numbers, three thousand times more farm animals than companion animals were abused and killed each year.

Pete listened, thought it over, and made a commitment to join us.

With Pete on board, MFA had now stepped into a new era of undercover investigations—a tactic that carries a rich history of exposing cruelty and corruption, while also driving change. This crucial moment forever changed our organization—as well as the American meat industry.

||||||||||||

STILL IN THE JUNGLE

5.

Undercover

Sunlight is said to be the best of disinfectants.

—Louis D. Brandeis, former associate justice
of the Supreme Court of the United States

n 1904, an ambitious young investigative journalist rolled up his sleeves and for seven weeks prowled the streets of Chicago's Packingtown, a residential district next to the stockyards and meatpacking plants. Donning overalls, he posed as a worker and slipped into the slaughterhouses to gain firsthand knowledge of the work. He soon witnessed the inhumane treatment endured by pigs and cattle, the dangerous and dehumanizing conditions faced by workers, and the filthy, unsanitary conditions, from severed fingers to tuberculosis and blood poisoning.

This undercover investigator was Upton Sinclair, who went on to write about the nation's largest slaughterhouses in disturbing detail. His manuscript contained fictional characters and plot lines, but the conditions Sinclair exposed in the meat industry were anything but fictional. Suspicious of the unsavory slaughterhouse details and worried about potential lawsuits from meatpackers, his publisher, Frank Doubleday, of Doubleday, Page and Co., agreed to release the book only if he was able to verify Sinclair's gruesome accounts. One of Doubleday's editors then traveled to Chicago and interviewed a former government meat inspector, who confirmed that Sinclair's version was, in fact, quite truthful. Still not satisfied, the editor secured his own inspector's badge and prowled through the sprawling packing plants. His conclusion: Things were as bad as Sinclair had reported, and perhaps even worse.

The book, titled *The Jungle*, was published on January 25, 1906. It was an immediate sensation, reaching all the way to President Theodore Roosevelt. After reading it, Roosevelt consulted with the United States Department of Agriculture (USDA), which assured him that meatpacking was carefully inspected and meat was safe to eat. Unconvinced, Roosevelt launched his own investigation and found, in the president's own words, that "the method of handling and preparing food products is uncleanly and dangerous to health."

Just six months after *The Jungle* was published, Roosevelt signed into law both the Federal Meat Inspection Act and the Pure Food and Drug Act—the first federal laws aimed at improving food safety and conditions inside meatpacking plants. Roosevelt described these laws as marking "a noteworthy advance in the policy of securing Federal supervision and control over corporations."

More than 110 years have passed since *The Jungle*'s publication, but the darkness, secrecy, abuse, and corruption still exist not only in our nation's slaughterhouses but in our factory farms. And animal-cruelty laws in the United States remain thoroughly inadequate. At the federal level, there is practically zero protection for farm animals. The federal law that you might think would protect farm animals—the Animal Welfare Act—in fact does not. Enacted in 1966, this law focuses on the treatment of research and exhibition animals and commercial breeders. It has an egregious shortcoming: Animals raised for food are exempted from its scope. In other words, nine billion animals killed for food in the United States every year are not protected by the most significant piece of federal animal welfare legislation in American history.

There are only two federal laws that do govern how farm animals are treated, and both of them are toothless with gaping loopholes. The first, the Humane Methods of Slaughter Act, enacted in 1958, requires that livestock be "rendered insensible to pain" before slaughter. The USDA's Food Safety and Inspection Service is required to send inspectors to slaughterhouses to make sure this basic mandate is being followed. Shockingly, however, the USDA has decided to exempt birds and fish, meaning that about 99 percent of the animals who are slaughtered for food receive absolutely no protection under the Humane Methods of Slaughter Act. The law also says nothing about how animals should be treated on the farm. As its name suggests, it applies only at the time of slaughter, a mere fraction of an animal's life. Moreover, enforcement of the law by the USDA is sorely lacking, with countless violations forgiven and no meaningful action taken against the most egregious and repeat offenders.

The second federal law is the Twenty-Eight Hour Law, which prohibits animals from being transported across state lines in a "common carrier," such as a vehicle, for more than twenty-eight hours without being unloaded for a minimum of five hours of rest, feeding, and watering. Once again, birds are excluded, so the overwhelming majority of farm animals are still exempt from basic protection. And violations are subject to a maximum fine of merely $500, easily absorbed as a "cost of doing business" by most producers.

Shamefully, Congress has not enacted a single federal law addressing the welfare of farm animals living on the farm. Instead, this task has been left to the states, which, too, fail to protect farm animals by routinely allowing cows, pigs, and chickens to be subjected to abuses that would land the perpetrator in jail if the victims were dogs or cats. Just nineteen states and Washington, DC, require that farm animals even be provided water, food, and proper shelter. Only Washington State and Puerto Rico require that animals be provided light, and only Maine and Wisconsin mention clean living conditions in their statutes—and even then, the laws are ambiguously worded. Meanwhile, the majority of states have "common farming exemptions," the same exemptions that permitted the piglet at my local high school to be slammed headfirst into the ground.

Unsurprisingly, the states that have baked the most glaring loopholes into their anticruelty laws are also the states with the most animal agriculture. For example, Iowa, ranked first in egg and pork production, amended its anticruelty laws to explicitly differentiate between "injury to livestock" and "injury to animals other than livestock." Under the new law, criminal prosecution can only occur if farm animals are injured "by any means which causes pain or suffering in a manner inconsistent with customary animal husbandry." This language gives the green light to horrifically cruel, yet "customary," practices. North Carolina, the third-largest poultry producer in the United States, amended its anticruelty statute in 1998 to exempt "lawful activities conducted for... purposes of livestock or poultry production" but failed to define what "lawful activities" actually means. Similarly, it is illegal in Vermont to "tie, tether and restrain" animals in an inhumane manner except when it comes to common husbandry practices for farm animals. On a state level, the only semblance of protection afforded to farm animals by cruelty status are often those aimed at preventing "malicious" or "sadistic" abuse, such as merciless beatings. These meager protections, which fail to address widespread systems and practices that cause acute and chronic pain for billions of animals, are often the only laws MFA is able to use when seeking prosecution in farm animal cruelty cases.

And because law enforcement officials don't have authority to actively monitor or inspect conditions on farms, cruelty flourishes out of sight and out of mind.

In short, politicians in Congress and all fifty states have made it clear that farm animals are not deserving of basic rights and are not worthy of compassion. The meat industry has written its own rulebook directly into the criminal code, allowing it to abuse animals with impunity.

This is why Mercy For Animals sends out our own versions of Upton Sinclair—undercover investigators like Pete—donning rubber boots and armed with pinhole-size cameras concealed in clothing, pens, and electronics. Their covert footage has captured images that shock consumers and corporations into action. If our government won't take action, then we will.

Their stories represent some of MFA's most challenging moments, but they are also moments that have changed the course of history, leading to new laws, prosecution of abusers, and adoption of international policies. But these changes don't come easy or without a heavy price to the investigators' physical and emotional well-being.

Pete

6.

"That Place Is Hell"

Pete lay paralyzed on his back. He was in shock and didn't feel any pain, but then it washed over him all at once. Next to him, the fender of his dirt bike was rammed ten inches into the sand. Pete was at his favorite supercross track, and he had hit an easy jump—the same one he had hit countless times before. Except this time his body positioning was slightly off and his speed was too fast, turning a twenty-foot bound into a sixty-foot free fall. Pete had landed directly on his heels and then on his ass and had never in his life been in so much pain.

"Think you can walk it off?" another motorcyclist asked him.

"Nope," Pete gasped. "Definitely can't walk it off."

Fortunately, the other rider was the head of radiology at a local hospital. He helped Pete to his truck and brought him for X-rays. The X-rays revealed that he had broken the right transverse process of his

L5 vertebra—more commonly known as the lower back. He would be out of commission for at least a month. The timing wasn't good. It was October 2006, and Pete was poised to undertake our very first undercover investigation.

At the time of his accident, Pete was in North Carolina working at a chicken processor called Mountaire Farms. He had taken the job expecting to be working in the slaughterhouse but instead was sent to the freezer room, placing bits of raw chicken onto freezer trays. He wasn't allowed anywhere near the slaughter floor. He had tried sneaking in twice, but he couldn't get any footage of the slaughter process.

I need to get the hell out of here, Pete realized.

Thanksgiving was right around the corner. If he could get undercover footage of cruelty to turkeys, it could be a major coup for the animal-protection movement. As the second-largest turkey-producing state in the country, North Carolina was a perfect place to try. Every year North Carolina slaughters approximately thirty-six million turkeys. The poultry industry has seen rapid growth: The rate of poultry consumption has easily outpaced red meat consumption over the past decade, and overall consumption of poultry has grown twentyfold in the last century.

Pete had heard rumors at Mountaire that House of Raeford Farms, a turkey slaughterhouse in nearby Raeford, was a grueling place to work. "That place is hell," he overheard a few of his coworkers saying.

Okay, Pete thought. *I've got to get a job there.*

The day before his accident Pete had walked into the manager's office at House of Raeford and inquired about a job. The manager glared at him and responded in a pronounced southern drawl: "You think you got what it takes?"

"Sure do," Pete said. "I want a job where I get paid to be on my feet and I hear that live hanging is a real workout." Pete was a master at talking his way into places.

"Well, I'm gonna tell you something," the manager said with a grin. "You go back there in that live-hang bay and see what these boys do. This is a *real* man's job. If you come back in here and still want a job, I'll give you one."

The live-hang bay is where live turkeys are shackled by their feet onto a moving cable, which brings them assembly-line style to a rotating blade that cuts their throats open, draining their blood. This is how hundreds of millions of turkeys meet their end every year—a killing method as efficient as it is brutal.

The first thing Pete noticed was the smell. Even after all these years Pete remembers it distinctly: blood, shit, and cooked meat. (The cooked meat smell came from a marinade factory directly next door.) To this day Pete can't be around a barbecue or burger joint without wanting to vomit.

Pete hadn't taken two steps into the live-hang bay when he saw a bird that had been run over by a truck. Her organs had spilled out and were still pulsating in a pool of blood. Workers were ripping turkeys out of cages and hoisting them onto live-hang shackles as fast as possible. Blood and feces were everywhere. Complete chaos.

This is it, Pete thought. *I think we found the spot for our first investigation.*

The next day, after crashing at the motocross track, Pete was sitting in a wheelchair, doped up on painkillers.

Fortunately, the House of Raeford manager was understanding. "Come back when you're ready," he later told Pete. Live-hanging is a very physical job, requiring a lot of strength and stamina, along with a willingness to be perpetually covered in blood and feces. In other words, there aren't many applicants, and they need to be in shape.

Pete was in a wheelchair for two weeks, and then on crutches for another two weeks. After a month he could walk, painfully, but that was good enough for him. There wasn't yet a job opening, but Pete was unfazed. He kept showing up until the manager had a spot on the line. Finally, in January, he was in.

While Pete was filling out paperwork on his first day, a worker walked by and said, "Hey, you're gonna be all right. You can do this job. Don't let anyone tell you otherwise." Another remarked, "Don't worry, you can do it. Don't think you can't." Now Pete was getting nervous. Surely this job wasn't *that* difficult, was it?

It was. Even today, with more than a dozen strenuous factory-farm investigations under his belt, that first day at House of Raeford Farms remains the hardest day of work Pete said he has ever experienced. By the time they arrive at the slaughterhouse, turkeys weigh about thirty-six pounds. They are large, they are scared, and it was Pete's job to take them out of cages, hoist them to about head height, and shackle them to a live-hang line. He had to do this for eight hours a day, not even a month after breaking his back.

Pete was barely surviving his first day, but the workers around him had endured this exhausting work for months and years. As the international nonprofit Oxfam reported in 2016, "Big Poultry treats workers as replaceable cogs in their machine. . . . To find workers willing to do these jobs, the poultry industry exploits vulnerable people who have few other options: minorities, immigrants, and refugees— even prisoners. Because of their precarious situations, most workers are afraid to speak out or do anything that might jeopardize their jobs." Pete remembers one worker, José, who said he was eighteen but was probably younger, with hands so swollen he could barely open them—a result of repeating the same motions thousands of times each shift, with few moments to rest or stretch. Finally the boy could no longer work and pointed out the injury to his manager, who sneered and said, "Just soak it in some hot water and get back to work." This story is no outlier: Oxfam calculates that the speed at which poultry companies run their processing lines has doubled in the past thirty-five years, and many workers are forced to repeat the same forceful motions more than twenty thousand times per day. A government report noted that among poultry workers, "the most common injuries are cuts, strains, cumulative trauma, and injuries sustained from falls, but more serious injuries, such as fractures and amputation, also occur." As a result, "labor turnover in meat and poultry plants is quite high, and in some worksites can exceed 100 percent in a year." It wasn't just the turkeys facing abuse; it was the workers, too.

After removing the struggling birds from cages on trucks, workers would shove their feet into hanging steel shackles that suspend the birds upside down. As Pete soon learned, the turkeys' knees blow out from the extreme force required to jam them into the shackling mechanism. Pete could feel the crunch reverberate in his arms each time. This happened with every single bird. At the same time, Pete estimated that 10 percent of the turkeys already had existing fractures and open wounds from their weeks spent crowded together at "grow-out" facilities.

Oftentimes, if a worker didn't thrust a bird hard enough, the shackles would fail. Their knees shattered, these birds would fall to the ground and lie there for the rest of the day, ignored. A new bird would be lifted in his place while the first one lay terrified on the floor, subject to relentless kicking and trampling. Only at the end of the day, when the rest of the birds had been loaded into shackles, would the downed turkey be hoisted back onto the line.

After being shackled, the turkeys would be whisked along toward the opposite end of the factory, to their deaths. What Pete remembers most distinctly about this step was the complete lack of noise. The birds fought and squawked when they were being thrown from their cages, but once they reached the hanging line they were completely silent. Birds do not have muscular diaphragms, which makes it extremely difficult and painful for them to breathe while upside down. Their wings splayed out, their heads became still—an endless procession of birds quietly awaiting their death, as if they'd known it was coming all along. The only sounds were the clanking of steel shackles and the scuffling of workers below.

Two minutes later the turkeys reached a "stun bath"—essentially electrified running water—which temporarily paralyzed them. However, oftentimes the bath merely gave the birds a painful shock, failing to render them unconscious. A moment later, a rotating blade cut their throats open. Farther down the line, a worker was stationed with a knife; it was his job to slice the necks of any birds who weren't cleanly cut by the rotating blade. Their blood quickly draining, the birds struggled and flapped their wings. And then, finally, they were still.

Even during the final minutes of life, many of the turkeys weren't spared abuse. Pete routinely watched workers—desensitized to violence by the sheer brutality of their jobs—use live turkeys as punching bags as they hung upside down on the slaughter line. Another time Pete was unloading turkeys from trucks when he saw a bird poke her head out of a cage. On a whim, another worker reached over and ripped it off. Then he laughed and threw the head over to another worker. At other times, workers would throw fallen turkeys up to eight-foot hanging platforms. The birds would often miss and fall back down to the floor. All in front of managers. For fun, some employees even shoved their hands into the vaginal cavities of live birds. And all the while, turkeys with broken wings and legs, bloody open wounds, tumors, and other untreated injuries were slaughtered for human consumption.

After five weeks of undercover filming, enough was enough. We were ready to go to law enforcement and present our case. I was also worried about Pete, who was thoroughly exhausted. Pete never complained, so I knew he wouldn't tell me just how bad things were. He would stick out any case, in any conditions, if it meant helping animals. But I could tell he was suffering. The physical labor, long hours, filthy conditions, fumes, and daily injuries were extreme. The thought of Pete doing all this right after breaking his back made me very concerned. Pete wasn't just an investigator; he was my friend, my brother. I wanted him out of there. By the end of the case he was taking 800 mg of ibuprofen three times a day for the carpal tunnel syndrome he had developed in his hands. He'd wake up in the morning and his hands would be locked in the position needed to grasp a thirty-six-pound turkey by the leg. At night he would massage and soak his hands in hot water, willing himself through the pain so he could open them sufficiently to cook dinner.

We prepared the case and mailed it to law enforcement. This was our very first investigation, and we knew that the odds of a prosecutor taking such a case were slim, even though the abuse was as repulsive as it was routine. No response. At the time, MFA was not well-known and was easy to ignore. We were pioneering this sort of work, and it would take many more investigations and immense fortitude before prosecutors would take the protection of farm animals seriously. But we had achieved something extremely important. With this case, we had developed a blueprint for litigating undercover investigations. We had pushed MFA into an exhilarating new era, and we would never look back.

It's remarkable how only a few years can make all the difference in the world. In 2007 we had just two employees. Four years later, MFA was beginning to morph into a successful nonprofit with a growing staff and expanding support base. By the time we pointed our hidden cameras back at North Carolina's turkey industry, we had already completed nearly a dozen investigations, hired a full-time lawyer, and opened offices in multiples cities across the country.

It was fast approaching Thanksgiving 2011. With a number of wins under our belt, we decided it was time to try another turkey case. Our investigator Liz had been trying unsuccessfully to find work in Minnesota, which is the number-one turkey-producing state in the country. So we made the decision to try again in North Carolina. As fate would have it, Liz found work at a farm just around the corner from where Pete had worked four years earlier. The facility was operated by Butterball—a name synonymous with turkey. Butterball is the largest turkey producer in the nation, raising and slaughtering 20 percent of all the turkeys sold in the United States every year (and nearly 30 percent of all Thanksgiving turkeys).

Liz is petite, unassuming, and nonthreatening. She has short brown hair and wears thick, black-framed glasses. She's sweet and incredibly smart, with a wonderful sense of humor and a giant, unforgettable laugh. In many ways Liz is your typical hipster, complete with colorful tattoos, a cool style, and piercings. I was worried she'd stand out on a factory farm, but Liz is like a chameleon. One moment she looks like a character from *Portlandia*; the next, she's knee-deep in manure and acting like a lifelong farmworker.

For as long as she can remember, Liz has felt compassion toward innocent and gentle beings, including children and, especially, animals. As a child she had an intense fascination with cats and dogs. Like most Americans, though, she ate meat. It's just what people did. But as a teenager she had a sudden revelation: *If I care so much about cats and dogs, why shouldn't I extend that compassion toward farm animals? What's the difference?*

After Liz attended an animal-rights conference in Portland, Oregon, she heard an MFA representative giving a talk about what we do. When he mentioned that MFA was hiring investigators, Liz decided to inquire. Liz was compassionate about many causes, though she didn't consider herself an activist. She couldn't stand the oil industry, but she wasn't about to hijack an oil rig with Greenpeace. But that was about to change: This was her chance to take a direct stand for animal rights.

Liz was trained in Chicago by Pete, who put her through a *Rocky-*

like program consisting of physical conditioning and technical instruction on the use of undercover cameras. Working in a factory farm requires core strength. Moreover, investigators need to be able to maintain proper filming posture while still laboring on the farm. This means keeping their torso straight while picking things up and setting them down. If the footage is too shaky, the case is ruined. Every day Pete made Liz perform hundreds of reps with weights from awkward angles until she had built up her strength sufficiently.

Liz also learned how to contextualize what she was filming. Investigators have to document not just the abuse of animals, but when and where it is happening, who is doing it, why it is occurring, and who is witnessing it, among countless other variables. For example, investigators cannot prove how long an animal has been suffering from an untreated injury by filming her for a few minutes. Instead, workers or managers must admit on camera that they were aware of the suffering animal yet did not act. Filming with a pinhole-size camera wired to your body is difficult. There is no viewfinder, so you're filming blindly. If Liz were bent over slightly, or standing too tall, she could miss a crucial shot. A lifelong photographer, Liz quickly learned to treat her gear as an extension of her eyes and body. Even though she could not see through the viewfinder, she could feel it with her body. She became an expert at getting the shot, every time.

Pete brought Liz to several livestock auctions—markets where animals are bought and sold for slaughter—where she familiarized herself with using her camera in real-life scenarios. There's a big difference between filming an inanimate object and the unpredictable movements of a live animal. She interacted with farmworkers there and learned how to ask the right questions. If our investigators are asking workers about how common abuse is on a farm, they can't seem obvious about it. It would raise suspicions. More important, Pete helped Liz understand that we are not trying to trick farmworkers. They are not our enemy. Farm laborers generally don't have a lot of options, and many are undocumented immigrants. Most are simply doing exactly as they are told by their managers. Pete helped Liz see them as our allies. It's the factory-farm culture—driven by corporate greed and consumer demand—that is the enemy.

Pete also brought Liz to live markets in and around Chicago, where animals are slaughtered for consumers in full view. At these places, hundreds of turkeys, chickens, ducks, and sometimes even rabbits are crammed into tiny cages awaiting execution. Catering to consumers who value freshly slaughtered meat, live markets are crazy, chaotic places. And they're extremely depressing. Customers walk up, choose an animal, and watch her being slaughtered for them. Visiting live markets is an extremely difficult part of undercover training, but it's crucial. If our investigators are going to be working undercover, they are going to witness a great deal of death. They must be prepared for it, because what they will see on factory farms will be far worse. As a lifelong animal lover, it was tough for Liz to see this, but she never wavered. She quickly became one of our top investigators.

Liz was employed at a Butterball turkey-semen collection facility, where the semen of male turkeys is gathered to later artificially inseminate females at turkey-breeding operations. It's not glamorous work: Workers are tasked with immobilizing turkeys' ankles and feet in a vice, turning them upside down, and then using a suction device to extract semen. It's an incredibly traumatic procedure for the large "tom" male turkeys, and it's one they must endure regularly. Fortunately Liz was not involved in this part of the job. Instead, she drove a truck around the farm collecting the semen and delivering them to other Butterball farms.

Because of their age and size—most of the turkeys Liz saw weighed as much as ninety pounds—many could not physically walk due to severe joint problems. One reason why turkeys are artificially insemi- nated is because they have been genetically manipulated to be so large and meaty that the act of mating is impossible.

Others suffered from open sores, eye infections from exposure to excess dust and ammonia, and wounds from other turkeys. The barns in which they live are dark and filthy. The facilities are rarely cleaned and cages are coated in thick cobwebs. With every breath these tur- keys inhaled a toxic cocktail of excrement and dust, a challenge to their delicate respiratory systems.

As Liz puts it, Butterball turkeys suffer from either too much or too little attention, sometimes all at once. Males are naturally territo- rial birds, and placing them in close quarters—as many as fifteen birds crammed in cages—guarantees they will fight. As a result, many wounded turkeys were quite literally picked apart by their cage mates. Butterball employees would often let the carcasses rot for days before bothering to remove them. The turkeys were also handled aggres- sively by the exhausted workers. Liz witnessed employees bashing birds over the head with metal pipes, violently kicking and stomping on them, dragging them by their wings and necks, and slamming them into transport crates. In one instance, Liz filmed a worker pick- ing a bird up by his wings, slamming him against a truck, and then kicking his head repeatedly.

Often the birds who received the most abuse were the ones who were least capable of enduring it. As they age, male turkeys produce less semen, making them less useful to the farm. By this point, most of the aged birds can barely walk and are suffering from any number of crippling health conditions. When they are considered spent, they are removed from their pens and marched to transport trucks. For many, this is the longest walk of their lives. Scared, in pain, and blinded by the sun, these birds are trucked to the slaughterhouse where their meat, not fit for high-grade products, is processed into hot dogs, turkey burgers, sausages, and dog food.

For Liz, the hardest moments were the early mornings. She'd often sneak in when the barns were quiet to closely document the conditions in which these animals spent their lives. Liz remembers checking on one bird in particular. He was smaller than the others and covered in open wounds. His filthy pen was grossly overcrowded and he had been trampled by his cage mates. His wings were so beaten that Liz could see his tiny muscles.

"I'm sorry," Liz whispered, stroking him gently. "I'm working on it. Just give me a little while. It will be better soon."

Turkeys are among the most misunderstood farm animals, and most people don't know how sensitive and intelligent these beautiful birds are. Benjamin Franklin called turkeys "birds of courage" and adamantly believed the wild turkey should be our national animal instead of the bald eagle. Studies have shown that turkeys possess a remarkable spatial memory and develop strong social bonds with their flock. Turkeys have a sophisticated language of squawks and cackles, mourn when a friend dies, and clearly become distressed when other turkeys in their flock experience pain. Mothers will attentively raise their chicks and fiercely defend them.

Turkeys also have very expressive faces. Liz could read the anxiety on this bird's face, the sadness in his eyes. With the simple act of holding his wings and stroking his feathers, Liz was able to impart empathy and love to a being who had until then experienced only fear and pain. Animals receive touch just as we do. In those few moments, Liz knows she was able to soothe him, just a little bit.

Yet, the case was wearing Liz down. She wanted to do so much more for these animals, but she had to maintain her cover. On her way home from work one day Liz saw a bird lying on the side of the highway. When she pulled over, she realized it was a hen, probably from a nearby egg farm. She must have fallen off a truck. Her chest was shredded and one leg was dangling off to the side. Liz immediately brought her to a veterinarian, who managed to patch her up. Liz named her Tobias.

Liz stopped at a feed store to buy food for her new friend, and then at a thrift store, where she found a dog bed and some old blankets. She smuggled Tobias into her hotel room and made her as comfortable as possible. Tobias was happy and clucking when Liz left for work the following morning. Optimistic, Liz had even begun researching possible animal sanctuaries for Tobias to live in permanently. But when Liz returned that evening, Tobias had taken a turn for the worse. She was lethargic and refusing to eat. Liz called the vet, who told her that Tobias likely had a serious infection from the fall; her immune system was just too frail to fight it. Liz held Tobias for most of the night, feeling her tiny heart slowly weaken until finally she was gone. Liz broke down and cried. She cried and cried and cried—not just for Tobias, but for all the birds she had watched suffer over the past few weeks. All the emotion she had suppressed for the investigation—all the pain and death she had witnessed—was all coming out now.

Early the next morning Liz buried Tobias in a nearby park, under a nice shady tree. Then she went back to work to finish the investigation, grateful for the moment to help an animal who had never known compassion, to hold her close, to cry for her.

We didn't have much hope when we brought Liz's Butterball footage to the Hoke County, North Carolina, district attorney. It was the exact same office we had sent Pete's case to four years earlier. Turkey production is big business in North Carolina—what were the odds that this time around would be any different than our House of Raeford investigation?

But we had an important new advantage: Vandhana Bala, MFA's general counsel. To those who know her, Vandhana is gentle, funny, and kind. But the gloves come off when it comes to fighting for animals in the courtroom, where she is known for being intelligent, articulate, relentless, and incredibly shrewd. She had begun her law career at a huge law firm defending corporations against lawsuits. (Tyson Foods was a former client.) But Vandhana's heart was always with animals. She started as a volunteer with MFA, before we had the means to hire legal counsel. As we grew, Vandhana came on board full-time, landing, as she says, her "dream job."

We also had a second advantage: a law-enforcement official who cared. His name was Mike Hardin, an assistant district attorney for Hoke County. When Liz and Vandhana showed him the footage, the color drained from his face.

"I can't believe this is happening over there," Mike said. "I can't..." he trailed off.

"It's happening," Vandhana replied. "And we need to stop it."

Mike knew he had to take action. To this day, Vandhana calls him the best law-enforcement official she has ever encountered. He was appalled not only by the abuse they watched but by the horrendous neglect—the untreated open wounds, the broken bones, the bruises. Mike immediately began building a case. He contacted renowned veterinarians from North Carolina universities to review our footage and identify the worst abuse. Then he began planning a raid.

But it was only a matter of time before the investigation hit a wall— in this case, an unscrupulous government employee who learned of the investigation. The fox guarding the henhouse, Dr. Sarah Jean Mason—the director of animal health programs with the North Carolina Department of Agriculture—improperly leaked information about the investigation to a veterinarian at Butterball. Worse yet, when questioned by the authorities on whether she had, in fact, tipped off Butterball, she lied about it. Mike learned of the leak. He wasn't happy.

Nevertheless, the DA's office pressed on. On the day of the raid, the DA's office gathered veterinary experts, a half-dozen official vehicles, and then swarmed the Butterball facility just after dawn on a late December morning. Meanwhile, holding up the rear of the police motorcade was Vandhana in her tiny white compact rental car. Butterball refused her access to the barn, so she set up camp in the parking lot, providing support to the sheriff's office and offering an endless supply of sandwiches.

Over the course of two and a half days, the sheriff's deputies and veterinarians individually examined almost two thousand turkeys. Dozens of injured and suffering birds were humanely euthanized.

News helicopters hovered overhead, broadcasting the dramatic scene on television as it unfolded, while news vans lingered along the farm's perimeter.

Then, seven weeks later, it happened: The district attorney's office announced that it would bring criminal charges. Liz's work had paid off, and in a big way. Her investigation led to the first-ever felony conviction in US history for cruelty to factory-farmed birds. Four other Butterball employees were convicted of misdemeanor animal-cruelty charges. And Dr. Sarah Jean Mason, the state official who tipped off Butterball about the investigation, was arrested and pled guilty to obstruction of justice charges.

This was a historic victory for MFA, though the success was bittersweet. While it was satisfying seeing the workers who abused animals brought to justice, it was dispiriting seeing Butterball executives called as witnesses for the prosecution. They testified that what these farmworkers did was against company policy, that Butterball did not condone abuse. One hundred percent of the blame was foisted on the factory workers who were carrying out cruel and abusive work on Butterball's behalf. Meanwhile, the executives who fostered this abuse were never charged. Our undercover investigation demonstrated that Butterball was allowing a culture of cruelty to fester at its company-owned factory farms. It also galvanized our belief that in order to produce true change, we needed to find a way to go after the owners themselves.

7.

Three Hundred
Every Second

Every year more than 9 billion land animals are slaughtered for food in the United States. Of these, approximately 26 million are ducks, 30 million are cattle, 106 million are pigs, and 236 million are turkeys. The remaining 8.6 *billion* animals slaughtered every single year are chickens—that's nearly 300 per second.

It is impossible for us to truly comprehend these numbers. They are too massive. Yet each and every one of these animals is an individual who suffers pain, who has a family, who has a story.

America's love affair with eating chicken began in early twentieth century. In 1928, the Republican Party published a pamphlet promising that Herbert Hoover would put "a chicken in every pot and a car in every garage." Incidentally, the poultry industry was the first to truly mechanize. On traditional farms, domesticated chickens were easy to keep: They were very hardy and didn't require around-the-clock care. Chickens foraged on their own for scraps and insects.

They were raised mainly for their eggs, which kept for a long time and could be shipped across long distances. Without access to refrigeration, however, few people actually ate chicken meat. But this all began to change.

In Georgia, the legislature authorized a statewide program to increase poultry production through mechanization, and soon farms and hatcheries sprang up devoted solely to raising chickens. These state-of-the-art operations more closely resembled factories than farms. Instead of roaming the farm pecking at loose corn, chickens started being confined to wire cages stacked in tiers and in rows that ran the length of football fields. President Franklin D. Roosevelt's Tennessee Valley Authority, designed to jump-start the Depression-era economy, expanded electricity to rural regions of the South, enabling poultry farms to install automatic feeders. This dramatically increased the number of birds that could be confined in one location, and newly invented vitamin D supplements meant chickens could be kept inside without ever seeing natural sunlight. Of course, the animals suffered and their health declined, but the new industrialists of farming knew they could make more money by cramming more animals into a smaller space, even if it meant higher mortality rates for the birds.

During the early 1940s, with sky-high demand for meat and the labor force leaving for war in Germany and Japan, the industry took mechanization to a new extreme. Georgia poultry producers were shipping 1.6 million chickens by 1939, a number that jumped to nearly 30 million chickens just six short years later. At the same time, producers were experimenting with genetics in a quest to make chickens gain weight faster. After World War II, the supermarket conglomerate A&P created the "Chicken of Tomorrow" contest to encourage producers to breed meaty, fast-growing broilers. (The term "broiler chicken" derives from the cooking method. These chickens are bred and reared for their meat, which is tender and can be broiled on a stove.) Thanks to these new Frankenstein birds and advances in refrigeration, chicken meat went from a rarity to a staple of every American dinner.

According to an analysis in the scientific journal *PLoS ONE*, over the past fifty years, daily growth rates of broiler chickens have increased from 0.88 ounces to 3.52 ounces—more than 300 percent. Think about that. Broilers reach slaughter weight—referred to as "market" weight by the industry—three times faster than they did just fifty years ago. Today, most broiler chickens are killed when they are forty-five days old—mere babies. They suffer from debilitating leg problems, bone deformities, lameness, ruptured and malformed tendons, and horrendous diseases. The *PLoS ONE* study calculated that as many as 30 percent of broilers suffer from skeletal defects that impair their ability to even stand. By the time they are six weeks old, broilers spend more than 75 percent of their time lying down—often because they are simply unable to walk. This leads to painful open wounds, breast blisters, and foot lesions. These incredible animals deserve better.

Birds, including chickens, are just as intelligent and sentient as primates. According to an analysis out of the University of Bristol, chicks begin exhibiting intelligent behavior just hours after hatching. Chickens have about two dozen unique vocalizations that can signal danger, fear, mating, and food discovery, among other alerts. A high-pitched *eeee* signifies a threat from above, such as a hawk or an eagle, while the *cluck cluck* we all recognize signifies a threat from the ground. Moreover, virtual-reality testing has revealed that chickens are "functionally referential," which means that they can understand the concept of a threat without actually needing to see it. When a hen hears the *eee* call, for instance, the rest of the flock understands the threat and then acts accordingly.

Chickens also have amazing memories. In one study by researchers at the University of Bristol, hens were fed a combination of yellow and blue corn kernels. Yellow kernels were normal, but the blue kernels were laced with chemicals that made the birds sick. Not only did they learn to avoid the blue kernels, but when the mother hens later hatched chicks, they taught their babies to avoid blue corn when the experiment was repeated. In other words, chickens pass information along from one generation to the next. Other studies have shown that chickens can count and outperform cats, dogs, and even human toddlers on cognitive tests. This intelligence is rooted in an ability called transitive inference. In short, chickens can observe and use deductive reasoning to figure out the relationship between events and objects. In another study, hens observing confrontations among other hens could reason whom they could compete with in the "pecking order," and whom they should avoid.

Visitors to Woodstock Farm Sanctuary, an idyllic place nestled in the foothills of the Catskills about two hours north of New York City, see the unique personalities of chickens every single day. Starting with an empty, unfenced hay field, Woodstock Farm Sanctuary has grown into one of the largest and most successful sanctuaries in the United States. Kathy Keefe is the shelter director there, where she oversees the care of all animals.

"People tend to think of chickens as being stupid and purely instinctual," Kathy told me. "Having worked closely with them for many years, I can tell you how wrong and damaging this myth is. People do not realize how individual chickens are. This one might be bold, while that one is a bit shier. This one likes sunflower seeds, that one doesn't. If you spend just a little bit of time with these animals, you'll even see how distinctive their physical features are. These animals are curious and inquisitive."

Kathy told me about a rooster named Clyde, who was found roaming the streets of Brooklyn, New York. He had most likely escaped a nearby live market. "I've never seen an animal with so much personality," Kathy told me. "If you come on the property, if you park up the hill and walk toward the barn, Clyde will come hauling across the lawn to say 'hello' and assess you. He is hardwired to protect everyone on the farm. Clyde needs to know who everyone is and what they're doing here. If it's a woman, he will do a little rooster dance. If it's a man, he'll fluff himself up to prove he is in charge.

"He also adores being held. When you stroke him in your lap, he closes his eyes and he settles right in. He adores the attention. I hope one day everyone realizes how special these birds are."

Until a 2013 Duke University study of avian brains, scientists believed that bird brains were mostly primitive and instinctive. However, we now know that their brains are very much like our own with large regions devoted to complex cognitive thought. In fact, researchers at Vanderbilt University found that birds have proportionally more neurons in their forebrains—the center for emotions and other complex thoughts—than many primates do. A study in the journal *Animal Cognition* found that chickens experience positive and negative emotions, including empathy, anticipation, anxiety, and fear.

. . .

Sadly, these amazing animals face cruelty on an unimaginable scale. MFA investigators have been there to expose and challenge it. In 2015, our undercover investigator Maria secured employment at Foster Farms, one of the largest chicken producers in the country.

If you were to see Maria in her native Southern California environment, you'd never guess she is an undercover investigator. Her image is all about fun: She loves wearing dresses and high heels, doing up her hair, tooling around in her Mini Cooper. She even has a bright pink iPhone—think a cheerleader straight out of the San Fernando Valley. But when you talk to her you discover a more serious person: wildly intelligent, articulate, and thoughtful. Of Mexican descent and fluent in Spanish, Maria can easily pass as an immigrant, a primary workforce on factory farms.

As a teenager, Maria volunteered with numerous animal-rights groups in Southern California, but her focus soon turned to farm animals. For her, the paradox was always clear: We would never think of eating a dog or cat. So why should pigs and chickens and cows be any different? The idea repulsed her. As Maria began screening some of MFA's early undercover videos to the public, she was struck by how quickly many people were moved to give up meat all at once. "Oh my God," they would say. "I can't believe this is where my food comes from." As she witnessed the impact of these videos, Maria decided to go undercover herself. One night, she and some friends snuck onto an egg farm. All the misery that she had seen in MFA's videos was suddenly right in front of her. Soon after that, she contacted MFA, determined to become an investigator. She quickly landed the job.

In 2013, Foster Farms began being certified as "humane" by the American Humane Association (AHA). This meant that Foster Farms could slap on a cheerful label that declared its poultry "American Humane Certified." Foster Farms played up AHA's endorsement at every turn, including big-budget TV commercials.

Despite its name, the AHA does more to protect animal abusers than animals. Famous for their "No Animals Harmed in the Making of This Film" program, the AHA has routinely been accused of putting the profits of animal-using industries ahead of animal welfare. Animals have died, nearly drowned, been abused, exploited, and injured on sets of movies and TV shows that the AHA was tasked with monitoring. The *Hollywood Reporter* slammed the AHA in a damning 2013 exposé titled "Animals Were Harmed," bluntly stating: "The AHA has not lived up to its professed role as stalwart defenders of animals." On nearly every animal-welfare issue, the AHA finds itself on the opposite side of every other national animal-protection organization. To the astonishment of many, the AHA has even come out in favor of bullhooks, the sharp metal-hooked weapons used to force elephants to perform circus tricks.

Maria began working at a Foster Farms broiler facility in Fresno, California, an enormous facility comprising nearly a dozen barns, each roughly two hundred feet long and eighty feet wide. Blankets of cobwebs coated the steel rafters above the animals. Looking down, you'd see a sea of chickens—more than twenty thousand per barn— clustered around the feeders, which were suspended from the ceiling.

Broilers' lives are short and brutal. Arriving from when they are no more than a few days old, the goal is to fatten them as quickly as possible. Injuries and deformities among broiler chickens are so common that Foster Farms employed an entire team to what was called "mortality." These workers spent their mornings pacing the barn, looking for birds who were too sick to be slaughtered or otherwise considered inferior.

It was Maria's job to find these chickens. "You're gonna see birds who just drop dead," Maria's supervisor warned on her first day. "Just like that. Dead."

"Why?" Maria asked.

"Heart attacks. Happens all the time. You'll just see them freak out and then keel over."

Maria was skeptical that this could happen to animals so young, but just minutes later she saw it occur. She watched a bird who suddenly had trouble breathing. He stopped, flapped his wings, and then his chest convulsed. He staggered involuntarily. Then, as quickly as it had started, it was over: The bird fell over dead. These birds' tiny hearts were simply not big enough to support the massive weight they'd been genetically manipulated to pack on. As many as 50 percent of all broiler deaths are the result of sudden heart failure and ascites, a condition in which a chicken's heart and lungs simply do not grow fast enough to distribute oxygen throughout their bodies.

The mortality team was also tasked with identifying and killing undersized birds. Broiler farms are often penalized for each bird that does not meet size requirements. This meant it was mortality's job to locate and snap the necks of birds who were healthy but too small. The first time Maria was instructed to kill a bird who was too small, she walked over and peered down at the tiny creature. The chick was perfectly healthy and gazed back up at Maria, peeping cheerfully. His only crime was his small size. Maria, small herself, could relate.

"I'm not going to kill you," Maria said quietly to the chick. "There's nothing wrong with you. You're just a little small, aren't you?" Quickly she ushered him away and watched as he disappeared into the sea of yellow peeping birds, hoping the little bird could find some joy in what little time he had left in this world. Maria remembers how broiler chickens would huddle around and protect downed birds whose bodies could not support their weight. When she attempted to pick up an injured bird, the others would peck at her, as if desperately trying to help their friend.

Other injuries were caused when the chicks were delivered. When a small team of workers are told to unload twenty thousand peeping chicks as fast as possible to keep up with the frenetic pace required by the industry, birds are going to get injured. At Foster Farms, workers took boxes of chicks from trucks and simply dumped them onto the floor. Many birds were stepped on or trampled by the overwhelmed workers. One time Maria saw a worker hurtle an entire crate of chicks onto the ground. When she returned later, they were all dead.

Birds who were deemed too sick for slaughter were killed by having their necks snapped and then were tossed into a bucket. At the end of the day, the full buckets were driven around to the Dumpster behind the barn. Often the carcasses would rot for days—Maria couldn't walk within fifty feet of the Dumpster, the smell was that bad. But she had to document it, so she held her breath and peered in. It was full of festering birds. The ones at the bottom had started to turn green. Maria nearly gagged, but she stood strong and methodically recorded it all.

Birth of the Superbugs

Alexander Fleming, the Scottish biologist who discovered penicillin in 1928, once wrote: "The time may come when penicillin can be bought by anyone in the shop. Then there is the danger that the ignorant man may easily under-dose himself and, by exposing his disease-causing organisms to nonlethal quantities of the drug, make them resistant." Fleming was worried that too much of a good thing—in this case, an abundance of easily accessible, lifesaving antibiotics—could ultimately be harmful. While we can't go to our local CVS and buy antibiotics without a prescription, factory farms are doing the next worst thing.

Since the 1950s, factory farms have been using vast quantities of nontherapeutic antibiotics to make animals grow faster and to keep them alive in disease-ridden conditions. This creates opportunities for disease-causing organisms to adapt and develop immunity to antibiotics. Once these "superbugs" evolve, our medicine becomes useless and people die from otherwise treatable infections.

According to the Centers for Disease Control and Prevention, antibiotic-resistant superbugs kill at least twenty-three thousand people every year in the United States and could kill as many as ten million American *annually* by 2050. It appears these fears may be well founded: In January 2017, a Reno, Nevada, woman died from a superbug infection that was resistant to all twenty-six known antibiotic medications. The infection was even resistant to the powerful class of antibiotics called carbapenems, the last line of defense when all other medications fail. "I think this is the harbinger of future badness to come," said Dr. James Johnson, a professor of infectious diseases medicine at the University of Minnesota.

Thanks to factory farms, the effectiveness of lifesaving antibiotics is quickly coming to an end.

After barely six weeks of life, the surviving Foster Farms chickens were packed into trucks and brought to the slaughterhouse. This was the job for a specialized crew who arrived in the dead of night and left before morning. One day the birds were in the barn, the next day they were not. All that was left for Maria to see were the remnants of this carnage: blood, feathers, and the carcasses of birds who had been run over by trucks. Maria could tell because they were covered in tire marks.

Thanks to Maria, we knew just how traumatic and short the lives of these poor creatures were. There was only one more piece of information needed to complete the investigation: what went on in the slaughterhouse. If we could get footage of a Foster Farms slaughterhouse, we could show the public exactly how the animals they eat are raised and killed. We had been trying for more than a year to get one of our investigators into one, with no luck.

Our director of investigations, Matt Rice, had an idea.

Standing six foot four with a ruddy goatee and a nearly bald head, Matt is the doppelgänger of comedian Louis C.K., with the quick humor and intellect to match. In fact, Matt looks so much like Louis that after moving to Los Angeles to head up MFA's investigations department, he was frequently stopped in the streets by tourists asking for autographs and photos.

Matt served in the United States Marine Corps for four years in the mid-1990s as a corporal in the First Battalion First Marines. He carried out special amphibious raid operations as well as search-and-rescue missions. His unit's main specialty was to launch small zodiac boats from land, from sea, and even from helicopters. Matt was a machine-gun section leader, boat pilot, and engine mechanic all at the same time.

After the US Marines he went to college and received a degree in biology and anthropology with a minor in chemistry, hoping to become a geneticist. But his life was about to take a dramatic turn.

It was the winter of 2002. Matt, still in college, was newly married. One evening, his wife, Tammy, came home from work and told Matt she had decided to go vegan because of an undercover investigation she watched online. She pointed to their beloved boxer-retriever mix, Tessa, and said, "You would never let anyone hurt Tessa. You would put yourself in front of one hundred angry people to protect her. Yet you are paying people, three times a day, to hurt other animals who are not that different from Tessa, just to eat them."

Matt sat there, stunned. Of course, she was right. Who was he to say which animals could be eaten and which could not? He immediately went vegan, and then he decided it was his duty to do more. He had joined the US Marines because he felt compelled to serve and protect. Now he knew it was his moral obligation to start speaking out against factory-farm animal abuse. He abandoned his plans of working in human genetics and started working full-time for animal rights—first by fighting to end animal abuse in the fur, leather, and wool industries, and then by working directly with rescued cows, pigs, and chickens at an animal sanctuary. In 2009 Matt joined MFA, first as a grassroots outreach coordinator, then as the operations manager. Finally he settled into the most stressful, high-stakes position within the office: director of investigations. The leadership skills he learned in the US Marines, not to mention his quick wit and strategic intelligence, help guide our field investigators through their most difficult and trying times.

Matt had recently hired a young guy named Robert who was in his early twenties: smart and thoroughly passionate about animal rights. Robert approached Matt at an animal-rights conference in Los Angeles.

"I already submitted my application to be an investigator," he told Matt, "but I wanted to meet you face-to-face and tell you how much I want to do this."

Matt was a bit hesitant. Robert was certainly dedicated, but maybe a little *too* dedicated. He worried that maybe Robert was an industry mole trying to infiltrate MFA. Nevertheless, Robert had all the right answers and the energy that drives our movement.

"I knew we had gold when I hired him," Matt said later. In fact, Robert was so good that we decided to send him to Foster Farms. Robert was big and muscular, and if anyone could handle the grueling work, it was him. It was a Hail Mary pass, but we had a special feeling about him.

Robert managed to secure a live-hang job at a Foster Farms slaughterhouse located in Fresno, just down the road from the farm where Maria worked. It was horrendous work. Robert spent eight hours a day hoisting live birds into the shackles, every time smashing his knuckles into a metal bar. Every night he would dip his bloodied and bruised hands into an ice bath to numb the pain. Then he'd wake up at the crack of dawn and do it all over again.

Robert witnessed workers hitting, punching, and beating shackled chickens. Other birds were passed around workers' bodies like basketballs. In another instance, he saw a worker ripping feathers out of a live bird, just for fun. Another time he saw an irritated employee beating live chickens with a chicken leg. The cruelty was constant and unrelenting. All this at a slaughterhouse certified as "humane" by the AHA.

To meet market demand, the pace was frantic: Robert estimated that each worker shackled a live chicken every three seconds, oftentimes improperly fastening the birds so they hung from only one leg. They would then be whisked along the slaughter line dangling by one leg, flapping and struggling the whole way. As a result, they often missed the kill blade and were subjected to the entire slaughter process fully conscious. These birds were scalded alive and drowned in hot-water tanks. Robert could easily see which birds had met this fate—since their necks were not cut and their blood could not drain, their skin turned bright shades of purple and red. The US Department of Agriculture estimates that one million chickens and turkeys are scalded alive and drowned every year. As awful as it was, we now had our footage. Our proof.

Because both Maria's and Robert's cases were of the same company and fell within the same jurisdiction, Vandhana consolidated both into one complaint to law enforcement. The sheriff of Fresno County recommended to the DA that charges be brought against several Foster Farms workers. The DA, however, did nothing for more than a year, seemingly apprehensive about going after the megacorporation, a politically powerful institution that employed more than ten thousand people and boasted more than $2 billion in annual revenue. After months of persistent follow-up, animal-cruelty charges were eventually filed against one Foster Farms employee who was caught on hidden camera maliciously abusing birds. He was convicted.

A few months after this investigation wrapped up, Robert headed to Mississippi. He had been hired at a Tyson Foods slaughterhouse located just outside Carthage. With more than 115,000 employees and revenue exceeding $30 billion, Tyson is the world's largest producer and marketer of chicken, beef, and pork products. Every year, Tyson slaughters more than *two billion* chickens—meaning about one in every four chickens eaten in America comes from Tyson. The facility where Robert worked is one of the largest poultry slaughterhouses in the entire world.

Here, he saw the same types of horrors he observed at Foster Farms. And just as at Foster Farms, he noticed that birds often missed the kill blade.

"How come so many of these birds aren't killed by the blade, like they're supposed to be?" Robert asked his supervisor, Sandra.

"Sometimes they aren't shackled the right way," she replied indifferently. "They miss the blade."

When he asked what happens to those birds, Sandra gestured down the line to two workers named Nita and Roy. Sandra explained that it was their job to kill birds who were not cut by the blade. Nita used a small knife to saw the birds' heads off, while Roy used his hands to rip off their heads.

Robert also saw poorly trained and unsupervised workers routinely tormenting birds, throwing and slamming them to the ground.

In addition to the deliberate cruelty, the frantic pace required by Tyson often resulted in workers breaking the wings and legs of fragile birds, all in the name of efficiency. Chickens were also dumped en masse onto conveyor belts, causing many to suffocate under the weight of other birds. Robert reported the abuse to his supervisors on numerous occasions, but no corrective action was taken. We quickly wrapped up the case. When Vandhana prepared our legal complaint, she realized we could take advantage of a unique provision in Mississippi's animal-cruelty statutes. Instead of presenting our case to law enforcement, as usual, and hoping they'd take it, we could have Robert fill out sworn affidavits against Tyson and a number of their workers. This would force a judge to look over our case and, if he or she agreed that the evidence of criminal animal abuse was sufficient, issue arrest warrants. Robert completed affidavits seeking misdemeanor charges against Tyson itself and six employees, for a total of thirty-three counts of animal cruelty. The judge issued arrest warrants against six of the workers.

But we weren't done with Tyson.

A few months later we sent one of our new investigators, Andy, to a Tyson supplier in Tennessee. A native of Seattle, Andy is tough, wiry, and at home in the outdoors. For eight years he worked as a police officer, where he was routinely in challenging and dangerous situations that required thinking on his feet. Andy soon became one of our top investigators, due predominantly to his phenomenal professionalism. An investigator needs to be meticulous. When we hand our investigation over to law enforcement, they need to see thorough, painstakingly precise notes. If we gather evidence or compile notes in a sloppy, unprofessional manner, law enforcement has an excuse to toss the case.

As a former police officer, he knew exactly how to prepare detailed notes. Even better, Andy had a background in interrogation, which meant he knew how to get animal abusers to confess. He accomplished this not by asking direct questions but by making people feel at ease and comfortable saying whatever was on their minds.

Andy had grown up hunting with his father and grandfather. For two decades he remained an avid hunter, but he slowly began to question his favorite pastime. He realized that hunting was special because of how it brought him close with his family and with nature, and he loved the natural beauty of animals in their habitats. Why did he have to kill animals to experience those feelings? One day while duck hunting and holding a dying duck in his arms, it dawned on him: There was no meaningful difference between the ducks he killed and his beloved dog at home. He soon went vegan and swore off hunting for good.

Andy, who grew up in a working-class home, fit in well with the farmworkers. He found a job at T&S Farm, a longtime broiler-chicken supplier for Tyson and McDonald's. T&S was Tyson's golden child, having been named "grower of the year" by Tyson five years in a row. But conditions there were bleak. Birds lived by the tens of thousands, crowded together in maggot-infested sheds. Many had severe injuries including uterine prolapses and leg deformities. But what shocked Andy most was how the farm owners, Thomas and Susan Blassingame, killed chickens who were too sick, injured, or simply not growing fast enough to be profitable.

"You don't work for PETA, do you?" Susan asked Andy his first day on the job.

"No," Andy answered.

Susan then grabbed a long, makeshift club with a nail spike sticking out of the end. She lifted it over her head before forcefully striking and stabbing an injured chicken. Then she did it again. And again.

And this was the horrific way nearly every bird on the farm was killed. But Thomas had his own technique. As he made his way through the crowded barn, he would beat chickens and impale them with a spiked club before dumping them in a bucket.

"You didn't see that," Thomas would tell Andy, as if to acknowledge that what he and Susan were doing was both cruel and illegal.

"Thomas added a couple of birds to the bucket in the middle of the barn and this one here, she's still alive," Andy later said aloud, filming a dying bird while alone at the farm. She was bloody and badly injured. "You can see her blinking."

The cruelty was sickening.

Unlike Mississippi, Tennessee does not have a sworn-affidavit system to report animal cruelty, so we had to approach Weakley County law enforcement and convince them to take the case. Vandhana and Andy met with the sheriff and showed him the footage Andy had captured. The first thing Vandhana noticed was the sheriff's expression: sheer horror.

He immediately picked up the phone and called the DA's office. That same day, an assistant district attorney drove over and viewed the footage, too. He agreed that action had to be taken, that the cruelty had to end. The wheels of justice often move slowly, if at all, when it comes to animal rights—and often intentionally. But things were different in this case. The DA's office swiftly brought charges against both owners of T&S Farm, one count each of animal cruelty. Not long afterward, Thomas and Susan Blassingame pleaded guilty. The farm has since closed down altogether.

Just months later, in October 2015, Andy was ready for his next assignment: going undercover at two Perdue contract farms in Rockingham, North Carolina, operated by a father and son. Perdue is another massive poultry producer, with nineteen thousand employees and revenues exceeding $6 billion. The company raises and kills nearly seven hundred million animals each year. Just like with the birds used by Tyson, generations of genetic manipulation had left many of Perdue's chickens unable to walk, leading them to die slowly of starvation, dehydration, heart attacks, organ failure, or any number of other painful ailments.

One afternoon Andy returned from his lunch break to find his coworker Danny beating the chest of a chicken with a hammer. Then he started pounding her with his fists.

"Why are you doing that?" Andy asked.

"Heart attack," Danny responded, finally giving up. He tossed the lifeless chicken onto a pile of dead birds. "Figured I'd try to revive it with CPR. You never know."

But heart attacks weren't the only suffering these birds endured. Andy's hidden camera also caught Danny cruelly kicking and throwing chickens, hurling them against walls and into trucks, and stomping birds to death in clear violation of North Carolina law. Evidence in hand, we sprang into action.

Vandhana assembled a complaint and, along with Andy, met with local law enforcement at the Richmond County Sheriff's Office. Immediately, the office called in a member of their animal task force to review the footage. The department was so appalled by the cruelty that within two hours of our meeting they had arrested Danny and charged him.

Danny eventually pleaded guilty to three misdemeanor counts of animal cruelty. After the conviction, I thought back to our very first undercover investigation with Pete, when law enforcement wouldn't even respond to us. Times were changing.

While the prosecution was important, it did nothing to change the systemic cruelty endured by the hundreds of millions of other chickens raised by Perdue each year. We needed a major policy change to do that. After the conviction, we launched an aggressive campaign to pressure Perdue to improve animal welfare. More than 180,000 consumers signed our petition urging Perdue to make life better for birds. Then, following extensive negotiations with Mercy For Animals, Perdue announced in June 2016 the most comprehensive animal welfare policy ever adopted by a major chicken producer. Perdue's policy alone would reduce the suffering of nearly 680 million birds on twenty-two hundred farms every year.

The new policy outlined the company's efforts to implement on-farm improvements such as environmental enrichment and natural light; curb malicious abuse; and address the unnaturally rapid growth rates of chickens, which cause incredible suffering to birds. Additionally, the policy mandates annual third-party audits and increased video surveillance to deter instances of malicious animal abuse. But the most notable changes were to be made at Perdue slaughterhouses. The policy committed to replacing live-shackle slaughter methods with less cruel controlled atmosphere stunning (CAS), which uses inert gas to put birds to sleep while in their crates. This will spare millions of birds from the horrific suffering caused by dumping, shackling, shocking, and slitting the throats of conscious animals at the slaughterhouse. The types of cruelty Robert and Pete had exposed.

The dominoes were starting to fall. Following the commitment from Perdue, we shifted our focus to pressuring other key players in the food industry. After we threatened protest campaigns, Aramark, Compass Group, and Sodexo—the top three food service providers in the country, collectively serving hundreds of thousands of meals each day at colleges, hospitals, and other institutions—quickly agreed to adopt similar policies.

We now had momentum on our side. Next we turned our attention to the restaurant sector, pressuring Burger King, Chipotle, Shake Shack, Jack in the Box, Tim Hortons, Red Robin, Noodles & Company, and others to do away with the worst abuses faced by chickens in its supply chains. Although far from creating a life of utopia for birds, these commitments will dramatically reduce the suffering of an additional two hundred million chickens each year—animals just like the little chicken Maria met who was deemed "too small" and ordered to be killed. Chickens just like the ones Andy witnessed being clubbed to death on the Tyson contract farm in Tennessee. Because of their brave work, change was finally happening.

8.

Behind the Carton

t's 2008 and I'm in California—ground zero for the largest battle in the history of the American animal rights movement. George W. Bush is president, the economy is in free fall, and no one has ever heard of Justin Bieber. The November elections are nearing. In addition to voting for the president of the United States, members of Congress, and state legislators, California voters will be presented with a dozen ballot propositions ranging from high-speed rail funding to abortion restrictions to the notorious Proposition 8, a constitutional amendment that would ultimately ban same-sex marriage in the state. (Proposition 8 was, of course, later struck down by the United States Supreme Court.) While defeating Proposition 8 was very dear to my heart, my energy was focused mainly on passing a different voter initiative: Proposition 2.

Proposition 2 was simple in language but vast in scope. The initiative would require that egg-laying hens, breeding pigs, and calves used for veal be given "enough space to stand up, turn around, lie down, and extend their limbs." In practice, the initiative would outlaw battery cages, gestation crates, and veal crates. With essentially no pork or veal production in California, though, Proposition 2 was mainly intended to protect the state's twenty million egg-laying hens. The question was to appear before voters on November 4. Animal-protection groups needed to gather footage of how animals were being mistreated and put it out there quickly. If voters could see how hens were abused, there was real hope of passing this landmark animal-protection legislation.

Various animal-protection groups had already sent investigators into the field to try to acquire video evidence from egg facilities, but they'd not succeeded. Despite our small size at the time, I knew that MFA could help. We had Pete.

To get the video, we sent Pete to Stanislaus County, an area of California saturated with egg farms. We thought this was the most likely place for him to find a job, although we were worried about exposure; Pete had already undergone a few legal name changes so he couldn't be traced after his puppy-mill-investigating days. Given the hype surrounding the Proposition 2 campaign and all the money being spent against it, egg farms were on the lookout for undercover investigators. Pete had to be extremely careful.

He reached out to dozens of farms before finally hearing that Gemperle Enterprises in Turlock, California, needed help immediately.

But there was a problem.

"We only need mechanics," the hiring manager told him. "We don't need any help in the egg barns."

Being a mechanic meant that instead of spending time in the barns gathering vital footage, Pete would be fixing egg-packing machines where no hens could be seen.

"But I don't have any mechanical experience," Pete insisted. "I really would be most useful in the egg barns."

The manager laughed. "That grunt work is for the monkeys," he said—meaning the Hispanic workers. "We'll train you to be a mechanic." An unfortunate reality at factory farms is that jobs largely fall along racial lines. Mechanics are generally white.

There was nothing else Pete could do. At least he had a job. Knowing he would raise suspicion if he insisted on working in the barn, Pete tried another tack. He began befriending members of the predominantly Hispanic cleaning crew. He helped them clean up eggshells, grease machines, and pick up trash. Most mechanics typically sat around for most of the day, but Pete insisted on being useful.

"Stop hanging out with the wetbacks," his manager often chided him, but Pete persisted. Fluent in Spanish, he'd joke with the Hispanic workers about how racist their bosses were. Then Pete approached the farm supervisor—his boss's boss.

"Thanks for the job," Pete said. "You really treat me well here. But I don't like being a mechanic. There's too much standing around. I prefer to work with my hands. Do you think you could find me something else? Maybe working more closely with the animals?" Then he added: "If not, I think I'll need to start looking for another job. But I want to do the right thing by telling you."

His supervisor thought it over. Pete was an excellent employee and was very popular with the workers.

"All right," he agreed. "We can find you something on the construction crew."

In this new role, Pete was responsible for building pullet barns and leveling concrete, but he also had part-time access to the egg barns, where he was tasked with fixing feed troughs, repairing cages, and sewing egg belts. Most important, he finally had the access he needed to see the hens.

The egg barns at Gemperle were enormous, about the size of a football field. When Pete walked into one, he was overpowered by the smell of ammonia. He had to wear a mask or else he'd gag. The barns were rarely cleaned; there was so much dust in the air that Pete couldn't even see the end of the barn. All surfaces—the cages, the floors, the machinery, everything—were covered in this dust and smeared with excrement. Cobwebs on the ceiling were so thick and ancient that even industrial blowers couldn't budge them. Pete's crew had to scrape them away by hand. Once Pete felt something thud onto his back. His coworker swatted it off and laughed. "Black widow!"

It had been four years since we'd seen the inside of an egg factory farm, but watching Pete's footage immediately brought back memories of our Open Rescues in Ohio. Along the sides of the barns were wire cages filled with hens stacked to the dusty ether. One hundred thousand hens in cages stacked like stairs—these are the world's largest prisons. Just as I saw in Ohio, Pete routinely documented decaying, mummified carcasses in cages surrounded by live hens still laying eggs for human consumption. Many hens also suffered from prolapsed uterus, in which their vaginal cavity essentially turns inside out from laying too many large eggs. Most were left to die in pain; others were tossed alive into disposal bins. Individual veterinary attention was virtually never provided.

Pete was also able to obtain disturbing footage of so-called depopulation, which no animal-protection group had ever before obtained. When hens are worn out from constant egg production, they are no longer of any use to the farm, so they are pulled from their cages and killed, or "depopulated." While well-treated hens can live for as long as fifteen years, at factory farms most are killed before their second birthday. By this point they often are missing feathers, are covered with infected sores, and have grotesquely swollen eyes. To Pete, these hens looked like battered zombies.

When the workers had crammed as many "spent hens" as possible into a bin they called a "kill cart," they wheeled over a tank of carbon dioxide and slowly began poisoning the birds with CO_2 gas. This method is inefficient since the gas can't reach all of the birds in the bin. Hens inside the kill carts would scratch and claw for air, slowly suffocating inside a trash can.

"The screams of the birds being pulled from their cages and slammed into the kill carts will stay with me forever," Pete recalls.

After these hens were removed, their cages were pressure-washed to remove as much filth as possible. While on the construction crew one day after a depopulation, Pete noticed that a sole hen had been left behind in her cage, huddled in a back corner. She was soaking wet, nearly featherless, still breathing. Her skin was beet red from the pressure washer. Pete knew fear when he saw it.

"Hey," Pete said to a coworker. "Este pájaro está vivo." This bird is still alive.

The worker yanked the bird from her cage, tried and failed to break her neck, then threw her to the ground. As she flailed around frantically, the worker stepped on her head. Then he stretched her neck in another attempt to break it. When this, too, failed, he kicked the thrashing bird under an egg belt and into a manure pit below the cages. There she finally drowned in a pool of liquid feces.

"She gave her entire life to that company," Pete later said. "And this is how she was honored. To be power-washed, haphazardly strangled, and then drowned in a manure pit."

In spite of the daily horrors these hens endured, their compassionate nature never wavered. Pete recalls approaching a flock of hens who had fallen into a dried manure pit. When the birds spotted Pete, they all ran away together except for two hens who were asleep at the far end of the pit. Instead of leaving them, fearing that Pete could be dangerous, one hen left the flock and bolted across the room to wake up the two sleeping hens. She then led her friends back to the safety of the flock.

It took a lot out of Pete to continue filming the brutality these hens were subjected to, knowing that evidence of abuse like this would one day make life better for countless other hens. But on egg farms, any semblance of compassion is suspicious. If Pete would have acted, his cover would have been blown.

Finally, Pete was able to secretly film the repopulation of the barn. This was the final piece of evidence we needed before breaking the case. Pete and the rest of the construction crew were given the task of unloading cages with young chickens who had just reached egg-laying age. The cages were brought to the egg barns, where Pete filmed the chaotic repopulation process. Workers were grabbing hens by their necks, their wings, their legs—anything they could get a hold of—and stuffing them violently into cages. The hens screamed and writhed in terror. Wings were broken, legs snapped, beaks smashed. Pete stood watching the next generation of hens begin to meet more cruelty at the hands of the egg industry. He wanted so badly to rescue each and every one, but he had to press on with the investigation.

After about five weeks we had enough video footage to tell the disturbing story of egg factory farming to California voters, so Pete left Gemperle. We brought the footage to Emmy Award–winning reporter Dan Noyes at ABC 7 News in the Bay Area. Sympathetic to the welfare of animals, Dan helped break the infamous Westland/Hallmark Meat slaughterhouse story, in which an investigator uncovered workers illegally abusing sick cows and sending their meat into the National School Lunch Program. The story led to the largest meat recall in US history and an eventual $500 million fine.

With his ABC team, Dan put together a compelling, in-depth story that featured much of Pete's undercover footage, which aired across California. ABC ran commercials and put up digital billboards advertising the segment.

MFA then held multiple press conferences around the state, including simultaneous events in Fresno and Sacramento, where I was joined by California state assemblyman Lloyd Levine and California state senator Carole Migden, who declared: "I am horrified to see that farmers and workers would treat animals with such disregard."

The next day we held a press conference in San Francisco, where we called out Trader Joe's, a major purchaser of Gemperle eggs. This gave a huge boost to the Proposition 2 movement. Until then, the idea of cruelty at egg farms seemed abstract to most people. Who knew anything about the egg barns in rural California with names no one had ever heard of? Trader Joe's, however, is a beloved California institution. When people could actually see the horrific conditions inside a Trader Joe's supplier, it was a game changer. Within a day Trader Joe's had dropped Gemperle Enterprises. Meanwhile, the Proposition 2 campaign began using Pete's footage in TV commercials that aired day and night. Momentum was on our side. Millions of people were seeing Pete's video.

Months passed and the campaign waged on.

Finally Election Day arrived: The moment of truth. The results were staggering. Proposition 2 passed with 63 percent of the vote—a massive victory. In fact, more Californians voted for Proposition 2 (8.2 million) than any other citizen-driven ballot initiative at that time in California's history. There were more votes for Proposition 2 than for Barack Obama. Because of Proposition 2, California's egg producers must now give hens enough room to turn around and extend their limbs. It was a powerful turning point in our work to protect hens.

I knew that helping pass Proposition 2 was an important landmark, but it was only the beginning. What about hens in New York and Pennsylvania? What about hens in Vermont? Until the federal government passes legislation, it's up to these states to pass their own laws. After wrapping up his California egg cases, Pete traveled east and began applying for jobs on egg farms in Connecticut. By this point Pete had completed numerous investigations for MFA and his identity had been circulated among the industry do-not-hire lists. In one instance, Pete was about to interview at an egg farm when he saw a "Gemperle Enterprises" sticker in the manager's office. They apparently owned this facility. Pete spun around and hopped back into his car.

After a month of this, Pete finally found an opportunity at Quality Egg of New England in Turner, Maine. After four phone calls, Pete interviewed in person for a job with HR.

"I can speak Spanish," Pete stated. "I get along well with the workers, I know how to run eggs, I can operate the machinery. Basically, I can do anything you need me to."

The HR rep was not impressed. "We're not really looking for anyone," she replied. "Be sure to check in again soon."

Desperately, Pete offered, "I'm really good at sewing egg belts."

And with that, a man poked his head into the office. "I'll take it from here," he said. This was the owner's son, Jay, who immediately had two managers take Pete down into the egg barn.

They gave him a needle and thread. "If you can sew this belt," one said, "you've got the job."

Pete quickly took care of business and was hired on the spot.

Within hours Pete had seen some of the worst abuse in all his years of investigations. He had one word for it: "Nightmare." Thick layers of dust and excrement coated every surface. The flickering lightbulbs were swathed in cobwebs, giving off a dim, haunting glow. Pete could smell the rot: of birds, of eggs, of the entire facility. Broken egg belts that hadn't moved in days, mummified hens, disintegrating eggshells. Drunk employees. Filth and neglect everywhere.

The production manager responsible for several egg sites, David, explained the culture at Quality Egg of New England. "Everyone drinks on the job. Most of these guys are alcoholics. No one cares." Once Pete's manager, a man named Chava, went on a bender and didn't report to work for three days. No one besides Pete seemed to notice.

Pete's first task was to get the egg belts moving, which he accomplished in a few hours. Workers took the old, blood- and shit-covered eggs that had been sitting on the belts for days and likely sent them off to grocery stores. In this environment, it didn't take long for Pete to acquire the evidence he needed: workers throwing live hens into trash cans. Pete filmed the birds taking their final agonizing breaths under the crushing weight of their former cage mates.

At one point Pete said to David, "Hey, I'm seeing sick and dying birds everywhere. They're even in the trash cans. No one seems to be helping them. Should we do something?"

"Nah," David replied. "Don't fuck with them."

"Even if they're still alive?"

"Yeah. Don't worry about it."

Then Pete went to Jay, the owner's son. On camera, Pete asked him what he should do about the sick birds in the trash cans.

"Don't worry about them," Jay responded.

Pete pressed him further. "If they're still alive in there, I don't have to worry about it? They all count as dead?"

"Yeah. If they are thrown away, the USDA counts them as dead."

That was the smoking gun we needed. We had management and ownership admitting that they were throwing live birds into trash bins. And they didn't care. This was in direct violation of the Maine anticruelty statute.

When Pete and I brought the footage to the district attorney, the mayor of Turner showed up along with the sheriff and the Maine state veterinarian, both of whom we feared were trying to sabotage the case. They didn't want this going to the press. But we persisted.

Finally, the DA's office capitulated. Not long after, Maine's Department of Animal Welfare raided Quality Egg of New England, the first time in US history that an egg facility had been raided by state authorities on the basis of an animal-protection group's investigation. Immediately afterward we released our footage to the press, and within days numerous New England grocery chains including Hannaford, Stop & Shop, and Shaw's severed ties with Quality Egg. Soon after, Eggland's Best, the nation's number-one specialty egg brand, terminated its relationship with the facility as well.

In June 2010, as part of a landmark civil settlement stemming from our undercover investigation, Quality Egg of New England's affiliate, Maine Contract Farming, pleaded guilty to ten counts of cruelty to animals. Several years later the owner of the factory farm, Jack DeCoster, was ordered to recall 550 million eggs after a massive salmonella outbreak at another farm he owned, which the Centers for Disease Control and Prevention estimated may have sickened as many as fifty-six thousand people. DeCoster was later sentenced to three months in federal prison along with his son. (He had previously been fined for numerous violations ranging from poor working conditions to employing child laborers.) Quality Egg admitted that workers knowingly shipped eggs with false expiration dates in a ploy to fool state regulators, and the company even bribed a US Department of Agriculture inspector at least twice to approve potentially contaminated eggs. No one at Mercy For Animals was surprised by any of this.

The farm was also ordered to pay more than $130,000 in fines and restitution, as well as hand over authority to the state of Maine to conduct unannounced inspections of the factory farm for the next five years. This was an important precedent. Until then, the few animal-cruelty convictions were almost entirely against individual workers, not the farm itself. But in the case of Quality Egg, the company itself pleaded guilty. No longer could factory farms blame their cruel practices on low-level workers. The case was historic.

B y 2010, MFA had now helped pass watershed legislation on the West Coast and had successfully helped bring landmark charges against a factory farm on the East Coast. Yet our work was far from over. We had shown the public the appalling conditions in which millions of egg-laying hens lived but still hadn't shown where these birds came from. Where did they hatch? And, most troubling of all, what happened to the males?

Egg-laying chicks begin their lives at enormous facilities called hatcheries—or, as Pete would later call them, "places designed by Dr. Seuss if he got possessed by the Devil." A little bit of research helped Pete determine he needed to travel to Spencer, Iowa, home of Hy-Line International, the largest hatching facility in the world. This company was shipping more than thirty million chicks a year to 120 countries.

Pete applied for a job at Hy-Line. When he showed up for his interview, he thought the place looked like a military base: immense, sprawling, and cold. Spencer is close to numerous universities, so the population skews young and transient. They likely assumed Pete was a student and didn't do a background check. Hy-Line hatched hundreds of thousands of egg-laying chicks every week, and they were constantly in need of help. Pete landed the position.

Hy-Line is a compartmentalized hatchery, so it was tough for Pete to see what workers in another section were doing. He couldn't exactly prowl around to check on conditions. As a result, he had to use his head to gain the information we needed.

His first job was working in "transfer," where all the chicks are hatched. Hy-Line hatches approximately three hundred thousand chicks every twenty-four hours. Instead of being nurtured under the warm feathers of their watchful mothers, these chicks were incubated in a hermetically sealed environment surrounded by cool, flickering fluorescent lighting. In nature, incubation is crucial to the bonding process between mother and chick. While sitting on their eggs, hens will cluck and baby chicks will peep and squeak back. When the chicks hatch, they are already bonded to their mothers. But at Hy-Line, the chicks' peeps were met instead by the steady buzz of machinery. Pete said it felt like he was walking through the set of a science fiction movie. Even Hy-Line's corporate slogan, "Genetic Excellence," sounds like something out of a dystopian novel.

Each egg was incubated for twenty-one days before hatching. When time was up, the incubator doors popped open and the workers swiftly unloaded trays of yellow peeping chicks, shell fragments still clinging to their bodies. From a distance they looked like tiny rows of potatoes. Entire shelves of chicks were loaded like office supplies onto enormous trolleys and rolled out of the incubation area.

But where did they go next? Pete didn't know, so he would have to ask for another job, one that would let him wander around. He'd observed that the cleaning crews seemed to float in and out of the various stations without being noticed, and at all times of day. So he went to his boss. "Hey, is there any way I can work extra hours with the cleaning crew?" he asked. "I could really use the money."

"Sure," his boss replied. Everyone liked Pete, and they were happy to help him out.

Now a newly minted member of the cleaning crew, his first stop was an RV-size machine called "the separator."

After they left their incubators, the chicks were dumped hundreds at a time into the top of the separator machine. This contraption was designed to remove the eggshells more efficiently than a team of workers.

With his hidden camera rolling, Pete stood behind the separator and tried to film it.

"Get the hell out of here!" screamed the machine operator. "Out! Out!"

Pete quickly left, but moments later he crept back with a ladder and placed it behind the machine. Pete pretended to clean the walls as he positioned the camera toward the separator. Now he could see everything: The trays of chicks arrived on a conveyor belt and then were dumped into the top of the machine. As they tumbled down, they smashed and bounced into a series of rolling bars designed to knock away eggshells. Some chicks broke their fragile bones during the process; others got jammed between the rolling bars. Any chicks who were injured or trapped were later blasted away with high-pressure hoses.

Suddenly the machine operator noticed Pete staring down at him. "Son of a— *Get the hell out of here!*" Pete jumped off the ladder and left, but the old man followed. He found his manager and angrily reported what Pete had done.

Oh shit, Pete thought. *My cover is blown.*

Calmly, Pete said to his manager: "Sorry, I just wanted to watch how the machine works. I'm on the cleaning crew and I want to make sure I do the job right. If I watch how it works, I can make sure to clean the parts I wouldn't otherwise know were there."

The manager looked at Pete suspiciously, but he bought the story. He smiled and took Pete aside. "Listen," he said. "Just leave that guy alone. He's a bit . . . *off.* There's a reason he's been doing this job for sixteen years."

"Sure thing," Pete replied. He had gotten the footage he needed.

On the cleaning crew, Pete would see the rest of the process, and the next stop on the conveyor belt was the "sexing room." Professional "sexers," as they are called, separate the male chicks from the female chicks by looking for distinctive markings on their feathers. While females continue along the conveyor belt, males are violently tossed into a metal chute on the wall. The workers segregated the fragile chicks at a frantic pace, flinging the tiny birds through the air like Vegas card dealers dealing out a deck.

Think about this for a second: The Hy-Line hatchery sends off 750,000 female Leghorn chicks every week to egg-laying farms like the ones Pete had investigated. So what happens to the roughly 150,000 male chicks that hatched each day?

We knew that they were being killed, but we did not know exactly *how*. Grainy video footage from Israel showed males being suffocated with carbon dioxide and thrown into Dumpsters, but no one had recently documented how males were killed in the United States. Although Pete was considered by Hy-Line to be an excellent employee and was even a member of the cleaning crew, he was forbidden access to the secret room male chicks entered but never left. Pete knew he had to find a way inside.

During his lunch breaks, Pete began chatting with employees he knew worked in that room. Pete is a charming guy, and before long his coworkers were enthusiastically inviting him to their "Wasted Wednesdays" pub night. That night Pete was able to finagle the invitation that mattered: a peek inside the secret room.

The next day Pete's new friends allowed him to observe their work in the sexing and de-beaking room. He saw a conveyor of discarded male chicks leading under a shut door. Inside was a large, dimly lit space. He watched as male chicks tumbled through shafts in the wall onto a conveyor belt, and then into a machine shaped like a truck transmission.

Pete had found the macerator.

A manager soon kicked him out, but Pete only needed a few minutes to capture the footage. Male chicks—healthy, chirping, curious—dropped from the belt onto an auger, and then into a plastic disk filled with blades, where their bodies were reduced to a pink slime. This was how over two hundred million male chicks met their end every single year, industry wide. The pink slime was later sold to processing facilities for use in fertilizer and pet food. At MFA, we were absolutely devastated by this footage. Male chicks were being pulverized and turned into goo by a machine specifically engineered to kill as many birds as possible, as cheaply as possible.

The surviving females weren't treated any better. For them, the next stop on the conveyor belt was a spinning machine where their sensitive beaks are jammed into tiny holes so a laser could burn a portion off. This incredibly cruel practice is tantamount to removing a human's fingers. Chicken's beaks are packed with nerve endings, enabling them to grasp and distinguish among objects while eating, nesting, and exploring. Later in life, pink scar tissue often develops at the wound sites, making it difficult for these chickens to eat or drink. The egg industry claims that they trim the beaks to keep the birds from injuring each other in their overstuffed cages. Of course, instead of subjecting them to this painful procedure, the industry could simply not confine hens in the first place.

But this is the industry standard. Letting prematurely hatched chicks die—standard. Power-hosing live chicks stuck in the separator—standard. De-beaking chicks with a laser—standard. And, of course, a single facility grinding up 150,000 male chicks alive every single day—standard. We knew a district attorney would never touch this case, but we truly felt the public deserved to know what goes on inside hatching facilities.

The Associated Press broke the story, and Pete's undercover video of the macerator went viral. Their powerful headline declared: "Video shows chicks ground up alive at Iowa egg hatchery." From Cleveland to China, Austin to Australia, consumers worldwide were given an eye-opening look at the cruel and violent truth behind the modern egg industry. In less than a day, more than two million people logged on to YouTube to view Pete's gut-wrenching footage, making it officially the number-two most "viral" video of the day. Their rotten secret exposed, the industry struggled to defend the practice. "If someone has a need for two hundred million male chicks," a United Egg Producers spokesman later sputtered, "we're happy to provide them to anyone who wants them."

No legal action was taken against Hy-Line International. As abhorrent as it sounds, it's perfectly legal for the industry to grind up hundreds of millions of "useless" animals a year. Referred to by Hy-Line corporate leaders as mere "genetic products," these chicks are treated just as they are viewed: as inanimate objects rather than as sentient creatures.

In the face of massive outcry, United Egg Producers, an industry group that represents 95 percent of all eggs produced in the United States, announced in June 2016 that its members would end the practice of destroying male chicks by 2020. Instead of macerating them, the industry will employ a new technology called "in-ovo sexing," which can determine the sex of a chick while still in the egg. Males will now be discarded before they even hatch, or simply sold as eggs.

The cruelty we have documented in hatcheries egg barns is a symptom of an out-of-control industry—as evidenced by a case involving a McDonald's Egg McMuffin supplier, Sparboe Farms, infiltrated by our investigator TJ.

Undercover investigators can be an eccentric bunch, and TJ is no exception. He's covered in colorful tattoos, wears ear gauges, and has long flowing hair and piercing blue eyes. Standing six foot three with a slim, muscular build, TJ is a gentle giant, and like so many of our best investigators, he's the last person you'd ever expect to be carrying out an undercover job. TJ is a total "dude" and loves rock 'n' roll, drives a beat-up truck, and adores the South. But he's sensitive, emotional, and intense in conversation.

At Sparboe, TJ saw the usual abuse: hens jam-packed into filthy wire cages and workers burning the beaks off young chicks. He witnessed employees violently heaving birds into cages, often missing the cage door entirely, leaving a crumpled heap of hens on the floor. TJ's footage was even worse than Pete's, with decomposing hens rotting amidst live hens laying eggs destined for store shelves. TJ watched one worker tie a string around a bird's feet and then spin her around over his head. Abuse like this was so commonplace that one of TJ's coworkers referred to the hens' living environment as "torture." Meanwhile, some depopulated birds weren't even gassed but were simply tossed into plastic bags to suffocate.

TJ's work paid off. His footage reached millions of people when it broke on *Good Morning America*, *20/20*, and ABC's *World News Tonight*. Soon Hollywood celebrities got in on the action: Ryan Gosling, Zooey Deschanel, Alicia Silverstone, Bryan Adams, and others signed on to an open letter demanding that McDonald's stop purchasing eggs produced by hens who live in tiny wire cages. All of this, along with an avalanche of animal supporters who bombarded McDonald's executives, led the conglomerate to drop Sparboe Farms as a supplier.

But McDonald's refused to implement more sweeping changes, such as banning cages altogether, that would make life easier for hens across the entire supply chain.

We pressed on. Next, we sent an investigator to a McDonald's egg supplier in Canada. Once again, we exposed sickening abuses. Once again, we released it to the media. Once again, consumers were outraged.

Then it happened. In September 2015, McDonald's announced that they were phasing out cages over the next nine years from both their US and Canadian egg supply chains, improving the lives of nearly eight million birds every single year. McDonald's is a major player in the egg industry, with their US stores purchasing 2 billion eggs every year, and Canada's another 120 million. The move was hailed by animal-protection organizations as a watershed moment for the movement.

Just months later, the Retail Council of Canada, which represents all the leading grocers in the country, announced that 100 percent of eggs sold in its member stores would be from cage-free hens by 2025. This means fifteen million hens annually will no longer suffer in tiny wire cages.

Meanwhile, following an aggressive campaign and discussions with Mercy For Animals, Safeway, the second-largest grocer in the United States, publicly declared that it, too, would sell only cage-free eggs. Then, Kroger, the nation's largest supermarket chain, announced that it would switch to 100 percent cage-free eggs. Within months, all twenty-five of the largest grocers in the United States had succumbed to the pressure, and each adopted similar policies.

Then, more than one hundred restaurants, food-service companies, and food manufacturers fell in line. The commitments, which affect over 70 percent of all eggs sold in the United States and Canada, mean that more than 190 million hens will no longer be crammed in cages. We then took the momentum to other countries, prompting dozens of companies in Mexico, Brazil, and Asia to do the same. Hundreds of millions of hens around the globe were impacted. What seemed like an impossible dream fifteen years earlier, when I first risked arrest to step foot inside Ohio's largest egg farms, was finally becoming a reality.

Yet, despite our successes, there is much work to be done. Cage-free represents meaningful improvements in the lives of birds who otherwise would be crammed in cages. (A review of science on the topic suggests that removing hens from cages increases their welfare by nearly 600 percent.) But it's far from ideal—cage-free does not mean cruelty-free.

The term "cage-free" means that birds are not confined inside individual cages. However, within the cage-free industry, conditions for the birds can vary greatly. For example, "free-range" and "pasture-based" birds have varying degrees of access to the outdoors, while conventional "cage-free" eggs often come from massive, factory farm–style operations where tens of thousands of birds are crowded into windowless sheds (similar to broiler chickens). Filth, stress, and overcrowding present serious welfare concerns. Unable to establish a proper pecking order as a group, smaller, weaker birds are often pecked by stronger, more aggressive birds.

Male chicks like the ones Pete met at Hy-Line hatchery are still ground up alive, regardless of whether the females are destined for cage or cage-free operations. The end is just as grim for cage-free birds, too, who are killed when their production declines. Like the birds Pete saw thrown into carts and gassed at Gemperle Enterprises, hens in cage-free operations face the same deaths. Their lives end violently, filled with fear.

Despite this inherent cruelty, MFA understands that change doesn't happen overnight. As long as people consume eggs, I believe it is our moral obligation to reduce as much suffering as possible for the birds unlucky enough to be born into this harsh reality. To that end, liberating hens from tiny cages that deprive them of their most basic freedom of movement is an important step in our journey toward a more compassionate society. But there is so much more to accomplish, so much more abuse to end. And not just for hens.

Supersized Cruelty

The burgeoning fast-food industry represented a major source of skyrocketing beef and chicken demand, further cementing and accelerating the rise of factory farming in America. Founded in 1940 by two brothers, Richard and Maurice McDonald, McDonald's began as a single restaurant in San Bernardino, California, emphasizing speedy service. When businessman Ray Kroc later assumed control of the company, he realized that the fast-and-cheap model could revolutionize how America ate. Between 1955 and 1965, McDonald's expanded from 1 location to nearly 230. By this point, Americans were eating one-third of their beef at restaurants like McDonald's and Burger King.

The first KFC franchise was founded in 1952 by Harland Sanders. As he expanded his business, Sanders grew dissatisfied by the thirty minutes it took to cook his chicken in a frying pan. Aided by high-volume factory farms, along with the advent of the pressure cooker in 1939, KFC could drastically increase production speed. Latching on to the fast-food model, in 1957 KFC introduced its famous "bucket meal": fourteen pieces of chicken, five bread rolls, and a pint of gravy. By 1963, KFC was the largest fast-food operation in the United States, with more than six hundred restaurants.

Largely driven by McDonald's and KFC, the fast-food industry exploded by nearly 80 percent between 1965 and 1970, with more than four hundred chains and tens of thousands of restaurants. Thanks to factory farming, the fast-food industry transformed chicken and beef from occasional luxuries into cheap, everyday staples of American cuisine. Their rise dramatically increased the amount of meat consumed—and with it the number of animals raised and killed.

Liz

9.

No. 2640

L iz pulled her car over to the shoulder of the highway before she
began sobbing. She couldn't see the road through her tears. It
had been one of the worst days of her life.

She was driving home from her first day on the job at Iowa Select Farms in Kamrar, Iowa. The stakes were high; we needed her to
succeed. At the time, in 2011, no retailer had yet adopted an anti-
gestation crate policy for its pork suppliers, and we needed to obtain
footage of this inhumane practice. Gestation crates—often referred
to euphemistically as "individual maternity pens" by the pork industry—are the extremely small metal enclosures inside which mother
pigs are forced to live nearly their entire lives, unable to turn around
or even lie down comfortably. Though Liz had spent months training
for this day, nothing had prepared her for the horrific abuse she had
seen—abuse that went far beyond confining pigs in gestation crates.

Liz identified regions in Iowa that were permeated with the most hog farms. She also researched each farm to figure out which large companies they supplied. From there she ranked them based on priority. Her target soon became clear: Iowa Select Farms, the largest pork producer in the state and, at the time, the fourth-largest in the country.

Liz got lucky. She called Iowa Select and they invited her for an interview. The next day she had a job.

She quickly learned how the facility operated. It was divided into two sections: gestation (pregnant pigs) and farrowing (pigs who have just given birth). Mother pigs, known as sows, spend most of their lives in windowless gestation sheds, where they are artificially inseminated and kept for the majority of their 115-day pregnancies. Gestation crates, which are about 6.5 feet by 2 feet, are designed to keep sows packed together as tightly as possible and are barely larger than the pigs' own bodies. Pigs are highly intelligent and extremely social animals who enjoy open fields, forests, and sunlight. They are natural sprinters who love running and following their noses for miles and miles. Confining mother pigs to cages in which they are unable to even turn around or lie down comfortably is so patently cruel that gestation crates have been banned by the entire European Union, New Zealand, and ten states, including Florida, Arizona, Oregon, Colorado, California, Maine, Massachusetts, and Michigan.

When sows are close to giving birth, they are moved from the gestation barn to the farrowing barn. This short walk across the facility is the closest these sows will ever come to freedom, the soppy manure under their hooves the closest they will come to having grass under their feet. Once they reach the farrowing shed, the sows are placed in tiny enclosures called farrowing crates. Within a day or two these sows give birth to a litter of eight to twelve piglets who are permanently separated from their mothers by cold steel bars. They can stick their heads between the bars to nurse, but no further contact is possible. Piglets derive comfort from the warmth of their mother, her steady breathing, her soft skin. But in factory farms like Iowa Select, piglets are deprived of even these minimal motherly comforts.

New hires often spend their first few days at work shadowing other employees, getting a feel for how the facility operates before doing any real work. This was not the case on Liz's first day. After filling out her employment paperwork, she was sent to a farrowing barn to begin working with newborn piglets. Liz's supervisor explained that there was a very specific routine to perform when piglets are born. It began with checking the farrowing crates to ensure that any piglets who died during the night were removed. This was a normal occurrence on factory farms, as piglets routinely died from sickness, disease, and outright neglect. Others were crushed by their mothers, who couldn't properly maneuver around them in the restrictive crate. Liz also had to look out for prolapsed uteruses among the sows, common due to repeated births. By their third or fourth birthdays, these sows, who had spent their entire lives either pregnant or nursing piglets, were typically deemed "useless" by the company and marked for slaughter.

The prolapses were difficult for Liz to see on her first day, but it was nothing compared to what she was asked to do next. Standard industry practice called for removing the tails of piglets, a process known as tail docking. The pork industry claims that the procedure is necessary to prevent pigs from biting one another's tails, a behavior propelled by boredom and stress. At ten a.m. on her first day, Liz witnessed the tail-docking procedure. With one hand workers picked up piglets by their hind legs, and with the other hand they cut off their tails with shears. The piglets screamed in agony as blood spurted from the wound. Then they were dumped back into the pen.

Liz's supervisor performed the procedure a number of times. Then she handed Liz a pair of shears: "Your turn!"

Liz's heart dropped. She took a deep breath and reached into the pen and grasped a squirming piglet by his hind legs. She then allowed herself a brief moment of introspection: She was a lifelong animal lover devoted to improving the lives of farm animals, yet here she was about to cause pain to the very animals she was trying to protect. She knew tail docking was legal: The Iowa anticruelty statute explicitly makes an exception for standard farming practice, and tail docking was certainly considered standard. And Liz knew that in order to one day end these horrific practices, the public needed to be aware of them. And if she didn't dock these piglets' tails, someone else would. She'd be as gentle and fast as she could.

She squeezed the shears and felt the crunch of cartilage and bone. The piglet squealed in pain. But the tail was still there—the shears were so dull that they had failed to sever it entirely. She had to try a second time, and it took every ounce of fortitude to do it. Liz squeezed again. This time she succeeded, and she gently set the squealing baby animal down.

"I need to go to the bathroom," she said calmly.

Once alone, Liz collected herself. She felt dizzy, overheated, exhausted—and thoroughly miserable. She told herself that this was all for a reason. One day, because of the horrifying work she and her fellow investigators had to do, farm animals would no longer have to suffer like this. She left the bathroom and returned to the tail-docking station.

The day did not get easier. The next procedure for the males was castration. Some claim that castration calms male pigs who are confined in pens, but the main reason the industry does it is to prevent "boar taint." As male pigs get older, their testes produce a compound called androstenone, which is stored in their fat and creates a foul urine- and feces-like odor when cooked and eaten. Removing the testes prevents this. Just as with tail docking, the procedure is performed not by vets but by hired, poorly trained hands, and without anesthetic.

Liz watched as one worker restrained a days-old piglet while another worker made an incision. She became light-headed as she watched the piglet squirm and squeal. A trickle of blood became a river as the worker reached into the incision and grabbed the piglet's testicles. The worker then ripped them out and then sliced them off with a scalpel. Liz was trained to keep her cool during moments like these, so she watched as the piglet was tossed into a pen, screaming. She watched as the procedure was repeated again and again and again.

And then it was her turn.

As you would expect, this crude operation was often botched. Piglets often bled out and died, while others suffered hernias so severe that their intestines spilled out from the incisions. At Iowa Select, sick and injured pigs were left to die without proper veterinary care. It simply wasn't worth the time or money to help them.

Liz could barely function by the end of that first day. The noise, the abuse, the blood, the *smell*—it was all so overwhelming. All she could think about were the squeals and cries of the piglets. It usually takes a while for our investigators to witness the full scope of abuse at a farm, but for Liz, she saw it all on her very first day. She took out her phone and called her mother. Fighting back tears, she recounted her day.

"And this is all for fucking *bacon!*" Liz exclaimed.

"You're going to be fine," her mom said. "You made it through the hardest part. I love you."

She got back on the highway, headed to her motel, and took a long bath. This was partly to calm her nerves, partly to remove the smell of pig shit that had set into her hair, skin, and clothes. Then, over the next several hours, she downloaded her footage and meticulously documented it. Like all of our investigators, despite how angry she was about this abuse, she had to be judicious with how she phrased her notes. Instead of writing, "The worker bashed the animal over the head with a pipe," she would write, "The worker struck the head of the animal with a steel rod." She had to remove her emotion. No editorializing. Liz knew this was going to be a tough investigation.

The investigation lasted three months, and each day the abuses only seemed to get worse. Liz's mornings typically involved moving— or "pushing," as workers called it—the older piglets to a grow-out facility where they would be housed for five months until they reached their slaughter weight of about 250 pounds. Pushing involved herding four hundred terrified piglets down a hallway and onto trucks. The piglets were scared and the workers were fatigued, overworked, and fed up—the perfect recipe for abuse. Piglets were trampled by other piglets and workers. Others were kicked and punched. It was uncontrolled chaos, every day.

Liz was instructed to toss piglets like footballs, a technique taught by management. They considered it faster and more efficient.

"Isn't throwing the piglets like that bad for their health?" Liz asked.

"Oh no, they're fine," the head of the farrowing department replied. "Pigs are very bouncy." The piglets' daily experience—from being thrown to being frequently dropped—wasn't actually painful, she said, but was "like a roller-coaster ride for piglets."

There was one sow in particular whom Liz still remembers. She was old (at least by industry standards) and very sick. She was sprawled out in her stall, her snout resting in a mound of old feed. She wasn't eating, barely drinking. Her skin had a gray tinge and her mouth hung open. Farmworkers had spray-painted a red "X" on her back. Every sow who could no longer bear piglets received this designation eventually. In a couple of days—whenever they got around to it—the workers would send over a "cull truck" to haul her to the slaughterhouse to be made into low-grade pork products.

Liz remembers the look in the sow's eyes, one of pain and resignation. Over the course of a week, she watched as the sow wasted away. When she was alone and had free time, she'd stop by her cage, sit down next to her, and quietly talk to her.

Liz knew that things would never be better for this pig. This animal had known nothing but pain and suffering for her entire life. But if Liz could impart to her a tiny bit of warmth, a tiny bit of compassion in a life otherwise devoid of it, she felt the investigation would be worth it, no matter what happened. When Liz came back the next day, the sow was gone. All that was left was the little mound of food, still untouched.

After Liz's last day at Iowa Select, we packaged her footage and brought it to law enforcement. She had done an unbelievable job.

Unsurprisingly, the district attorney's office declined to take the case, claiming it was all standard industry practice.

So we decided to go right to the public. We learned that Iowa Select Farms supplies pork to Safeway, Costco, Walmart, and Kroger—the four largest grocers in the country. We set up press conferences in various cities in Iowa and states where these retailers are headquartered. *Time* magazine covered Liz's case with a story titled, "Could a Barbaric Pig-Handling Video Hurt Major Grocery Chains?" Nothing happened immediately, but the video did land us numerous in-person meetings with top executives at Costco. The pressure was building.

Meanwhile, Liz was ready to leave Iowa. It had been a long, grueling case. She had been on that farm for three months, longer than most of our investigations. Three months of watching piglets losing their tails and their genitals. Three months of watching piglets being thrown and beaten. Three months of feces and blood and nauseating conditions.

When Liz reflects on the case, she stresses that factory-farm owners deserve as much (or more) blame as the workers who commit the abuse. For laborers, it's either do what the company tells you to or get fired. Most people don't want to work at a factory farm. These people often have no other choice and will take whatever job they can get. Liz shared a bond with many of these workers. They looked out for each other and shared food with each other, and they were warm and welcoming toward Liz. She befriended one man named Gastón who brought her candy and snacks and helped her understand the internal workings of the facility. He took the job out of desperation and needed the work to support his family. He didn't enjoy abusing animals, but that was what the job description entailed. It's what the pork industry required in order to meet consumer demand for cheap meat.

The factory-farm ethos—applying industrial techniques to the mass production of animals—means that caring for individual animals is nearly impossible. On some hog farms, only three or four full-time employees are tasked with overseeing five thousand pigs. With so many animals, it is far more efficient and cost-effective to simply let sick animals suffer and die than provide medical care. As farms become more mechanized, the animals themselves become viewed as mere machines. "Forget the pig is an animal—treat him just like a machine in a factory," *Hog Farm Management* magazine suggested in 1976. Two years later, *National Hog Farmer* recommended, "The breeding sow should be thought of, and treated as, a valuable piece of machinery whose function is to pump out baby pigs like a sausage machine."

In the days before industrial operations, on small farms like my family's, pigs spent many hours of their day playing, sunbathing, and exploring their surroundings using their powerful sense of smell. But as land and labor became scarcer and more expensive, hog farmers began depriving pigs of this basic freedom of movement. By the 1960s, pork producers were reducing labor costs while exponentially increasing output. In 1950, about two million individual farms were raising pigs; by the 1970s barely five hundred thousand remained despite huge increases in pork consumption. This meant that many more pigs were being squeezed into far fewer farms. This trend has only accelerated. According to Food & Water Watch, a Washington, DC–based nongovernmental organization, between 1997 and 2012 the number of pigs on factory farms grew by 37 percent, while the average size of hog farms grew by 68 percent.

Our investigators often say that working on hog farms is the most difficult of all the factory farms. Pigs are so vibrant and full of life, and they're not only some of the smartest farm animals in the world but some of the smartest animals, period. As a study in the journal *Animal Behaviour* proved, pigs are one of the few species that can learn how mirrors work—they can recognize their own image, use the mirror to scope out their surroundings, and discover new sources of food. Research has shown that pigs have an understanding of time and can anticipate future situations based on past experiences. Other studies have found that pigs have excellent long-term memories, can become skilled at complex puzzles and mazes, and love to play. It's easy to spot when a pig is ready to have fun: He bounces on his legs, twists his head, and nuzzles up to potential playmates. Pigs can understand simple sign language. They have complex social cognition and can recognize other individual pigs. Scientists at Wageningen University in the Netherlands found that pigs can even empathize with other pigs who are enduring stressful situations and adjust their behavior accordingly.

One of my favorite stories that illustrates this empathy involves two pigs, Nikki and Rose, who escaped their gestation crates when a massive flood hit their factory farm in Iowa. Volunteers organized to help out. First they found and rescued Nikki, who was thoroughly exhausted and near death, yet still cuddling and nursing her healthy newborn babies. Rose, unfortunately, had given birth prematurely due to the overwhelming stress caused by the flooding. Her piglets did not survive. The volunteers found Rose severely emaciated, desperately urging her lifeless babies to suckle her milk—they tried to move Rose to safety but she refused to leave her piglets. Rose agreed to follow only when the rescuers picked up her babies and brought them into a warm trailer, where Rose finally received medical attention.

The volunteers brought the survivors of the flood to Farm Sanctuary in Upstate New York. There Nikki labored day and night to build and maintain a nest for her piglets. As they grew strong, Nikki overcame the trauma of the flood and her warm personality delighted everyone on the farm. Every day she greeted volunteers by nuzzling her mouth against their chins. She was also incredibly strong—before long, Nikki had taken over as top pig among a herd of more than twenty females. But Rose remained stricken with grief. She was depressed and would not touch her food. Farm Sanctuary workers introduced Rose to the other pigs, who attempted to socialize and play with her. But she rebuffed them each time. Rose was heartbroken.

Then something miraculous happened: Nikki invited Rose into her family and allowed her to help raise the piglets. Rose began to eat and play with other pigs. She was happy. At MFA, we want all of the pigs involved in our investigations to find happiness like Nikki and Rose, but that is not possible. It's our job to expose the horrors of the hog industry so that one day pigs will not need to be rescued. The hellholes that imprison them won't exist.

We have taken steps closer to that goal. After holding numerous high-level meetings with animal-protection organizations including MFA, and after public outrage from investigations including Liz's at

Iowa Select, McDonald's released its plan to phase out the use of gestation crates for mother sows. Not long after, Safeway, Kroger, Burger King, and Wendy's also agreed to phase out gestation crates. But other retailers including Costco, Kmart, and Walmart weren't budging. It was time to increase the pressure.

In late 2011 we sent TJ to start another investigation, this one at Christensen Farms in Hanska, Minnesota. Just like Liz, TJ saw thousands of mother pigs confined to filthy metal gestation crates so small that they were unable to even turn around or lie down comfortably for nearly their entire lives. He found pigs suffering from large, open wounds and pressure sores from rubbing against the bars of their tiny cages and the hard concrete flooring. He saw workers rip testicles out of male piglets and slice off their tails—all without anesthesia. Sick and injured pigs with severe wounds and infections were left to suffer and die.

TJ was also introduced to the horrendous—and entirely legal—process of "thumping." When filth and excrement cover almost every surface, including the underside of sows where piglets nurse, illness is routine. Because piglets' immune systems are so underdeveloped, and veterinary attention so rare, infections spread quickly. Sick piglets often suffer from horrendous diarrhea and grow so weak that they cannot even move. Many are left alone to die; at other times, workers are instructed to kill ill piglets by "thumping" them. The animal agriculture industry is clever with their euphemisms, but this tactic is as barbaric as it sounds: A worker picks up the piglet and slams his or her head against concrete. Though thumping is supposed to deliver an instantaneous death, TJ routinely documented workers slamming piglets into the ground and leaving them to suffer and slowly die with fractured skulls. While watching TJ's footage, my mind raced back to my high school days, when I heard about the piglet who was slammed into the concrete in full view of students—the incident that led me to found MFA. Thirteen years later, it was still happening, and on a massive scale.

Armed with this footage, we prepared elaborate campaigns against Costco, Kmart, and Walmart. The video opened with "an important consumer warning" about the pork sold at the retailers. We were ready to launch protests all over the country. But before we did, we decided to approach each retailer privately. Out of concern for their brand image—if not animals—maybe we could convince some of them to ditch gestation crates, along with so many of their competitors.

It worked. Kmart, the third-largest discount store in the world, immediately announced that it would phase out gestation crates among its suppliers. Despite Costco's reputation for progressive politics and its existing ban on confining calves in veal crates, the company was slow to embrace change, so I arranged an interview between the Associated Press and Matt, our director of investigations. During the interview, Matt explained that Costco was allowing pork suppliers to cram pigs in restrictive gestation crates. The animals were suffering terribly, and we had the tapes to prove it. Shortly thereafter, I received a phone call. Costco was now on board. They would end the use of gestation crates.

In an urgent letter sent to all their pork suppliers, Doug Schutt, Costco's executive vice president of merchandising, declared: "We want all of the hogs throughout our pork supply chain to be housed in groups. All of us at Costco take animal welfare seriously and consider humane animal handling a business imperative."

The story the AP was about to publish, which was intended to serve as an exposé and would coincide with MFA's national campaign launch, quickly turned into a victory announcement. Newspapers around the country ran the AP article titled, "Costco Joins Cause Against Use of Small Pens for Pregnant Sows."

The meat industry also took notice. The headline in *Pork Network*, the industry trade publication, read, "Gestation Crate Pressure Builds; Costco Buckles."

This left Walmart as the sole remaining holdout. It was crucial that we get them on board. As the world's largest company by revenue—they sell a quarter of all Americans' groceries—we knew that if Walmart changed, entire industries would have to change along with it.

It was time to launch a full-blown campaign against Walmart. But we needed another investigation of a Walmart pork supplier. We needed a new investigator, one who hadn't been overexposed or "outed" within the pork industry.

And along came Jess.

Jess started as an intern for Mercy For Animals in Chicago and then interned again in New York back in 2010. A blond former high school cheerleader from Texas with a hint of a Valley Girl accent, Jess was someone I would never have predicted would be capable of rolling up her sleeves and diving into the muddy, shitty, bloody world of factory farming—much less that she would become a prolific undercover investigator. After coming out as gay, though, Jess completely changed her appearance. She lost weight and ditched the blond hair and the makeup—but not her quirky, kind, and fun-loving personality.

By 2013 Jess had gone through investigator training and was

ready to hit the field. Her first assignment: Pipestone System's Rosewood Farms in Pipestone, Minnesota—a major Walmart pork supplier.

The stakes were high. Pipestone was owned by Randy Spronk, president of the politically powerful National Pork Producers Council—the pork industry's primary trade association and ardent defender of gestation crates. It would be a major coup if we could expose abuse at a farm that represents the face of the pork industry. As it turned out, Jess's footage revealed a situation even worse than we had expected. In our video, narrated by James Cromwell (nominated for an Oscar for his role as Farmer Hoggett in the classic 1995 film *Babe*, which featured a loveable, talking pig), we exposed workers violently slamming conscious piglets headfirst against the ground, ripping out their testicles, and confining pregnant pigs in filthy, fly-infested gestation crates. Sick and injured pigs with bleeding wounds or infections were left to suffer without veterinary care. Thumped piglets, still convulsing violently, were tossed into bins. Other piglets were crushed to death after being caught between their mothers and the narrow bars of their cages. And workers viciously beat animals.

We decided to report the cruelty to the authorities. Vandhana knew of a little-used provision of Minnesota law that would allow us to go directly to a judge. The law was so obscure that even the judge's clerk hadn't heard of it, and Vandhana had to send a copy of the law to them. Jess and Vandhana met the judge, a kind man who took the time to hear the gruesome details of the case and watch the video evidence. We provided him with the footage, pinpointed the abuses that violated Minnesota's anticruelty laws, and delivered statements from veterinary experts. He was so appalled by what he saw that he immediately issued an order for the district attorney and the sheriff to investigate the facility.

In a perfect world, this information was all they needed to take action. But Pipestone was governed by typical good-ol'-boy politics. It was a major employer in a town of barely four thousand people. Instead of catching them by surprise, the county sheriff let Pipestone know we had incriminating evidence. Then he arranged to tour the factory farm on a predetermined day. He even brought along a pork industry veterinarian. The sheriff interviewed a worker Jess had filmed beating pigs mercilessly. The worker denied it all, of course, and that was all the sheriff needed to hear. The sheriff wasn't able to open our footage on his computer; there was something wrong with the file, he claimed. Never mind that MFA offered to fly someone down immediately, laptop in hand. Never mind that Vandhana was on the phone with them describing exactly how they could view the footage online. The Pipestone "county attorney," who was in fact a partner at a private law firm in the area, sent MFA a letter stating that he was declining prosecution in the "interest of justice." He hadn't bothered to watch the video, either. That was it. Case closed.

I felt nauseous. We had done everything right. We had gift-wrapped this case and put a bow on it for the sheriff's office. The footage demonstrated horrendous abuse clearly in violation of the law. It did not get more obvious than this. Here was a classic example of law-enforcement bias and small-town politics, two reasons that farm abuses often go unpunished. The factory farm was a major employer in a heavily agricultural community. Mr. Spronk had power and clout, and the pigs did not.

Despite the legal setback, we weren't done yet. We released the Pipestone footage to the public and dispatched mobile billboards with giant images of pigs locked in crates that cried, WALMART: STOP TORTURING PIGS, to circle Walmart's headquarters in Bentonville, Arkansas. We organized more than 150 protests around the country—complete with a ten-foot-high replica of a battered pig suffering in a crate to drive the point home. We needed to keep chipping way. After we aired the Pipestone case, we finally got Walmart's attention as they sent representatives to the farm to investigate the abuses that were occurring. But as the world's largest retailer, Walmart moves slowly. We still needed another big case. It was time to bring back Pete.

If you ask Pete what pigs smell like, he'll smile and say, "Maple syrup." That's not the smell most people associate with pigs, but it's true. Pigs are not able to sweat, so they naturally seek out cool places like mud and water when temperatures rise—that's why people associate them with being dirty. But when these naturally clean animals are held by the thousands in tiny gestation crates encrusted with feces, that sweet maple syrup smell turns sickly. Beneath the gestation barns are manure-retention ponds that are flushed into open-air lagoons. The lagoons fill up quickly and turn pink as bacteria colonizes the stagnant water. Often, workers will hook up high-pressure hoses and spray the manure over nearby fields. In fact, one of the biggest environmental nightmares for pork-producing states is what to do with the monumental amount of waste produced every year.

Cesspools of Waste

Mark Devries is a thirty-year-old attorney and filmmaker who helps produce MFA's investigative videos. Before that, Mark produced the documentary *Speciesism*, which explores the dark side of factory farming. Along the way, Mark discovered how to use drones for filming. He flew a drone over a hog farm in North Carolina and gained a vantage point rarely seen. He learned how the animals' feces falls through slats in the concrete floor and is flushed into giant open-air cesspools the size of multiple football fields. As a result, people living nearby are forced to smell what is similar to millions of gallons of untreated human sewage.

More disturbing, when the lagoons overflowed, workers would hook up hoses and pump the liquid waste into giant misting machines. Instead of paying to transport millions of gallons of waste elsewhere, these factory farms drained their cesspools by simply spraying the waste into the air, allowing the wind to carry the noxious mist to nearby communities.

Mark interviewed scores of neighbors affected by these cesspools. They mentioned not being able to catch their breath due to the sewage smell, and many other health issues. Numerous studies back up what Mark and his drones discovered. One North Carolina analysis of more than fifty-eight thousand children found a 23 percent higher prevalence of asthma symptoms among students attending schools near these factory farms. Other studies have linked the waste to neurological and respiratory problems and increases in dangerous bacteria in drinking water, such as *E. coli*, salmonella, and cryptosporidium.

The toxic mist from open-air lagoons carries into neighboring yards, sickening residents. Elsie Herring, a senior citizen who lives near the lagoon, told *National Geographic* that the odor was "very, very offensive. I don't feel comfortable even having people over, because it's embarrassing and humiliating that, you know, you're trying to entertain someone and there's someone eight feet away spraying animal waste on you." She described physical symptoms including headaches, stomachaches, excessive coughing, watery eyes, and the urge to vomit.

There isn't much these residents can do. People who live near factory farms are often very low-income and cannot afford to move. Considering that pig farming earns North Carolina almost $3 billion per year, these red lagoons are creating green pockets for a select few. Like the plight of animals inside factory farms, it's easy to overlook the plight of humans living beside them.

It was to a farm like this that Pete showed up for work in 2013. West Coast Farms was a typical hog farm comprising six barns—three for gestation and three for farrowing. Off to one side was a large structure that Pete later learned was a cooler for piglets who had died overnight or had been thumped. It tended to fill up fast.

West Coast Farms was a bit of a misnomer, considering it was located in Henryetta, Oklahoma—about ninety miles due east of Oklahoma City. It's a parched, pancake-flat place dotted by the occasional stunted brown tree. Apparently, the farm's owner, Lonnie, had a soft spot for California.

A major supplier to Tyson Foods and Walmart, every week some of West Coast Farms' twenty-one hundred sows birthed roughly one thousand piglets. The facility was kept to a precise schedule to meet Tyson's high demand. If a sow could not be re-impregnated within thirty days of giving birth, she was removed from the shed and sent to the slaughterhouse. At West Coast Farms, twelve sows were sent for slaughter every week for this reason.

When Pete reported for work, Lonnie told him that if he were caught abusing an animal he would be fired and reported to law enforcement. Later that day, as Pete was removing manure from farrowing crates, he noticed piles of feces covered with maggots. He also noticed that many of the pregnant sows had open wounds on their cheeks and heads, and yet more had large blood sores on their shoulders and hips. Then, later, a sow tried to run from two workers who were trying to shove her into her crate.

"Watch this," Pete's coworker Daniel called out. He then took a three-foot-wide wooden board and slammed it into her face. When that wouldn't subdue her, he jammed his fingers into her eyes until she backed up. Not long after, Pete watched workers inject dozens of pigs with antibiotics using needles that were rarely changed or even cleaned.

Pig enclosures were supposed to be cleaned out every day, but that rarely happened. These tiny prisons are designed so that excrement can fall through slats into manure pools below, but the slats often became clogged. Feces would pile up to such high levels in the crates that workers couldn't even open the cage doors.

At West Coast Farms, Pete regularly watched workers thump piglets and walk away before ensuring they were dead, ignoring convulsing piglets. With his camera rolling, Pete approached Lonnie.

"I've noticed that the workers aren't thumping piglets correctly," Pete told him. "They're still thrashing on the ground. They're obviously still in pain."

Lonnie gave him a bored look. "Well... no... I'd get in big trouble for that," he sighed. "It has to be blunt-force trauma, and you have to verify death." Then he changed the subject. As far as Pete could tell, Lonnie never looked into the situation. Pete didn't see Lonnie talking to any of the other workers about this, so he asked around. The other workers told him that Lonnie never talked to them. And unfortunately, Pete never saw the situation improve; workers continued to incorrectly "thump" the piglets and just leave them, causing them to endure horrific suffering until they eventually died.

Other abuse bordered on pure sadism. One worker, José, was just eighteen years old, but his time working on hog farms had thoroughly desensitized him to cruelty. Sometimes he would shake the piglets and growl at them. Once he saw a piglet with a tail he had forgotten to remove, so he took a metal spade designed to scrape manure off the floor, held the piglet between his feet, and hacked off her tail with the filthy tool. Bowling balls were kept in a few of the group pens, ostensibly for the pigs to play with. Once, when he was bored, José heaved one of the balls at a sow's head. Another worker, Lewis, would routinely punch, kick, and poke sows in the eye to get them to move.

One day a veterinarian employed by Tyson showed up to inspect the farm. Eyeing an opportunity, Pete shadowed the vet while secretly cataloging severe medical problems with the pigs—including open sores and prolapsed uteruses. He needn't have bothered—the vet only spent about half an hour inspecting the twenty-one hundred pigs.

"This is my fifth inspection today," he told Pete. "I like to be in and out fast so I can move on to the next farm."

"Did you see any problems with the animals?" Pete asked.

The vet looked taken aback. "Of course not. They're all fine. This was just an easy walk-through. Just make sure everything looks good."

The vet then had a forty-minute conversation with Lonnie about how best to deal with dying pigs. Lonnie wanted to know how long they could keep these pigs alive until enough drugs had left their system so they could be legally slaughtered.

Before Pete left for the day, he approached Lonnie and told him that two pigs were dying in one of the barns, but the vet hadn't noticed.

"He doesn't care," Lonnie chuckled. "I once saw him do an inspection in under fifteen minutes."

Pete remembers one sow in particular. Like all the others, she wasn't given a name—just a tag number. She was No. 2640. She was heavily pregnant and was being moved to the farrowing side of the facility. On the way she collapsed and wasn't able to get up, because her legs were so wobbly and weak from atrophy. A worker named Tino began beating her until blood trickled down her face. Then he slapped her back and ripped out patches of her hair, slammed a wooden board into her front feet, pulled her ears, and kicked her in the face. She still didn't budge, so she was left on the ground, alone, overnight.

When Pete arrived the next morning, 2640 was still lying in the same spot. Finally, she was moved back to her crate, but she wasn't touching her food or water. She was sick and depressed. The next day Pete found that she had entered labor. Pete and another worker helped deliver her piglets: eleven alive, one dead. When Pete arrived the next day, he found 2640 still in labor, lying by herself, a dead piglet by her side and another barely alive. Pete never found out what happened to her after that. The last he saw her, she was lying alone in her crate, a few food crumbs by her snout.

Pete also saw the intelligence and empathy of pigs firsthand. He was fascinated by one particular sow who figured out how to escape from her gestation crate. He watched as she wiggled her rear end under the gate and then casually lifted it up over the latch. But more remarkably, each time she escaped, she would begin unlatching every gestation crate around her until there were half a dozen pigs running around trying to make a break for it. And each time workers would wrangle them back to their crates and beat them.

At West Coast Farms—like nearly all industrial pig operations— pigs were kept indoors for their entire lives except for several fleeting moments when they made the short walk from the gestation barn to the farrowing barn. Pete remembers how this moment always annoyed the workers. For just a few seconds, these pigs could be outside. They could smell fresh air. They could see countryside. Pete even thought he could see them smiling. They'd look up and gaze at the brilliant blue sky, and then they would sit down and refuse to move. "These pigs knew they would be beaten," Pete recalls, "but they didn't care. They were outside. They could be in the sunlight. They never wanted to go back inside."

The West Coast Farms investigation lasted a little more than three weeks. Pete, Matt, and Vandhana met with an assistant district attorney just days later. They were armed with the footage of workers kicking, throwing, hitting, and body-slamming baby piglets to the ground, among countless other abuses. The cruelty was so bad that both the National Pork Producers Council and the Oklahoma Pork Council issued statements condemning the cruelty and even recommended that charges be brought. This was one of the most appalling cases we had ever completed. Even the pork industry admitted that those committing the abuses we documented should be prosecuted.

When Pete, Vandhana, and Matt entered the ADA's office, they saw several framed aerial photographs of hog farms and a "Young Hog Farmers of America" display on the walls. *Oh boy*, Vandhana thought. *We're in the lion's den.* Pete later joked it was like a Drug Enforcement Administration agent paying tribute to meth labs.

The ADA watched the footage with her thumb under her chin, lips pressed tightly together in an expression that barely concealed her anger at being disturbed. "Well," she said when they had finished their presentation. "We'll be sure to look into it for you." And with that, she shuttled them out of her office.

Pete couldn't help but laugh. He had been here before, and he knew that nothing was going to happen. Even though the abuse at this Tyson supplier went far beyond what is standard—not even the pork industry could find a way to defend workers throwing bowling balls at pigs' heads—the DA's office sat on their hands and ran out the clock. Of course, if this sort of abuse happened to cats and dogs, we would be talking extended prison sentences and psychiatric evaluations. But farm animals? Often no action is taken at all.

We pressed on. In 2014 and 2015, we investigated two factory farms in Colorado operated by Seaboard Foods, the country's third-largest pork producer. There it was more of the same: pregnant pigs locked in tiny metal gestation crates unable to turn around; workers tail-docking and castrating piglets with dull blades; workers hitting piglets with rock-filled gas cans to force them into overcrowded walkways and transport trucks; workers punching and violently hitting pigs in their faces and bodies with boards and heavy cans; and workers snaring animals and firing captive bolts into their skulls in full view of other pigs. And just like other cases, the local district attorneys refused to take any action against the wealthy and powerful pork industry.

Eventually, Walmart had had enough. A few weeks after our final case in May 2015, it happened. Walmart publicly committed to improving farm animal welfare across their supply chain. At long last, Walmart agreed to end some of the cruelest, sanctioned abuses, including the confinement of pregnant pigs in gestation crates. But they went further, also agreeing to end the confinement of baby calves in veal crates and egg-laying hens in battery cages. Walmart also announced that it was working to end the needless mutilations of animals without anesthesia, such as castration, tail docking, and dehorning. Theirs was one of the most comprehensive animal welfare policies of its kind. I felt so grateful to our brave investigators when Walmart made its historic change—especially Liz, who endured such a long investigation and had to participate in these standard industry practices. Because of her hard work, life is a little easier for millions of pigs.

This campaign hadn't been easy. It took three years and six investigations; more than 150 protests and 640,000 petition signatures; full-page newspaper ads and billboards; and celebrity support from the likes of Joaquin Phoenix, Sia, Pamela Anderson, and many others. It took six gritty, relentless investigators. It took countless hours at MFA headquarters to review and package the cases.

With Walmart's announcement, it was becoming clear that the days are numbered for many of the factory-farming industry's cruelest practices. But our battle wasn't over.

Cody

10.

"You'll Learn to Hate Them"

We're not hiring."

Cody was crushed. He was looking for a job at Kreider Farms, New York State's largest egg farm, and they wouldn't even let him submit an application. This was supposed to be his very first undercover investigation for Mercy For Animals. He'd been working as a research analyst for a private investigation firm in New York City, helping to run the pro bono department. A lifelong animal lover, Cody was horrified by Pete's undercover video from Gemperle Enterprises. After seeing it online, he gave me a call offering his firm's professional services to help us trace suppliers to producers, along with other investigative work. But I had other plans.

I told him we didn't need corporate investigators. We needed undercover investigators.

Cody and I are nearly the same age. He's intelligent, articulate, and a strategic thinker. I could tell immediately that he was driven, fearless, and free-spirited. Raised in New York, Cody fits the bill of the post-punk intellectual. He is athletic and his arms are covered in vibrant tattoo sleeves; he has dark blond hair and sometimes scruffy facial hair. His smile is electric. In other words, Cody was the ideal candidate to be an investigator.

Not long after our conversation, Cody quit his job and boarded a plane to California for undercover training. We paired him up with Pete. Cody learned how to set up and use concealed cameras and, more important, how to blend in with other farmworkers. A city kid, he didn't exactly resemble your typical farmhand. Pete coached Cody on how to keep his cool and how to make quick decisions: When they are alone in the field, investigators need to be able to improvise on the spot. If not, they risk having their cover blown and finding themselves in serious danger.

Cody was physically prepared for the manual labor and mentally prepared for the abuse he would see, but he never thought the hardest part would be simply finding a job. He had quit his career, said goodbye to his girlfriend and to his New York City apartment, essentially putting his life on hold—and for what?

But the next day he got a call from Willet Dairy, the largest dairy farm in all of New York. They needed a maintenance technician and they were only about thirty miles south of Syracuse. Cody hopped in his truck and drove down for an interview. The farm was located in the tiny town of Locke in the Finger Lakes region of New York. It's a beautiful place, but cold and quiet in the winter—nothing like the busy streets of New York. The ground was hard and specked with snow. Like the land around it, Willet Dairy was cold and gray. Four sprawling concrete barns housed the facility's forty-five hundred cows. After assuring the hiring manager that he didn't mind getting dirty or learning how to weld, Cody was hired.

His job at Willet was to perform basic maintenance, such as unclogging milking lines and repairing manure scrapers. Trudging through knee-deep fields of manure is not glamorous work, but it allowed Cody to be near the cows. And that meant being close enough to document abuse. Many people think that cows used for dairy live in peace and comfort, frolicking in open, lush pastures. As Cody would reveal, the lives of these cows were brutal.

On the first day of the job, in the dead of winter 2009, Cody was helping to repair trough heaters, which prevent cows' water from freezing in the subzero temperatures. As he was working, a curious cow strolled over to Cody and sniffed him. Cody reached out his hand to greet her.

Phil, Cody's manager, pushed his hand away. "Believe me, you'll learn to hate them. I learned that ten years ago." Then he screamed at the cow, whipping her with a frayed steel cable, and charged at her with his wrench.

Cody was stunned by the cruelty, but the other farmworkers just laughed it off. "Yup, that's Phil," one said. "He's definitely got anger issues. He can get a bit rough."

At Willet, the cruelty began within moments after the birth of calves, when these babies were dragged from their mothers. Cody's hidden camera video recorded the mothers bellowing in distress, which could last days, and workers admitted that cows "become crazy" when their babies are taken. "Oh yeah," one of the workers said. "Once you get the calf out of there, the mother will be running around looking for it for days." To subdue them, workers kicked and hit the cows.

On a dairy farm, cows' milk is intended for humans—not calves. The more a calf drinks from his or her mother, the less profit the farm makes. This is why calves are separated from their mothers shortly after birth. The effects are devastating on the animals. Imagine if your own child were literally dragged from you minutes after birth, never to be seen again—like any of us, you would surely be hysterical with rage. That bond is no different in cows. One day, Cody watched as workers dragged a calf by her legs away from her mother, who had just given birth. They placed the calf into a nearby pen. The two stared at each other, mooing loudly. Early separation has lifelong consequences for calves. One study revealed that calves who stay with their mothers longer put on healthy weight up to three times faster than calves who are separated from their mothers at birth. Another study found that calves who are separated from their mothers at birth have difficulty as adults navigating stressful situations and socializing with other cows.

I've heard countless stories from around the world of mother cows grieving just like humans do. As is well-known, cows are considered sacred in India, and in much of the country it is illegal to slaughter them. They're even allowed to roam free among the roads. Several years ago, a bus driver ran over and killed a calf who was walking beside his mother. From then on, the mother grieved for her baby by returning every day to the spot of the accident. Day after day, for years. Amazingly, she recognized the driver and the bus, even after it had been painted in an attempt to disguise it from the distraught bovine. Every day she waited until she spotted the bus and then chased it down the road. Then she would run in front of the bus to make the driver slow down—as if she were ensuring the tragedy could never happen again.

Cow intelligence was beautifully illustrated by a veterinarian named Holly Cheever, who had a practice in Upstate New York—not far from Willet Dairy. One day a client, who ran a small dairy farm, called her with a bizarre mystery: One of his cows, who had recently given birth, was not producing any milk. New mothers produce around fifty pounds a day, but this cow was completely dry. A few days earlier she had gone out to pasture—these were the days when cows were afforded fragments of a natural life—delivered her calf, and returned with the baby to the barn. Holly couldn't figure out what was wrong; the mother seemed perfectly healthy. Finally, the farmer followed the mother as she walked out to the periphery of the pasture. There, hidden in the woods, was another calf. She had delivered twins, and every night she came to feed her second, secret baby, who drank all her milk. It turns out that four previous times she had given birth, and each time her baby was taken from her. She knew this time would be no different, and she had a *Sophie's Choice* moment: She had to give up one calf in order for the other to live in secret. She had the memory of her previous losses, and she had the intelligence to formulate a plan and the heart-wrenching wisdom to know she had to give one child up to fool the farmer. Despite Holly's pleas, the farmer took the calf and sent him to a veal factory. Holly later wrote, "All I know is this: there is a lot more going on behind those beautiful eyes than we humans have ever given them credit for, and as a mother who was able to nurse all four of my babies and did not have to suffer the agonies of losing my beloved offspring, I feel her pain."

Cows don't just experience sorrow, but joy as well.

All of us have experienced the eureka effect—that sudden, revelatory moment in which you finally understand a previously incomprehensible problem. Scientists say that this euphoric thrill of solving complex problems is a hallmark of human intelligence. Cows, too, can problem solve and experience eureka moments. Recent research out of Cambridge University revealed that young female cows, known as heifers, demonstrate behavioral signs of excitement after solving complex problems. In addition, research shows that cows are highly individualistic and respond to personalized attention. A study from Newcastle University found that cows used for dairy who are given unique names yield more milk than cows who are not given names. They also appear to be happier and more relaxed the more they are treated as individuals. And just like humans, cows have very distinct moods. They are happy when the weather is nice and they can graze with their friends. Cows can even hold grudges and develop social hierarchies. They are sad when it's raining or when they are not around friends. In fact, a study out of Northampton University found that cows are far more stressed when they are alone or around unfamiliar animals. But they immediately relax when reunited with their best friend.

At Willet Dairy, these emotional, social, intelligent animals were denied any semblance of a natural life. Cody observed perhaps the worst example of this abuse on a day he wasn't even supposed to be working. He had heard that on his day off, dozens of calves would be "disbudded," a benign-sounding industry term that disguised horrendous abuse. He had to be there to document it. So he showed up, claiming he had forgotten his cell phone somewhere in the calf barn. With his camera rolling, he wandered until he spotted workers herding a large group of calves. He watched as a worker harnessed a panicked young calf—her ear tag number reading 7531—then restrained her by tying her head to a gate post. The worker then grabbed a hot iron and began digging it into one of the budding horns to prevent it from ever growing. Smoke billowed up as the red-hot iron met flesh. Eyes wide, 7531 struggled and moaned before buckling under the pain and collapsing. Her head firmly tied to the post, the worker then moved to the second bud and began digging the iron into her skull again. As 7531 struggled, the worker jammed his fingers into her eyes to restrain her. She kicked, gurgled, fell over again, and vomited from the extreme pain.

Next, without using anesthesia, the worker cut off the calf's tail using bull castration shears, twisting violently until the end of the tail snapped off. Then the worker cauterized the exposed vertebrae with a hot iron. After the traumatic ordeal, 7531 was untied and half led, half dragged back to the pen.

At Willet, newborn calves were kept in frigid tin sheds. (Temperatures in Upstate New York regularly stay below freezing during the winter months.) One day Cody found a calf who had frozen to death. She was lying near two other calves who were close to death themselves.

When he pointed them out to his coworker, he agreed. "Yup, she died during the night. But don't worry, the others are still alive."

"Won't they die, too?" Cody insisted.

"Don't worry about it. It's fine."

Not far away, Cody found two other dead calves buried in straw. It was as if death were coming for each calf, one at a time, in the frigid night. Cody spent a lot of time with one calf in particular who was no more than a few days old. He would sit down next to her in the freezing, filthy pen, softly stroking her. She would bellow whenever he got up, as if pleading with him to stay. She had grown weaker each time Cody visited her. "I could see the light draining out of her eyes," Cody later said. The next time Cody visited her, he knew she was about to die. He remembers thinking that he wished he could scoop her up, whisk her to safety, and nurse her back to health. He wanted to save her from this frozen hell.

Our investigators face this dilemma every single day. Why work so hard on undercover investigations if they can't even save the animals in front of them? But, like Liz and Pete, Cody knew that he had to push on with the investigation and expose these abuses to the world. He left the calf alone. When he returned later in the day, she was dead.

Cows used for dairy are kept in a constant cycle of pregnancy, birth, and lactation, and the harsh reality is that the dairy industry has little use for their calves. Some females are kept alive to be grown into replacement cows for their mothers. However, as Cody saw, many are neglected and left to die. When they are only a few weeks old, most males are shipped off to be auctioned and slaughtered for low-grade beef products. Others are immobilized in tiny pens and raised for veal. This keeps their flesh tender, which means a higher price at slaughter.

Female cows are milked twice a day by industrial machines. When they are not hooked to the milking apparatus, they mainly live on manure-coated concrete floors in overcrowded sheds. Factory farms have made a science out of milk production. For a cow, milk production peaks about sixty days after giving birth, at which point she is artificially inseminated. Nine months later, she gives birth again and the process is repeated. According to the USDA, the average cow produces more than twenty thousand pounds of milk every single year for human consumption. That's more than four times what was produced in 1950.

As you can imagine, this makes life extremely strenuous for cows. While a cow's natural life span can exceed fifteen years, at factory farms they are typically "worn out" and sent to slaughter by the age of five. By then most can barely stand, constant pregnancy and lactation taking a huge toll on their bodies.

At Willet, eight workers milked about five hundred cows per hour in parlors coated in filth. Cows' legs and udders were layered in excrement and rarely, if ever, washed. Cody noted many cows with painful and life-threatening prolapsed uteruses, a condition that, with prompt veterinary care, is very treatable. During Cody's third week on the job, he noticed a cow with a severe prolapse.

"What should we do about it?" Cody asked another worker.

The other worker merely smiled and said: "She won't be having another calving cycle, so she'll probably be hamburger soon. The only way a cow won't become hamburger is if she dies in the lanes or is too sick to walk to auction. Then she's dog food." Weeks later, the cow still had not been treated.

On his third day on the job, Cody noted in his diary: "Cows never leave their lanes, except when herded to and from the milking parlor. They will not see the outdoors until they are loaded onto a truck and sent for slaughter." For nearly their entire lives, the cows were either standing in manure or lying down in so-called free stalls, a thinly padded slab of concrete separated into compartments by steel bars.

The industry calls the cows "free" because they are not chained to the bars by their necks. But the stalls are too small, and cows cannot move freely. Pressure sores from the concrete were common and were rarely treated.

Another day, Cody counted twenty-two cows with swollen hocks (joints near their rear hooves), some swollen larger than a baseball. Many had open sores caked with manure, infected and oozing pus. Meanwhile, all the cows were drinking murky brown water teeming with chunks of feed, manure, and other debris. When he asked a mechanic if workers ever washed the troughs, he was told: "No, they're too fucking lazy.... They don't ever wash them, not even in the summer."

During one particularly slow day, Cody's manager, Phil, entertained himself by punching cows in the head. Then he laughed and bragged to Cody about how often he battered animals, telling him it was "probably why I got arthritis big-time in this hand."

He took sadistic glee in detailing the pain he caused. "What do you think that wrench did to her?" he asked Cody giddily, referring to a cow.

"I don't know," Cody responded. "What did you do with it?"

"Cracked her right over the fucking skull."

One year, Phil claimed, he even broke his hand by punching a cow in the eye. Another time, he ripped his hand open when he punched a cow in the nose. He also said that he once locked a cow's head in a gate and cracked her over the head with a wrench, dropping her to the floor.

Cody stuck it out at Willet for more than a month. Even though it was his first investigation and every day offered sad lessons, Cody battled through it and methodically documented each and every abuse. Every day he drove back to his motel covered in filth—bleary-eyed, exhausted, trying to blank out what he had seen. Then he'd upload his footage and type up the details—every kick, every punch, every injury, every beating with a blunt object. He would go to sleep, wake up, and do it all over again. Cody had nightmares, he lost a lot of weight, but he stuck with the investigation until we had enough evidence.

It wasn't hard getting media attention. After we wrapped up the case I happened to get a call from Paul Shapiro, the vice president of public policy for The Humane Society of the United States.

"Hey, Nathan," he said, "I just got a call from ABC's *Nightline*. They want to run a segment on dairy cows. Do you know of any good cases they can feature?"

"You know what, Paul?" I replied. "I think I have just the one they're looking for."

Paul quickly set us up with ABC. Soon after, we were sitting down with Brian Ross and the investigative team at *Nightline*.

The footage broke simultaneously on *Nightline* and ABC *World News Tonight* with Diane Sawyer. Cody gave a fantastic interview on *Nightline* (and a few years later he discussed the case on *The Daily Show* with Jon Stewart). ABC News had also contacted Temple Grandin, the famed animal welfare expert and professor of animal science at Colorado State University, for her opinion. She was outraged, declaring, "Dehorning hurts. It's a lot of stress and we should be giving them a lot of anesthetics. The research is clear. The dehorning is the single most painful thing we do." Following the broadcast, Leprino Foods, a cheese supplier to Domino's, Papa John's, and Pizza Hut, dropped Willet Dairy as a milk supplier. And soon after that, Willet Dairy announced it had ended its practice of tail docking and would be using anesthesia before dehorning. In the end, only Cody's supervisor, Phil, was arrested. He was eventually convicted of criminal animal cruelty, fined, and ordered to have no contact with animals for a year.

As the story broke, New York State assemblywoman Linda Rosenthal introduced a bill to ban tail docking. Tail docking is opposed by the American Veterinary Medical Association and widely considered cruel and outdated by the industry. It should have passed easily. Unfortunately, the bill stalled in the agriculture committee, which almost never goes against the interests of Big Ag. Matt later met with the chairman of the agriculture committee, who bluntly explained why the bill died.

"Matt, I agree with you about tail docking," he said. "It's cruel and inhumane."

"Then why won't you support this bill?" Matt was exasperated.

"It's a slippery slope. Where does it end? If we criminalize tail docking, then we'll have to criminalize disbudding. Then we'll criminalize the separation of mothers and calves. Before we know it, the dairy industry will be out of business. We can't have that."

Matt tried to explain that simple reforms would not bankrupt the industry, but the ag committee chairman doubled down. He vowed to never let the bill pass through his committee.

Because New York does not have a ballot-initiative process like California does, there was not much more we could do. But other states did. We quickly regrouped and refocused.

. . .

t was 2009 and right after the passage of Proposition 2 in California—one of the most successful moments in the history of the animal-rights movement. Factory farmers and the animal-ag industry started to get worried. *Feedstuffs*, the *Wall Street Journal* of agribusiness, published an editorial titled "California Dam Must Not Be Breached," urging industry to dig in and fight Proposition 2. The initiative "will affect all of livestock and poultry production across the entire U.S., if not North America," the publication warned. The animal-agriculture industry had spent $10 million in California, they had lost badly, and now they were scared.

And they should have been. California was only the beginning. The next battleground state would be one I was all too familiar with: Ohio.

That year, the Ohio Farm Bureau (OFB) preemptively pushed their own ballot measure to establish the Ohio Livestock Care Standards Board. Sounding like a pro-animal initiative, the measure passed easily. The board was to be composed of thirteen people, most of whom, not surprisingly, were representatives of the meat, dairy, and egg industries. MFA did not campaign against it because we were preparing for the real battle in 2010—passing our own animal-friendly ballot measure. We wanted action similar in scope to California's Proposition 2, in addition to a ban on strangulation as a euthanasia method and preventing downed, sick cows from being slaughtered.

Championing the effort was a coalition, Ohioans for Humane

Farms. MFA dove in—mobilizing our large support base around Ohio. I was tasked with overseeing the volunteers gathering petition signatures in a key area, northern Ohio.

The OFB fought back fast and hard. They knew their best chance to stop us from winning was to prevent us from getting onto the ballot in the first place. So they started running radio ads, warning people against signing any petitions. They also waged disruption campaigns—to the point of hiring people to circulate fake petitions in an attempt to confuse voters.

The stakes were high. Dairy is a huge part of Ohio's gross state product. According to the American Dairy Association, Ohio ranks first in the nation in Swiss cheese production, tenth in overall cheese production, and eleventh in total milk production. Meanwhile, dairy contributes $4.2 billion to the economy while directly employing more than fourteen thousand people. In other words, dairy is big business, one that the industry—and, as we learned, law enforcement—will stop at nothing to protect. In order to win signatures and combat the OFB's tactics, we needed to release undercover footage exposing the abuse animals faced behind the closed doors of Ohio's farms.

We put Pete on the case. As he was driving around one day looking for a job, he spotted Conklin Dairy Farms off the highway. It wasn't a large facility, but Conklin was unique in that they "trained" heifers (young female cows who have not yet borne a calf) how to be milked. Nearby dairies would bring their pregnant heifers to Conklin, where they would give birth, be trained to milk, and then be returned to the original dairy.

The appearance of the farm was deceptive. It was surrounded by lush, rolling hills. The machinery was well-kept and tidy. There were no noxious odors. The milking parlor was also pristine—metal tubes lined the walls alongside rows of blinking lights stacked between spotless milking machines that look like modern torture devices.

The farm's owner, Gary Conklin, hired Pete on the spot. Pete's role was to feed calves, clean out milking lines, milk the cows, and perform general maintenance and cleaning. He was told to shadow Billy Joe Gregg Jr.—a man who seemed warm and affable with his coworkers and by all accounts was an excellent employee. But like the Conklin facility itself, appearances were deceiving. Billy turned out to be the most sadistic animal abuser any of us at MFA had ever seen.

Many chronic animal abusers we've encountered are otherwise good people, but exhaustion from overwork and lack of training or oversight can cause them to do bad things. When you produce animal products at the frenetic rate required to meet demand, abuse is, sadly, commonplace. But Billy was in a league of his own. He didn't just abuse animals out of frustration or fatigue. He made abuse into a sport.

On Pete's very first day, Billy informed him that when cows don't cooperate, "we stab 'em with a pitchfork." Billy was true to his word. Soon after, a frightened cow ran the wrong way out of her pen, got her hoof stuck in a metal fence, and collapsed to the ground.

"You goddamned cow," Billy spat. First he kicked her hoof and slapped her face, then he took a pitchfork and jabbed her in the mouth with the wooden end. Then, using the spiked end, he repeatedly stabbed her in the head and abdomen. For good measure, he kicked her in the hindquarters until she finally freed herself from the fence. Later in the day, Billy administered oxytocin injections to the cows, a controversial practice designed to make cows "let down" more milk. Billy would inject a cow, wipe the used needle on his manure-encrusted sleeve, and then inject another cow with the same needle. "I like sticking them sometimes," he told Pete, "to get 'em back," presumably for all the distress they had caused him.

Pete remembers one cow in particular, a beautiful black-and-white Holstein, the kind you'd expect to see grazing on an idyllic family farm. She didn't have a name, just a tag number: 3761. She seemed happy and curious and always glad to see Pete. But she was also a little shy and was very afraid of the milking parlor. Every time workers would try to bring 3761 to the milking parlor, she would sit down on her hind legs, too afraid to move. Pete would stroke her gently, silently telling her that everything would be okay.

But Billy had other ideas. When she resisted, he grabbed a metal lug wrench and a set of metal clamps with handles and pincers designed to restrain a cow by her nose. While singing "around and around we go," Billy hit 3761 with the wrench repeatedly before grabbing her by the eye socket and applying the clamp. Secured to a metal fence by her nose, Billy said: "You're mine," and began to beat her with a crowbar, again and again and again. She bellowed and screamed in agony as Billy continued to smash her face and head. Forty-two times Billy struck her face. Sometimes he'd stop and then poke her eyes with his fingers. Her screams echoed through the barn.

Pete said he could feel it in his bones, yet he could only stand there and watch. It took every ounce of fortitude to restrain himself, but Pete calmly filmed the abuse, went home that night, cooked dinner, typed up his notes, and went to bed. But even after all of his years in the field, Pete was deeply shaken by what he had seen. He made it a point to check on 3761 over the next few weeks. To his dismay, she was no longer her happy, curious self. She was constantly terrified, as if she were bracing for the next beating.

Over the course of the investigation, Pete kept his composure as Billy and other employees stabbed cows with pitchforks and blasted them with water hoses. He kept his composure as Billy kicked and stomped on calves. He kept his composure when Billy force-fed calves while standing on their legs, grabbing their ears, and twisting their necks. He kept his composure when Billy bragged about dumping a live cow into a nearby pond and then shooting her twenty-five times with a rifle. He kept his composure when Billy smashed a cow's nose, ankles, and eyes with a crowbar. Every night he still went home, ate dinner, typed up his notes, and went to bed. But he was deeply disturbed.

We wanted to go to law enforcement right away, but we needed one last piece of evidence: proof that the owner was involved. There was more than enough evidence to implicate Billy, and we suspected the owner, Gary Conklin, was aware of and condoned the abuse, but we needed to be able to prove it. We knew we had to get the ringleader.

"Does Gary know that you're rough with the animals?" Pete had asked Billy one day, casually, early on in the investigation.

"Gary? Oh sure. He doesn't care. In fact, he taught me how to get the cows to move. Watch this." Billy grabbed the cow's tail and twisted it until there was an audible *crack!* Then he kicked her for good measure. Scared, the cow lurched forward.

"See?" Billy said. "That's what he taught me. Works every time."

But no court would take Billy's word for it. We needed to get Gary on camera abusing an animal. The problem was that he was rarely in the barns.

Finally Pete got what he needed. There was a downed cow in the barn and Gary happened to be there. Frustrated and cursing, Gary walked up to her. Pete knew that look on Gary's face, and he positioned the camera perfectly. It was the same twisted grimace that all workers make when they beat helpless animals. With the camera rolling, Gary kicked the downed cow in the face until snot flew from her nostrils.

Now we had what we needed. We were ready to approach law enforcement. The initial signs looked promising: The detective assigned to the case was named Mike Justice. With a name like that, surely we were in good hands! But after reviewing our footage, Detective Justice and the district attorney's office began interrogating Pete about the undercover video.

"Were you abusing the cows, too?" they asked Pete. "Were you punching and kicking them like Billy was?"

"No," Pete replied. "Of course not."

"Were you giving money to Billy to hit these animals? Why else would he willingly do it on camera?"

Even though it was abundantly clear that Pete had been wearing a concealed camera and that Billy had no idea his torturous acts were being filmed, law enforcement had the audacity to suggest that Pete was involved in the abuse.

Gary Conklin was on the Union County Central Committee. He paid significant taxes and was a generous donor to local charities. We had enough video to convict him on animal-cruelty charges. He had willfully ignored the abuse and clear evidence of injured animals

Billy and others were administering on his watch, and he had kicked a cow himself—but law-enforcement officials refused to touch him. The DA wanted to show that the Conklin case was isolated and not representative of the industry at large. And so he only arrested the smallest, easiest-to-catch fish in the pond: Billy Joe Gregg Jr.

After Billy Joe Gregg Jr. was arrested, the police were concerned that the farm would become the target of violent action by animal-rights activists. They'd read some online comments by angry activists who had seen our video (but who were not associated with MFA), so when they heard about a planned protest outside the farm, they sent more than 150 armed personnel to guard Conklin. This small army included sheriff's deputies, Ohio State Highway Patrol troopers, emergency management staff, and helicopter pilots. Ultimately, only a handful of peaceful protestors assembled.

Matters got worse after the DA summoned a grand jury. The DA's office was determined to portray Mercy For Animals as a radical, militant organization, and it became clear that they were also hoping to charge *Pete* with animal cruelty. Pete was now being accused of perpetrating the very acts he had worked so tirelessly to end. I was shocked, sickened, and in total disbelief. We had kicked over a hornet's nest. Fortunately, the grand jury was not persuaded. No charges were brought against Pete or MFA. On September 24, 2010, Billy Joe Gregg Jr. pleaded guilty to six misdemeanor counts of cruelty to animals. He was sentenced to eight months in jail, ordered to pay a $1,000 fine, and was barred from contact with animals for three years.

Yes, cruelty to farm animals in Ohio, no matter how egregious, is classified as a misdemeanor. The state has some of the weakest animal-protection laws in the nation, ranking forty-third out of fifty states. While it was encouraging for us—no one more than Pete—to see Billy spend time in jail, the victory was bittersweet because we knew so much more could have been done. Gary Conklin himself should have been charged, which would have sent a signal to all factory-farm owners that they are responsible for their workers' behavior.

Once again, though, ordinary citizens stepped up when law enforcement would not. Immediately after our first meeting with law enforcement, we released the investigative footage to the media and we held simultaneous press conferences in four cities. Billy Joe Gregg's horrendous treatment of cows made headlines across the state and the nation—and right when we were entering the most crucial stage of signature gathering for the Ohio ballot measure.

The campaign had not been going well. I had recently moved from Chicago to Cleveland to oversee the signature-gathering effort in the northern regions of the state. The clock was ticking, and life was becoming stressful. For the most part, people were anything but friendly. I'd been to church socials to gather signatures where I was told I wasn't welcome. I'd had doors slammed in my face by angry farmers. I'd been called names and threatened. I'd had people spit on me. All in all, we were bone tired. Worse, we still didn't have enough signatures. I was losing confidence that we would ever get there.

But the Conklin case changed everything. All of a sudden, it seemed that everyone had seen the footage of Billy Joe Gregg punching and pummeling and beating defenseless cows. Suddenly, we were getting the signatures. People wanted to help protect farm animals from cruelty. They saw the urgent need. But just hours before five hundred thousand signatures were slated to be filed, I received a phone call.

Ted Strickland, Ohio's governor, stepped in.

He knew that changing the state's constitution to protect animals would mean costly and contentious campaigning on all sides. It would be ugly, it would be long, and it was a fight no one wanted to wage.

Up for reelection the next year, Strickland, a Democrat, was wary of conservative farmers coming out specifically to defeat the initiative. So he proposed brokering a deal between the animal-protection community and farmers. He had brought Wayne Pacelle from The Humane Society of the United States and representatives from the Ohio Farm Bureau to the negotiating table. The talks were lengthy and emotional. However, at the eleventh hour, the two sides hammered out an agreement. It outlined important improvements for animals in Ohio, including:

- A ban on the transport of downed dairy cows for slaughter.
- A ban on veal crates by 2017.
- A ban on new gestation crates in the state as of January 1, 2011. Existing facilities were grandfathered in but must cease use of these crates within fifteen years.
- A moratorium on permits for new battery cage confinement facilities for laying hens.
- A ban on strangulation of farm animals and mandatory humane euthanasia methods for sick or injured animals.

The agreement also stipulated changes that would help protect non-farm animals, including the enactment of legislation establishing felony-level penalties for cockfighters, a crackdown on puppy mills, and a ban on the acquisition of dangerous exotic animals such as primates, bears, lions, tigers, large constricting and venomous snakes, crocodiles, and alligators as pets.

Ohio's largest newspaper, the *Plain Dealer*, covered the story, publishing an article titled "Strickland Strikes Better Deal for Animals."

"Although impossible to prove, it's likely that what dragged agribusiness to Strickland's table last week were undercover video recordings that surfaced in May of apparent—and sickening—abuse of cattle at a Union County dairy farm," wrote reporter Thomas Suddes. "The abuse was recorded by Chicago-based Mercy For Animals, self-described as an 'animal advocacy organization.'

"The Farm Bureau, in a statement about its deal with The Humane Society, said the agreement means 'the livestock industry will be less vulnerable to emotional video used to sway public opinion on farm animal care. Farmers, their organizations and allies will not be forced into a multimillion dollar media battle.'

"Arguable translation: That Mercy For Animals video killed us. So we called Strickland."

The compromise was important, but it wasn't anywhere near perfect. The biggest concession was on the treatment of the state's twenty million egg-laying hens—hens whose terrible fate I was all too familiar with. The phase-out time for gestation crates was also much longer than we had originally hoped for, and violations wouldn't carry harsh penalties. Nevertheless, this was a watershed achievement that marked the most comprehensive series of animal welfare reforms ever enacted by a single state at one time. It was a meaningful step toward a more humane society.

. . .

The Texas Panhandle is Cattle Country, USA, and the town of Hart, Texas, where Pete showed up in February 2011, is no exception. The land is brown and flat, dotted by the occasional twisted, stubby tree. Everything from the vegetation to the animals to the people seem to be struggling to survive. The wind is constant and often severe. The city of Amarillo, seventy miles north, has been deemed the windiest city in America by the National Weather Service. The smell of cow shit permeates the air and every dust particle in it. Farther north, slaughterhouses replace cattle ranches and the smell of blood and death is overpowering. Locals have another term for the stench: "the smell of money."

This investigation almost didn't happen. Pete, who was living in Texas at the time, was about to move to California. His bags were packed, his car loaded up. Then, one day before he was about to leave, he heard about a calf ranch up in the Panhandle. We had never investigated a place like that, nor even seen one, for that matter.

"Screw it," Pete said. "I'm going to go take a look."

The E6 Cattle Company, where Pete showed up the next day, reared calves for use on dairy farms. Nearby dairies would bring their newborns to E6, where they would be raised for about six months and then returned to the dairy. E6 made their money by "growing" as many cows as possible—in this case ten thousand calves at a time. The place was staffed by approximately fifteen poorly paid farmhands, and Pete had heard that abuse was rampant.

Pete drove up, found the owner, Kirt Espenson, and told him that he wanted to buy a calf. He replied, "Sure, I got some mixed breeds that are no good. You can buy those. No one wants 'em."

Mixed breeds are the offspring of Holstein cows, those picturesque black-and-white cows you see in the commercials, and Jersey cows, who are caramel with big brown eyes. Holstein cows produce most of the milk in the country, while Jersey cows produce creamier, richer-tasting milk, often used for cheese. Mixed breeds are typically unwanted, and they're often sold to rodeos for pennies on the dollar.

Espenson showed Pete the mixed breeds, who were segregated in the back of the ranch. Thoroughly emaciated, the calves wheezed and coughed and could barely stand. They were clearly dying.

"If I were going to butcher them," Pete asked a manager at the ranch, "would I have to worry about medicine in them? Like antibiotics?"

"Nah," the manager replied. "We never give them medicine." Espenson later told Pete, "If they manage to survive we'll sell them. Hell, I'll sell you them for ten bucks a head."

After taking a quick tour of the ranch, Pete saw that the mixed breeds weren't the only calves being neglected. Even the calves meant for dairy purposes were not doing well. Many had open wounds. Others couldn't walk. Some appeared to be freezing to death. Pete knew that Texas law dictated that dying calves had to be treated or properly euthanized, and here he was being told point-blank that they were being denied medical care and left to die.

Pete went for it. "Tell you what, Kirt. I could use a little extra money. Any chance I can get a job here?"

Espenson shrugged. "Sure. Show up tomorrow."

That was it. Pete was in.

Pete was hired as a carpenter. His job was to maintain the wooden hutches in which younger calves spent their lives (older calves lived in group pens). The hutches, thick with manure and urine buildup and barely large enough for calves to turn around, were constructed row by row as far as the eye could see—wooden grapevines in the barren Texas landscape. In addition to his carpentry duties, Pete would feed the calves in the morning and then perform what quickly became his main responsibility: removing dead and dying calves from the hutches.

At night, temperatures in the Texas Panhandle regularly dip below twenty degrees Fahrenheit during the winter months, and in the morning Pete would usually find frozen calves. Pete once told Espenson that a calf's hooves were quite literally freezing off. Espenson mumbled that someone would put her down the next day. No one did. Veterinary care was rarely, if ever, provided. The ranch employed one veterinarian technician who poorly understood the medications at her disposal. When Pete mentioned that a calf was sick, she shrugged and walked in the other direction. Mixed breeds were often neglected altogether.

If a calf could not stand on her own to eat in the morning, workers would turn her feed bucket upside down. This alerted Pete's crew that the calf was to be killed.

One afternoon, Pete was with a coworker who spotted an overturned bucket—indicating a sick calf. Standing between rows of crates, Pete watched as the worker approached the hutch. He grabbed the weak calf by her leg and dragged her out into the open. Then, using his carpenter hammer, he delivered blows to the baby bovine's head. With each hit, the calf's cries grew weaker, and after six blows to the head, the calf was dead. This was the way that all sick calves met their end at E6. While carpenter hammers were the tool of choice, some workers brandished giant pickaxes. Many of the calves would twitch and convulse for minutes until they finally slipped away.

One morning, as Pete was collecting dead calves from their hutches and piling them in the back of a truck, he noticed that one—tag number 7296—was still breathing. She was barely a few weeks old, mostly black except for a few patches of white. Pete watched as she struggled to get air in the truck bed, surrounded by rotting carcasses.

"¡Amigo!" Pete yelled to his coworker. "Ella no es muerta." She isn't dead. At first the worker, Christian, did nothing and continued to load more bodies on top of 7296. Finally, after Pete brought it up again, Christian found a hammer and hit the calf six times at the base of the skull. Yet her chest continued to rise and fall as she struggled to live. Smiling, Christian slowly beat her skull dozens of times until she finally stopped breathing. It was one of Pete's most difficult moments as an undercover investigator—to stand there helplessly as a calf was slowly clubbed to death.

Sometimes workers would use .22-caliber rifles to kill downed calves, but this method was often ineffective. Twenty-two-caliber bullets are small—a step above a pellet gun—and often fail to sufficiently penetrate calves' skulls, especially once the animals reach three or four months of age. Often Pete would find calves lying on the ground, bleeding from holes in their heads, still alive.

On numerous occasions Pete told Espenson about the abuses that were occurring at his ranch. He knew workers were torturing downed calves with pickaxes and hammers, yet Espenson did nothing. He knew the calves were living in squalid conditions in subzero temperatures, yet he did nothing. He knew the rifles weren't powerful enough to effectively put down sick calves. Still nothing.

And with each passing day, Pete thought about the very first calves he had seen at the ranch, the ones Espenson was willing to practically give away because they were so sick. Then we had an idea. What if we could rescue them? As much as it pains us, we normally can't entertain the idea of rescuing animals during an investigation. Doing so could constitute theft, get our investigators in serious trouble, and jeopardize our whole organization. But the E6 case offered a unique opportunity, because Espenson had already offered to sell Pete a few of the unwanted mixed breeds for mere dollars. Perhaps we could rescue the calves while still protecting the investigation.

I decided to contact Gentle Barn. Founded by Ellie Laks and Jay Weiner and based in Southern California, Gentle Barn provides a sanctuary for rescued farm animals and organizes events with children from the inner city, group homes, mental health care facilities, foster homes, and schools to teach respect toward animals. I quickly explained the situation to Jay, and he agreed to make the sixteen-hour drive to Texas in his truck and trailer. I jumped on a plane and headed to Texas to meet both Jay and Pete. Posing as Pete's uncle, Jay agreed to purchase four calves from Espenson for $10 each, saying he planned to raise them for slaughter.

Pete began loading up the calves he had picked out earlier. They were sick, but Pete felt they were strong enough to make the journey back to California.

"Wait a minute," Espenson said when the calves were loaded up. "Not those. They're too healthy. I can sell them to the rodeo."

Pete had to think fast. If he resisted, Espenson would get suspicious and we could blow a possible criminal case. But if he relented, Pete knew he was damning the calves to death.

"I'm sorry," Pete told him. "I thought they were pretty sick." Then he pointed out a few open wounds and sores. "Are you sure I can't just take these?"

Espenson sighed. "You know what? Keep them. Merry Christmas." Before he could change his mind, Jay paid him and drove off. I met Jay down the road, jumped in the truck, and began navigating our route back to California. Every few hours we'd stop to bottle-feed the calves, who were all suffering from severe diarrhea and other intestinal issues. The next afternoon we arrived at Gentle Barn. We were greeted by a dozen volunteers eagerly awaiting our arrival. They provided around-the-clock care and nursed the calves back to health. To this day Bob, Roy, Mercy, and Ari—as the four lucky calves were named—enjoy a happy, care-free life. Pete still visits them when he can, bringing him immense joy at times when the horrors of his job really get to him.

Meanwhile, we quickly put a criminal case together against Espenson and E6. We knew we had the evidence to convict him and numerous workers on cruelty charges. Texas may not be the most progressive state when it comes to animal-cruelty laws, but the Texas Penal Code does prohibit the inhumane treatment of domesticated animals. But we were worried, as we often are, that the local prosecutor wouldn't be willing to take the case. We arranged a meeting with the district attorney and the sheriff of Castro County. The sheriff was older and dressed like an old-fashioned cowboy, complete with cowboy boots. Pete later joked that he had ridden his horse to work that morning.

We showed them the video and methodically walked them through the undercover process.

"I don't get it," the district attorney said. "You did this for some sort of publicity stunt? For some Internet thing?"

The sheriff, meanwhile, sat stone-faced. The DA was sprawled back in his chair, his cowboy boots up on the table. Pete remained patient and calmly told his story, but the odds weren't with us. Castro County has fewer than eight thousand people and is situated in the heart of cattle country. Kirt Espenson, the DA, and the sheriff likely attended the same church. In a newspaper article about the investigation that was published a while later, the sheriff even praised Espenson as "a good guy." This was another good-ol'-boys club.

Then something very fortuitous happened. Vandhana had just joined MFA full-time as our general counsel. She immediately began working on the E6 investigation, calling the sheriff's office weekly to discuss the case. The initial conversations were not good. We looked like some big-city animal-rights organization coming into cattle country and telling old-school ranchers how to do their jobs. But Vandhana kept at it, always coming across as polite and respectful, with a special, nonthreatening charm.

At the same time, our investigative footage of E6 had gone viral. YouTube even temporarily banned our video from their site, claiming it was "too graphic" after it sparked massive controversy. The investigation also inspired national outrage, prompting countless consumers to consider for the first time the plight of calves born into the dairy industry. The Castro County Sheriff's Office was inundated with calls from angry people, and Vandhana knew that it was just a matter of time before the sheriff capitulated. After a while their conversations became less hostile. Before long they were friendly, even jovial.

Two months after our investigation ended, the sheriff drove to Kirt Espenson's home and arrested him. The district attorney later handed down a one-year probation and ordered Espenson to pay a $4,000 fine. The DA also charged six employees with felony cruelty to livestock animals, though they fled and were never tried for their crimes.

In the end, Espenson admitted that he did not train his employees properly and pledged to improve conditions at his ranch. The fact that we managed to secure criminal convictions this deep in cattle country was astonishing not only to us but to the industry. After the release of the investigation, the stock price of live cattle suddenly dropped—a warning sign to the industry that cruelty would no longer go unpunished, even on their own turf.

While it is satisfying to see animal abusers like Espenson convicted for their crimes, it's not enough. We need to prevent cruelty from the top down. Convincing a multibillion-dollar conglomerate to change its ways can seem extremely daunting, but sometimes enormous waves of change begin with the tiniest ripples, as our investigator AJ learned when he showed up at a factory farm in Wisconsin in 2013.

AJ grew up in New York but moved to Korea after falling in love with Soyoun, a kind and brave woman who has dedicated her life to advocating on behalf of animals. AJ's undercover work began in

Korea, where he documented conditions inside the country's dog-meat industry. AJ went to dog factory farms and slaughterhouses and filmed the horrific farming and killing of dogs for food. The conditions were grotesque and traumatizing.

AJ first reached out to me by e-mail to ask if I'd be willing to meet with him and a close friend, a fellow investigator named Kevin, to discuss their work in Korea. A few weeks later AJ and Kevin arrived at the MFA office. We sat together at our conference table for the next hour as they showed me heart-wrenching footage on their laptops of dogs crammed in filthy cages and being killed for meat. We talked about strategies to end the dog-meat trade in Korea, but then the conversation shifted to the treatment of farm animals in the United States. We all agreed that what pigs, cows, and chickens endured for the food industry was just as horrible, if not worse, than what AJ and Kevin had documented dogs suffering in Korea. But the numbers of animals affected here were so much higher. Before the end of the meeting, AJ was ready to return to the United States to put his undercover skills to use inside American factory farms.

Fluent in English, Spanish, and Korean, AJ is an intelligent, compassionate, sensitive person who had proven that he had both the motivation and the bravery to witness and document truly horrible animal abuse. We brought him on as an investigator.

In the fall of 2013, AJ went to work at Wiese Brothers Farm in Greenleaf, Wisconsin, a dairy farm about sixteen miles south of Green Bay and just northeast of Lake Winnebago. The grass is lush, the soil is rich, and even though the railroad was shut down decades ago, the town still has the hallmarks of a train stop: a restaurant, a post office, and a few bars where locals gather after a hard week of work. Over the years, the area has become a hub for dairy and cheese production. Wiese Brothers is one of the largest farms in the area. With about eight thousand cows, they supplied the milk used to make cheese for DiGiorno, the most popular frozen pizza company in America. DiGiorno is owned by Nestlé, the largest food company in the world.

Hired by the farm manager, Scott, AJ moved the slow, tired cows all day long, from shed to milking parlor. The workers were all under tremendous pressure—if the farm didn't produce enough milk in any given month, they might be shut out of the co-op that supplied companies like DiGiorno, putting employees out of work. While AJ was practically running to get the cows where they needed to go each day, he saw sick and injured animals lying on the ground, too weak to move. They had open, bleeding wounds from slipping and falling on the wet, feces-covered floors. Who had time to call a veterinarian when you had so much else to do?

And he saw the workers' frustration with the cows who just *wouldn't* move. It didn't matter that the animals were too exhausted— Scott still demanded they be milked. Over the course of four weeks, AJ documented his fellow employees kicking immobile cows in the head and sides or stabbing them with screwdrivers when they fell. Once, AJ entered the barn to find a team of workers standing over a cow. She was sick and couldn't get up. She lay in her stall, mooing softly as the workers prodded and kicked her, trying to make her stand. AJ then heard beeping, and he turned to find a tractor backing into the barn. The workers wrapped a chain around the cow's neck, then tied the other end to the tractor's plow. Slowly the tractor reversed, and the chain tightened as the tractor dragged the sixteen-hundred-pound animal out of her stall, choking her and placing immense pressure on her spine. AJ would routinely document cows clearly in extreme pain being dragged and hoisted into the air by tractors.

AJ wanted to be sure he was covering all his bases, so every time he saw someone kicking, dragging, or stabbing a cow, he went to his boss, Scott, and complained. He also wanted to implicate as many higher-ups as possible in his legal complaint, so he needed to document the fact that the abuses hadn't gone unreported.

After about four weeks, we had enough footage to file a legal complaint, and so Vandhana jumped into action. Greenleaf is an unincorporated district smack in the middle of the town of Wrightstown, which isn't that much bigger than where I grew up in Ohio. The sheriff's office in Wrightstown was as small an affair as you'd expect—Andy Griffith's Mayberry, plus Wi-Fi access and cars with cruise control.

When Vandhana walked inside, she was greeted by one of the deputies in the hallway. The deputy himself was a dairy farmer, which might seem like a coincidence, but it actually happens more often than you'd think. In any rural town, it's hard to get away from the farm. Many people with desk jobs that start at nine a.m. have been milking cows since sunup.

"Good morning. How can I help you?"

"I'd like to make an animal cruelty complaint," Vandhana responded. "Do you have a room where I can show you some video?"

The deputy paused and looked at her as if she'd just stepped off a spaceship. People came to the sheriff's office for domestic-violence complaints and to fight parking tickets. But animal cruelty? That rarely happened.

"Can you say that again? Where are you from?"

"My name is Vandhana Bala. I'm here with an animal protection organization called Mercy For Animals. We investigate factory farms. We've discovered some animal abuse locally, and I want to report it. There's a pretty big case of animal cruelty happening on one of the factory farms around here."

The dairy farmer/deputy stopped her short, blurting out, "Don't call them factory farms! They're not factory farms!"

And Vandhana thought, *Oh boy, this is going to be fun.*

He took her to a conference room, and despite their rocky beginning, the deputy patiently watched the video. Within minutes, Vandhana saw the expression on his face change—his jaw began to clench, and his stare became fixed—and she realized he understood. Regardless of the deputy's background or sensibility, he knew deep down in his bones that what he saw before him was criminal animal cruelty.

"Ma'am, can you come back with the investigator tomorrow so we can talk some more?" he asked, his tone friendly.

AJ and Vandhana did return, and their meeting lasted a full hour and a half. Within a few days, the sheriff and deputy forwarded their report to the DA.

This kind of efficiency was unusual for a small-town sheriff. In these rural areas it's not surprising to find out that the sheriff is a cousin of the farmer you're hoping to prosecute, or that the assistant DA is married to the owner of the farm. But this case was shaping up differently. Soon thereafter, the Brown County, Wisconsin, district attorney decided to handle the case personally and saw it through with a tremendous integrity. He was decent, honest, and committed to the proper discharge of his public duties. He wasn't swayed by politics, and he answered all of Vandhana's calls personally as the investigation proceeded.

But these things can take time, and we realized that we couldn't wait for charges to be announced before we took the case public. Our goal is not just to make sure the abusers are prosecuted; it's to stir public awareness, upgrade animal-protection laws, and get corporations to improve their practices. We knew we had a huge case on our hands, and we needed a full-court press to get the ball rolling toward real change. So we took to the media.

We gave NBC News an exclusive, and on December 10, 2013, the network featured our video on their Web site's home page. Just as the footage went live, we held four press conferences around the United States: in Green Bay and Milwaukee, Wisconsin; Chicago (where DiGiorno had its headquarters); and Los Angeles (where Nestlé USA, DiGiorno's parent company, is located). We also posted the graphic footage on our Web site, which rebranded DiGiorno as "DisGusting" and came with the tagline "Cruelty in Every Slice."

The news hit hard. Our Web site traffic shot through the roof, celebrities including Kate Mara and Mayim Bialik began tweeting about what they'd seen online, and our publicity team started getting calls from around the world. But we wanted more: Public awareness is essential, but meaningful change still had to happen at the highest levels.

That same day our director of corporate outreach, Jaime Surenkamp, picked up the phone to call Nestlé, and almost immediately reached Hannah Coan, the vice president of corporate and brand public relations. Nestlé was in a panic. This video was a public relations disaster—as the world's largest food company, they wielded enormous power and influence, yet they weren't even aware of abuses in their own supply chain. It was a grievous blow to their image.

The first call between Jaime and Hannah was contentious. At first, Hannah denied that Wiese Brothers was one of their suppliers, but after she showed her we had proof that it was, Jaime secured an in-person meeting with Nestlé. We wasted no time getting ourselves prepared, and a short time later Jaime; Dr. Jim Reynolds, one of the world's foremost experts on the welfare of cows in the dairy industry; and I walked into their Glendale, California, headquarters.

I've been through a lot in my thirty years. I've cried after seeing animals suffer and die in front of me, and I've spent years struggling to finance Mercy For Animals. I've felt the sting of people's criticism and outright rejection of my supposed "wacko" activism. Because of this, I've lived in a constant state of watchful anxiety. But rarely have I felt so many emotions as I did at this meeting. It's very unusual for a powerful multinational corporation to respond to us so quickly, so I was thrilled, terrified, and hopeful all at the same time. So much was on the line, and while I knew Nestlé had the power to change everything for millions of animals, in my experience, corporations tend to change very little.

The building housing Nestlé headquarters is a behemoth, topped with a helicopter landing pad. The iconic Nestlé logo, complete with a mother bird feeding her chick in a nest, adorns the enormous structure. When we entered a boardroom nearly a dozen floors up, three executives stood before us: Hannah Coan from Public Relations; Kevin Petrie, their chief procurement officer; and Patrick Drye, their dairy procurement manager. Calling in on the phone was Paul Bakus, the president of Nestlé Pizza, who oversaw the DiGiorno brand. The meeting started well enough. Coffee was offered, introductions were made, and everyone from Nestlé seemed cordial, if a bit guarded. In retrospect, I think they were trying to gauge who we were. If we were crazy and militant, it would be easy to shut us down. However, if we were reasonable and professional, perhaps just sitting with us and letting us know they were aware of the issue would be enough to appease us.

But we wanted real action and I presented our case.

"Mercy For Animals would like you to adopt a set of seven dairy cattle welfare requirements," I began. "These guidelines are no different from those adopted by other corporations, and they offer a baseline of improvements your suppliers should be required to follow." We weren't asking them to set their cows out into beautiful, grassy fields to live and eat the way nature intended them to—we knew that wouldn't happen yet. We just wanted them to act now to stop blatant abuses. Our demands included:

1. Establishing procedures to address the care and treatment of non-ambulatory cattle.
2. Ensuring proper animal care and handling, including banning electric shock devices and training employees in humane care practices.
3. Prohibiting painful and unnecessary procedures—this rule would outlaw tail docking and dehorning.
4. Providing group housing for calves with no tethering—this rule meant no more veal pens.
5. Providing a safe, clean, and sanitary environment for cattle—nonskid floors and grounds that are cleaned of manure twice a day.

6. Implementing and adhering to a comprehensive hoof-care and lameness prevention plan—cows would have their hooves evaluated regularly, be able to lie down eleven to fourteen hours a day, exercise four hours a day, and have access to the outdoors.

7. Installing video cameras in milking parlors, housing barns, and transport areas that live-stream to the Internet—this practice, recommended by animal expert Temple Grandin, deters people from committing acts of cruelty against animals.

The executives listened, and, judging from the looks on their faces, I could sense a tiny bit of compassion. They weren't just a bunch of stiff suits in a boardroom, and not a single one of them had looked at their smart phones since we started talking.

Then Kevin Petrie spoke up. "Nathan, thanks for everything you just said. I get it. I have children, and I wake up every single day wanting to do the right thing to make their futures better. That's one of the reasons I like working at Nestlé; we do good work, and we're proud of it. We're helping people." He paused. "But we're a principles-based corporation, and we just don't adopt or adhere to lists of rules like these. So while I'm sympathetic, we can't agree to take on a set of policies like these."

What Kevin had meant was that Nestlé relied on a broad, high-level standard of ethics rather than detailed lists of specific prescriptive measures. To me, this was just corporate doublespeak. Clearly, they *hadn't* been following these principles when they ignored practices in their supply chain.

"With all due respect, Kevin," I countered, "Nestlé just worked with Greenpeace to end some of the abuses with your palm oil suppliers." We'd done our research, and we knew that they'd recently adopted detailed regulations in reaction to Greenpeace's viral campaign against Kit Kat candy bars. Nestlé's palm oil suppliers were destroying portions of the Indonesian rain forest, which threatened the livelihoods of local people and pushed orangutans close to extinction. So Nestlé had agreed to a set of rules that banned importation from these places.

The executives didn't look surprised at what I'd said—after all, Greenpeace's efforts had been very public—but they remained tight-lipped. I'd put them in a corner, and I could tell they were almost ready to acknowledge that something had to be done.

Kevin finally spoke up. "Look, we're proud of that improvement. We did what's right. And we want to do the same here, but we can't do anything just yet. I can't disagree with you about anything you've said, and frankly, I'm mortified that you discovered such horrible things in our supply chain. So we'll schedule another meeting later to talk more. Just give us some time."

At that point, Paul Bakus, the president of Nestlé Pizza, hadn't said a word. We heard a rustle on the phone, and finally he spoke up.

"We'd like you to take the undercover video off of your Web site." The hostility and determination in his voice was all too evident. Then his voice dropped to a hushed tone. "As a business owner, I'm asking that you release my brand and stop your petition immediately."

Mercy For Animals doesn't seek to harm anyone or violate their trust, so I'm always careful to avoid showing any kind of hostility while remaining as straightforward as possible. What Bakus had asked was completely unreasonable to me, but I wanted to remain professional.

"We'd like nothing more than to take the video down," I responded, "but we simply can't do that unless Nestlé makes a commitment to adopt meaningful animal welfare standards that prevent cruelty in your supply chain. Once that's done, we'll end the campaign and praise Nestlé for making these changes." Paul Bakus didn't say another word.

After some pleasant good-byes and a few handshakes, we left the meeting feeling cautiously optimistic. As we stood talking outside the massive building, we took comfort in the fact that we'd been heard. And better yet, we knew we'd see them again.

In the meantime, Vandhana had been keeping us up to date on everything that was happening on the legal front. The news was better than any of us had ever expected. That winter, four workers at Wiese Brothers had been charged with multiple counts of criminal animal cruelty.

In April 2014, the four workers were prosecuted and convicted. They settled out of court, which wasn't unusual. In fact, in the ten years MFA has been conducting investigations, only three have ever gone to trial. Few defense attorneys would risk showing a jury our footage.

A few months passed and despite our attempts to follow up, we didn't hear anything from Nestlé. Then, in the spring of 2014, they scheduled a meeting but canceled it at the last minute. I grew nervous. Had we hit a brick wall? Had Nestlé run our proposal up the ladder and met insurmountable resistance? Finally, Nestlé set up another meeting for April 16, 2014, just under four months after our initial face to face.

When we returned to their offices and entered the boardroom, we saw some new faces, including a few executives from the Swiss parent company. People had flown *halfway across the world* to be here. For a brief moment Jaime, Dr. Reynolds, and I allowed ourselves to think something big was about to happen.

Kevin Petrie began to speak as handouts were passed around and the lights dimmed for a PowerPoint presentation.

"Welcome back, everyone, and thank you, Mercy For Animals, for coming here today. We've spent the last four months addressing our supply-chain issues. No corporation as big as ours should have suppliers who are breaking laws, behaving irresponsibly, or inflicting pain and suffering, and we're determined that's never going to happen again. We can run a company saying we have a strong ethical code, but if it's not upheld at even the lowest levels, we've failed. So after we met with you in December, we hired independent auditors throughout the dairy supply chain in order to find the cracks in the system. We visited dozens of farms in several states, and unfortunately, we found a lot. Now I'm going to turn the room over to one of our auditors to discuss how they proceeded. We want you to see how thorough we've been."

While we all pored over our handouts, barely believing what we were hearing, the auditor discussed the methodology his group had used, the abuses and systemic issues they'd looked for, and what they'd ultimately found. The auditors discovered that almost all of the farms in the Nestlé supply chain were docking cows' tails, and a large percentage of farmers weren't using anesthesia for dehorning.

Then Duncan Pollard, another high-level executive, took the floor.

"Nestlé is still shocked and dismayed that Mercy For Animals had more visibility into their supply chain than we had. It's embarrassing, unacceptable, and we're thankful to you for bringing it to our attention. In response, here's what we'd like to do."

For the last five minutes I had barely been able to breathe. Nestlé hadn't just acknowledged that the company had a problem. They had given us their own facts and figures documenting it and were prepared to do something to reverse it.

What happened next was the single most sweeping and far-reaching reform any food company has made—not just in the sixteen years I've been an activist but in the entire history of factory farming. Duncan Pollard told us that Nestlé was ready to change their policies in the United States *and* in the ninety countries where their suppliers were located. At that point they had seventy-three hundred suppliers, and their new standards would apply to all of them. That's half a million farms. That's millions of animals whose lives would soon be better.

Nestlé had decided to commit to the Five Freedoms of Animal Welfare:

1. Freedom from hunger, thirst, and malnutrition
2. Freedom from fear and distress
3. Freedom from physical and thermal discomfort
4. Freedom from pain, injury, and disease
5. Freedom to express normal patterns of behavior

These principles are supported worldwide by the World Organization for Animal Health, and nearly every animal-protection organization in the world holds the principles in high regard as a reputable base for animal care. Nestlé didn't want their support to be merely symbolic, though. The company committed on paper to real, groundbreaking changes. They agreed to end tail docking, dehorning, and castration of cattle and pigs without anesthesia, the intensive confinement of calves in veal crates, pigs in gestation crates, egg-laying hens in cages, an end to the use of growth hormones, and an end to live-shackle chicken slaughter. They also agreed to third-party audits to ensure compliance.

The presentation concluded, and Duncan asked me what I thought.

"Congratulations," I said, smiling. "And thank you. This represents the farthest-reaching and most meaningful animal welfare policy ever adopted by a food provider, and we look forward to praising it as such." At that point, I could have hugged everyone in the room.

When the announcement about these new standards was made public several months later, it was picked up by news media around the world. It was headline news in the *New York Times* and on NBC *Nightly News*. I spent many hours over many days on the phone with reporters talking about what progress this represented for animals. What had begun with AJ's brave work on a cold December morning at a factory farm in Wisconsin ended with a sweeping, worldwide policy change by Nestlé—the largest food company in the world.

The situation for animals on factory farms is slowly changing, as is public perception. Because of our work with Nestlé, we've also had victories with Leprino, the world's largest pizza cheese producer; Great Lakes Cheese; Saputo, the largest dairy company in Canada; and many others who have agreed to adopt groundbreaking corporate policies that begin to address the worst types of abuse within the dairy industry, such as tail docking. Feeling pressure from major dairy purchasers, the dairy industry's own trade associations are finally recognizing that change is needed.

But our victories have come at a price.

11.

Gagged

U ndercover investigations that expose abuses are increasingly leading to policy changes, criminal prosecutions, and headlines that reflect negatively on the meat and dairy industries. Consumers are quickly losing trust in the factory-farming ethos, and rightfully so. Hidden-camera exposés have brought transparency to industries that prefer to operate in the shadows, resulting in an escalating battle that recently erupted into an all-out legislative war.

At the behest of the animal food industry, almost half of all state legislatures have introduced "ag-gag" laws, a term coined in 2011 by then *New York Times* columnist Mark Bittman. These laws come in different forms, but all are intended to stop investigators from exposing abuses on factory farms. Kansas, Montana, North Carolina, Utah, and North Dakota have outright bans on undercover filming; Iowa has banned activists from applying for farm jobs under false pretenses; and Missouri requires that any evidence of animal abuse must be turned over to law enforcement almost immediately—blocking an investigator's ability to build a solid, comprehensive case that will stand up in court. By silencing whistle-blowers, ag-gag laws are designed to protect factory farms by ensuring that evidence cannot be compiled against them. This means undercover investigators like Pete, Robert, Cody, Liz, and Andy could be criminally prosecuted. Instead of cruelty, these states are going after compassion.

It's easy to see where these bills originate: Just follow the money. In 2012—after Liz's investigation at Iowa Select Farms—Iowa governor Terry Branstad signed a bill criminalizing undercover investigators who expose animal cruelty, corporate corruption, dangerous working conditions, environmental violations, and food safety concerns at factory farms. Governor Branstad and several other legislators supporting the bill received substantial contributions from influential agriculture groups, including the Iowa Pork Producers Association. The National Institute on Money in State Politics found that the agriculture industry provided nearly 10 percent of Governor Branstad's $8.9 million in campaign funding, while another leading supporter of the bill, Senator Joe Seng, received more than 25 percent of his campaign money from agricultural interests. Founders of Iowa Beef Products topped the donor list, contributing $152,000 to Governor Branstad's campaign. Cofounders of Iowa Select Farms, where Liz documented sickening abuse, were also among the top donors, contributing $50,000 to Branstad.

The same year Branstad signed Iowa's ag-gag bill into law, a Mercy For Animals investigation in southern Idaho was setting the stage for another ag-gag showdown.

. . .

We had sent Pete to a tiny town named Murtaugh to investigate Bettencourt Dairies, a cheese supplier to Burger King, Kraft Foods, Wendy's, and In-N-Out Burger. With more than ten thousand cows, the animal population at the dairy outnumbered the town's human population eighty-six to one. In most of our cases, it usually takes several days before our investigators witness sadistic abuse. At Bettencourt Dairies, it only took forty-five minutes.

The morning he started, Pete watched a Bettencourt manager take a Taser and shock a downed cow about twenty times in an attempt to make her walk. A worker then shocked the cow another fifty times. When she still wouldn't stand, the manager tied a chain around her neck like a noose and attached the other end to a tractor, which then dragged her more than two hundred feet across gravel. The footage was horrific, as bad as anything we've ever released. But it didn't stop there. Pete exposed workers and management viciously beating, kicking, punching, electrocuting, and violently twisting cows' tails in order to deliberately inflict pain. He also documented unsafe and unsanitary conditions, including feces-covered floors, as well as cows with open wounds, broken bones, and infected udders left to suffer without proper veterinary care. The hidden-camera video even showed a worker fondling a cow's vagina while making crude sexual references. Because of Pete's work, several employees were arrested and convicted on criminal animal cruelty charges.

The dairy industry was outraged—not because of the abuse uncovered but because we had exposed it for the world to see. It was only a matter of time until the powerful dairy industry fought back. Less than two years after Pete stepped inside Bettencourt Dairies, Idaho governor Butch Otter signed the Agricultural Security Act, which made it a criminal offense to film abuse on the state's factory farms. The author of the legislation, a registered lobbyist for the dairy industry named Dan Steenson, was clear about intentions: shielding Idaho dairymen from "the court of public opinion."

The law made the penalty for someone like Pete who *documented* abuse higher than the person *committing* the abuse. Why would lawmakers seek to protect animal abusers while punishing whistleblowers? Money. The legislators behind Idaho's ag-gag bill received massive campaign contributions from the dairy industry. In fact, Idaho's agricultural lobby paid more than a half million dollars to political powers in 2012 alone. Pro-factory-farming legislators were stooping to new lows in their efforts to pass the ag-gag bill—using fearmongering and lies to advance their agenda. One state senator compared Pete and other investigators to "marauding invaders centuries ago who swarmed into foreign territory and destroyed crops to starve foes into submission" and called investigations of animal abuse "terrorism." Another Idaho lawmaker accused us of "taking the dairy industry hostage."

Our country has a long, important history of journalists going undercover to expose abuses in the food system, similar to Upton Sinclair's time in Chicago's deplorable slaughterhouses back in 1906—an investigation that led to the first laws governing conditions inside packing plants. Even though Pete had exposed horrific animal abuse that led to criminal convictions of workers, under Idaho's new ag-gag law it was now illegal for someone to expose animal abuse at factory farms like Bettencourt. The American Civil Liberties Union and other organizations declared that the law was blatantly unconstitutional and an assault on freedom of speech. A lawsuit was filed, challenging it in federal court. The courts agreed. In August 2015, a judge in the federal district court for Idaho ruled that the state's ag-gag law violated the First Amendment protections for free speech and struck it down. In his ruling, US District Judge B. Lynn Winmill wrote, "Undercover investigations actually advance core First Amendment values by exposing misconduct to the public eye and facilitating dialogue on issues of considerable public interest. . . . Food production and safety are matters of the utmost public concern." In his ruling, Winmill specifically likened the work of Pete to that of Sinclair.

But the battle wages on. Newly passed ag-gag-type laws still stand in Kansas, North Dakota, Utah, Missouri, Montana, Iowa, Arkansas, and North Carolina—many passed in direct response to the cases outlined in this book. A growing number are now being challenged in court. The first ag-gag charges were filed in 2013 when a young animal welfare advocate named Amy Meyer used her cell phone to record a live cow being bulldozed by a tractor at a slaughterhouse in Utah. Appalled, she uploaded the footage to YouTube. Despite being on the side of the road, not on private property, the police arrived and later charged her with violating Utah's ag-gag law. (The prosecutors dropped all charges after massive public outrage two months later.)

Ag-gag laws are the animal agriculture industry's attempt to silence whistle-blowers and keep consumers in the dark about where their food comes from. MFA is a leading voice of opposition. From mobilizing local residents and holding news conferences to organizing public protests and working with a broad coalition of animal-protection, food safety, workers' rights, and civil-liberties organizations, we continue to fight these unconstitutional efforts to conceal the truth about food production in America. And while the passage of ag-gag laws represent setbacks in the battle against factory farming, it's clear that we are making huge progress in the larger war.

S tarted because of one poor piglet, MFA has grown into an ever-changing, powerful voice for animals. We've shifted from a small, all-volunteer-based organization to a sophisticated international institution with a multimillion-dollar budget employing more than two hundred people around the globe, from Canada to Brazil to India to China. Thanks to our undercover investigations, our support base has expanded from dozens to many millions of people.

The moment I knew Mercy For Animals had truly arrived occurred one April afternoon. My cell phone rang. The caller ID read "Private Number." The days of ignoring calls from unknown numbers after our late-night egg farm visits were long over. I answered.

"Hello, Nathan," said the deep voice on the other end. "This is Bob Barker. Do you have a few moments?"

"I always have time for you, Bob!" I stammered, trying to hide my excitement.

Like millions of others, I grew up watching *The Price Is Right* and had always loved Bob. He wasn't just the *Guinness Book of World Records'* "Most Durable Performer" and "Most Generous Host in Television History." He was arguably the world's most famous and powerful animal advocate. Bob had always ended the more than thirty-five hundred shows he'd hosted with an important message: "Help control the pet population: Have your pets spayed and neutered." After winning nineteen Emmys during his thirty-five-year hosting career, Bob Barker had the platform, and the resources, to help animals in a big way.

"I've seen your undercover investigations and I'm very impressed," he told me. "Can I help?"

"Sure," I said. "We need to raise two hundred and fifty thousand dollars to grow our investigations department. And we need to hire more investigators. It's crucial that we have more boots on the ground."

"Well, get started! I'm going to send you the money right away," Bob said.

"Wow! Thank you so much. This is the best birthday gift ever," I said, my twenty-sixth birthday just days away.

Bob soon became one of MFA's most generous and loyal supporters, not only by bankrolling our growing investigations department but also by narrating our investigation videos, standing beside me during press conferences, and sending letters to heads of corporations we were campaigning to change. With Bob's endorsement, other stars soon stepped forward to help: musicians from Moby to Sia, as well as hip-hop mogul Russell Simmons; television royalty, such as *Murphy Brown*'s Candice Bergen, Alec Baldwin, *Bones* star Emily Deschanel, and *The Simpsons* co-creator Sam Simon; and movie stars from Joaquin Phoenix to Ryan Gosling and Kim Basinger. I was excited, proud, and humbled.

By 2016, as the result of our work, animal abusers had been

sentenced to nearly twenty-six thousand days of imprisonment or probation. Factory farmers soon branded MFA "More Farmers Arrested." Factory farms were being forced to shut their doors—for good. Our high-profile investigations were also capturing the attention of media outlets around the world. We worked with reporters from CNN, NPR, *Dateline*, *20/20*, the *New York Times*, *USA Today*, and many other outlets to expose cruelty within our food system.

But we've achieved the farthest reach by harnessing the power of the Internet and social media. That includes running online petitions signed by more than four million people. And in 2016 alone, MFA's online videos—ranging from shocking hidden-camera exposés to mouthwatering vegan cooking demos to cute shorts highlighting the similarities between puppies and piglets—racked up more than 270 million views.

By rallying the support of millions of people, we have helped shift the landscape for farm animals, something that once seemed an impossible dream back when I founded the organization as a teenager in my small farm town. In the last decade, the tide has begun to turn toward compassion. And there is no better evidence of that change than in the marketplace. In the last decade, the retail market for vegetarian foods has doubled to $1.6 billion. The number of Americans who say they are vegetarian or vegan has risen to 7 percent. Of that number, more than 12 percent of millennials now consider themselves vegetarian (compared with just 2 percent of baby boomers).

From factory farms to corporate boardrooms, courtrooms to communities, Mercy For Animals will continue to confront cruelty and inspire compassion. Today there is real hope that the most abusive practices documented by MFA's investigators will soon be a thing of the past. Yet, animal welfare improvements and increased monitoring will only go so far.

At the heart of the agriculture industry is a view that animals are mere commodities and production units to be used and abused however humans see fit. As long as animals are deemed nothing more than property to be bought, sold, bred, and killed at our whim, they will continue to face abuse. It is only when we recognize that animals are our fellow inhabitants of the earth, with innate needs, personalities, and a fundamental right to freedom, that true animal liberation will occur. As Alice Walker so powerfully wrote, "The animals of the world exist for their own reasons. They were not made for humans any more than black people were made for whites, or women for men."

Never before in history have animals faced such extreme abuse at the hands of humans in such unfathomable numbers. Today, an undeclared war is being waged against tens of billions of animals around the globe.

But animals aren't the only ones suffering.

Working inside factory farms and slaughterhouses takes a severe toll. Pete, Liz, Cody, Ryan, and other MFA investigators have all told me that they continue to be haunted by the incidents they witnessed and participated in during their time working undercover: These investigators all had to sacrifice their emotional well-being (not to mention their physical safety) in the interest of helping animals. They experience nightmares and night terrors, waking up in the middle of the night screaming and gasping, haunted by visions of squealing, of faces, of eyes. They suffer through vivid dreams of animals staring back at them from slaughter lines or from their locked cages. They suffer from heightened anxiety and paranoia, to the point where some begin to avoid looking at themselves in mirrors. They endure prolonged periods of depression and feelings of numbness and emotional disconnect, leading to weight gain or weight loss. Many find that when they return home, they have trouble communicating their feelings with loved ones, leading to challenged or failed relationships.

For Ryan, the trauma revealed itself in unexpected ways. "Ever since I worked as a backup killer cutting the necks of chickens in a Tyson slaughterhouse," he says, "I have felt an extreme discomfort with anything touching my neck. This was especially hard during the past winter when working the night shift on a dairy farm. I remember preferring the feel of the freezing wind on my neck to that of my jacket's collar zipped around it. On my breaks I am only able to wear V-necks and tank tops because the feel of regular T-shirts is almost unbearable. I also can't bear the touch of my girlfriend's hand on my neck or inner shoulders."

For Liz, the effects of working at Butterball and Iowa Select brought long-term emotional trauma. She says, "One of the most surprising psychological changes was that I lost a lot of my ability to feel emotion toward animals, positively or negatively. It's as though the part of my emotional life that compelled me to veganism—compassion, empathy, love, and a desire to correct injustice—stopped working. I still feel politically and intellectually connected to those ideas of right and wrong, justice and ethics, love and protection toward animals, but the supporting emotional structure withered away. I'm sure this change was made in my head and heart out of necessity while I was doing the work, but it never occurred to me that I would just not be able to rouse those feelings again, even in civilian life."

The trauma experienced by these investigators is often shared by other workers on factory farms and in slaughterhouses. In fact, there's a term for it: perpetration-inducted traumatic stress (PITS), which is a form of post-traumatic stress disorder. PITS results from situations in which a person was participating in the creation of traumatic situations, such as killing animals, castrating piglets, debeaking chickens, and so on.

Psychologist Rachel MacNair, who studies PITS, says symptoms of the disorder can include drug and alcohol abuse, panic, paranoia, dissociation, anxiety, and depression. While MacNair's research has largely focused on combat veterans, MacNair includes slaughterhouse workers as a sector of population susceptible to PITS.

In her book *Slaughterhouse*, Gail A. Eisnitz interviewed many slaughterhouse workers, who described their trauma. Here is one account:

> The worst thing, worse than the physical danger is the emotional toll. If you work in that stick pit for any period of time, you develop an attitude that lets you kill things, but doesn't let you care. You may look a hog in the eye that's walking around down in the blood pit with you and think, God, that really isn't a bad-looking animal. You may want to pet it. Pigs down on the kill floor have come up and nuzzled me like a puppy. Two minutes later I had to kill them—beat them to death with a pipe. I can't care.

The violence inherent in slaughterhouse and factory farm work desensitizes workers, a physiological defense that allows employees to operate in harsh environments. Individuals who walk in the door kind and empathetic may leave the job hardened and cruel. Our investigations time and again reveal desensitized workers sadistically abusing animals or inflicting pain on animals "for fun," without any remorse.

Three sociologists, Amy J. Fitzgerald, Linda Kalof, and Thomas Dietz, wrote a 2009 paper investigating the effects of slaughterhouses on communities, testing the so-called Sinclair effect, a theory novelist Upton Sinclair proposed more than one hundred years ago after observing that neighborhoods near slaughterhouses had elevated levels of crime and unemployment. The sociologists' studies similarly suggest that lower feelings of empathy present in slaughterhouse workers may be responsible for higher crime rates in nearby neighborhoods (with some homicides carried out in a manner consistent with animal-slaughtering practices).

Workers in slaughterhouses suffer. They are victims as well. Many are undocumented immigrants who take these jobs out of desperation, hoping to provide basic support for their struggling families. They end up with the dirty, dangerous, traumatic, and demoralizing jobs that few Americans would dare accept. These workers are unable to demand even basic improvements in their treatment without facing termination or deportation. In short, the meat industry abuses and exploits these workers just as it does animals. The fact that such facilities not only cause pain and suffering to billions of animals but also extreme emotional trauma to workers, should give us all pause. Do factory farms have a place in a civilized and moral society? Can't we do better?

Our food system is in desperate need of reinvention and innova-

tion. From animal cruelty to worker trauma, environmental degradation to human health, our current methods of producing protein to
feed the world's growing population are in need of disruption.

Thankfully, a group of forward-thinking entrepreneurs are setting
out to do just that.

‖‖‖‖‖‖‖‖‖‖

A KINDER
TOMORROW

Clean meatbal

12

The Future of Food

You can't solve a problem on the same level that it was created. You have to rise above it to the next level.

—Albert Einstein

Consider the horse-drawn buggy.

In the late nineteenth century, Americans involved in the animal-protection movement were concerned that horses in city streets were forced to lead miserable lives. Placed in an environment in which they were never meant to live, these literal workhorses were separated from other horses and often mistreated by their owners. Furthermore, their presence created public safety issues, such as waste-disposal problems and the large number of equine corpses lining the streets, which cmanated noxious odors and spread disease. Using horses as transportation was clearly both flawed and unsustainable.

A small group of activists began to campaign to help these animals. Within a few decades, horses were no longer being used as transportation in American cities. What happened? Was the horse-and-buggy industry disrupted because of these campaigners? Did people listen to their ethical and health-based arguments? A few people certainly did. But the real game-changer was that, in 1908, the Model T automobile appeared. The new machine not only allowed people to travel as before, but it had many advantages over animal-based transportation. Within a short time, people chose cars over horses. Today, more than a century since the automobile changed how we travel, using horse and carriage seems antiquated, inefficient, slow, and inhumane.

The meat industry is in a similar place to where animal-based transportation was so many years ago. Wasteful, destructive, and cruel, it is thoroughly in need of disruption, just as the horse-and-buggy business once was. And, because I have felt so strongly about this for many years, in 2016 I was part of a group that conceived and launched The Good Food Institute (GFI), an organization that focuses on supporting innovation in the food sector by helping accelerate the development of alternatives to meat, dairy, and eggs.

GFI is, I believe, a new breed of nonprofit. It works with scientists, investors, and entrepreneurs to help produce "clean" and plant-based meat, milk, and eggs by providing marketing, legal, business, and other support to early-stage and established companies. Safer, healthier, more affordable, and cruelty-free—these products aim to outpace animal ones in the marketplace and, ultimately, to make factory farming a thing of the past.

GFI's executive director is my former mentor, Bruce Friedrich, who has been working to end animal agriculture for more than two decades. Another of GFI's board members is my friend Josh Balk, a devoted animal advocate who turned to the business world to solve many of the problems he saw on factory farms. The following is his story:

In 1990s suburban Philadelphia, two best friends, both named Josh, met while attending the same high school. Their intended careers at the time? Athletics. Josh Tetrick wanted to be a professional football player, and Josh Balk, a baseball player. Tetrick was the star linebacker on the team, known for his hard hits. Balk, a pitcher, was so good that he was chosen as an Adidas top 100 future Major League Baseball prospect and was his school's record holder for the most wins and strikeouts.

After high school, Tetrick played football at the University of West Virginia, where he continued to excel as a linebacker and was awarded the team's Rookie of the Year honor. As his time at WVU continued, however, he realized he'd never be good enough to reach the NFL, so he hung up his cleats.

Meanwhile, Balk enrolled at Keystone College, near Scranton, Pennsylvania, where he also won an award: Pitcher of the Year. However, after that promising first season, a shoulder injury put an end to his Major League aspirations.

Both Joshes steered what had been their athletic intensity toward other interests, becoming more concerned about the impact they could have on the world. Tetrick improved his grades and transferred to Cornell. Balk, an animal lover, started an animal-protection club while in college. His passion came about in high school when the Joshes watched two documentaries, one showing how animals are raised and killed for food, the other chronicling the inconsistencies in human behavior regarding the treatment of pets versus other animals, including those in food production. Balk found the images so disturbing that he immediately became a vegetarian, which he continued through college. He became vegan his junior year. But he wanted to do more.

In 2001, Balk, who had transferred to George Washington University, was walking down a Washington, DC, street one day, wearing ripped jeans and an old T-shirt, when he saw a building that he thought was an animal shelter. He decided to volunteer his time. But when he walked in, instead of seeing a messy lot of unkempt volunteers milling around, everyone was wearing suits and ties, looking profound and serious. The building wasn't a shelter. It was the national headquarters of The Humane Society of the United States (HSUS). Undeterred, Josh asked for an internship. He got one, right there, on the spot.

In the meantime, Tetrick had graduated from Cornell and, after being awarded a Fulbright scholarship to do work in Africa, spent time working in Liberia and South Africa to help on issues related to girls' education and homeless children. In the following years he worked for the United Nations and former president Bill Clinton, and he attended law school at the University of Michigan. Influenced by Balk, he, too, had become a vegetarian.

In 2009, Tetrick started working at a law firm that represented Smithfield Foods, one of the world's largest producers of pork products. This didn't work out well: Tetrick wrote an Op-Ed in Virginia's *Richmond Times-Dispatch* about how to make the world a better place and included one sentence about factory farming. Because of that sentence, a week later, the firm fired him.

Meanwhile Balk had been at HSUS for six years, making his way up the ranks to become the senior director of food policy, where he worked with companies to create farm animal welfare policies. One day in 2011 he had a meeting with the food conglomerate General Mills to discuss eliminating its use of eggs from caged chickens. Everyone in the meeting agreed that battery cages were wrong. Chickens certainly deserved better. However, because of cost issues, the company felt that it couldn't make a change.

A few hours later Balk was sitting on an airplane, waiting for take-off, when he suddenly thought, *Why not create a company with entirely plant-based products that taste just as good as or better than their animal-based counterparts? And what if these products were more affordable as well?* Balk's experience working with executives at major food companies had taught him that most food-industry executives wanted to do the right thing for animal welfare, consumers, and our world. However, these companies and their employees were caught up in a broken food system that they themselves didn't create. So why not create a company that could change the system?

Balk approached Tetrick with the idea. Tetrick loved it. The two quickly put together a team, including an animal-loving former head salesperson from Yum! Brands (which operates Taco Bell, Pizza Hut, KFC, and WingStreet) and a former bigwig from Unilever, the world's largest maker of food spreads, with products available in 190 countries. The Joshes named the new company Hampton Creek, after Balk's Saint Bernard, Hampton, who had recently passed away.

After breaking into the Silicon Valley scene, Hampton Creek rapidly captured investments from some of the most future-focused venture capitalists, including Khosla Ventures and Horizons Ventures—a Hong Kong–based firm that has supported the most recognizable technological innovations in recent memory, including Facebook and Siri. Prior to investing in Hampton Creek, the majority of these firms' Silicon Valley investments had been focused on technologies to improve and redefine the way we communicate and connect. With the arrival of Hampton Creek, this spirit of disruption found a new mission: revolutionizing the food system. Over the course of three years, the company raised more than $100 million and hired more than one hundred people, becoming the planet's fastest-growing food company.

By early 2017 Hampton Creek had a line of more than forty products made entirely of plants, including mayo, cookie doughs, cake mixes, and dressings sold on the shelves of thousands of Walmart, Target, and even Dollar Tree stores. And the company is just getting started: It is working on more than four hundred new products that redefine traditional foods with animal-free ingredients. Hampton Creek expanded its vision beyond reformulating individual products and is taking on the broader question that drives its founders: What would it look like if we started over? Would we produce food the same way we do today or would we rewrite the script? Through Hampton Creek, the Joshes are doing just that by leveraging markets and technology to re-envision the food system as one that produces healthy, humane, and sustainable foods. Nowhere is this mission more evident than in the company's massive headquarters in San Francisco's Mission District: ground zero for the fight against factory farming. This building houses chemists, data analysts, food scientists, and chefs hailing from Michelin-starred restaurants, all researching fresh approaches to plant-based food production.

One of its most ambitious ventures is to create an open-sourced database containing information on every plant protein in the world. As it stands, nearly 92 percent of plant proteins remain unexplored for use in food production. By analyzing the functional and chemical properties of each plant, Hampton Creek's scientists and chefs are discovering new formulations that function identically to certain animal products. "The Hampton Creek research databases contain botanical, molecular, and functional data across more than one hundred thousand plant species and varieties," Tetrick says. For instance, the company has been able to reproduce the egg patties that are popular at so many fast-food restaurants with a plant-based version that tastes identical, is equally affordable, and is cholesterol free.

Through their analysis of thousands of plants from forty-one countries, Hampton Creek's food scientists have found that a certain variety of Canadian yellow peas acts just like an egg in mayo, while sorghum—a grasslike plant—behaves just like an egg in baked goods such as cookies, muffins, and cakes. The goal is to find a plant that can replace animal products in everything, tasting exactly the same as well as binding, holding, and gelling in products.

Major chains and food-service distributors have plenty of reasons to consider these products, even if the message of cruelty-free and sustainable production doesn't take the main stage within their operations. Purely from the perspective of their bottom lines, these companies stand to benefit from sourcing products that don't rely on factory farming. As an example, after the avian flu epidemic of 2015 decimated the chicken population on factory farms, where tight quarters and unsanitary conditions accelerated the spread of the disease, companies were calling on Hampton Creek in droves in search of a plant-based replacement for the eggs used as ingredients in baked goods, sauces, and more. By being able to supply this reliable replacement product, Hampton Creek became a true threat to conventional egg producers and demonstrated the strength of its disruptive model.

Hampton Creek is not alone—companies similar to it, and people similar to the Joshes, are leading what may be one of the biggest revolutions in human history: a healthy, inexpensive, and delicious diet based primarily on plants.

J ust a few miles from the Hampton Creek building across the Golden Gate Bridge, another innovator is taking on the artisanal cheese industry, introducing a plethora of new products made with cashews, not cows.

Classic Double Cream Chive. High Sierra Rustic Alpine. Fresh Loire Valley in a Fig Leaf. Aged English Sharp Farmhouse. These all sound like cheeses worthy of a high-end wine-pairing dinner. And they are. But they're not made with dairy. They're made with cashews, and they're just some of the offerings from a company called Miyoko's Kitchen, founded by acclaimed vegan chef, author, and TV host Miyoko Schinner, who is determined to turn the cheese world upside down and save animals along the way.

In the late 1980s, Miyoko opened a restaurant in San Francisco to re-create the gourmet French and Italian delicacies she so adored, and later she started a natural food company. As a former self-described cheese addict, Miyoko eventually set her sights on creating a plant-based alternative to satisfy her cravings for "rich, creamy, unctuous premium cheeses like Brie, Gruyère, Roquefort." Soon cheeses became her primary focus, and she started Miyoko's Kitchen in 2014.

At Miyoko's Kitchen, employees grind cashews into a heavy cream before culturing, aging, smoking, and flavoring the nuts to achieve the taste and texture that *Food & Wine* magazine says "mimics the real thing." In under two years, Miyoko's Kitchen outgrew its original production space and the company signed a lease for a 28,000-square-foot facility down the road to accommodate its rapidly growing demand. In 2016, Miyoko's plant-based, cultured butter launched at Trader Joe's stores nationwide.

By ramping up production, Miyoko is reaching even more consumers with her mission, which she says is simply "to get people off of dairy. I love it when people come up to me and say that they no longer have any excuses not to go vegan. And that's why we do what we do. We are out there to save the world. We see ourselves as solutions providers that help people transition away from products."

Miyoko is an advocate for growth in the entire plant-based foods sector, and she sees other companies on the market as collaborators, not competitors. In recent years, the number of these plant-based collaborators has been steadily growing, while some of the earliest companies in the dairy-alternative market are pushing out innovative new products. Among the first of these companies was WhiteWave Foods, founded by Steve Demos in Boulder, Colorado, in 1977. White-Wave revolutionized the plant-based, nondairy market when it introduced its Silk brand of soy milks; by 2001, more than 80 percent of all supermarkets in America carried the brand. Blue Diamond, a company known primarily for their almonds, introduced its first line of almond milk, Almond Breeze, in 1997. In a five-year period ending in 2016, almond milk sales surged by 250 percent, while dairy milk sales sagged by 7 percent. Today these substitute milks constitute almost 10 percent of the $26 billion milk market.

Daiya, a Vancouver, British Columbia–based company established in 2008 by Andre Kroecher and Greg Blake, is the most well-known of the nondairy cheese makers. Its products are made primarily from cassava and arrowroot and can be found in grocery stores, restaurants, and some packaged foods including the Amy's Kitchen brand. Daiya (pronounced "day-ya") products are perhaps most famous for their use on vegan pizzas due to their ability to melt like dairy cheese.

MEAT FROM PLANTS

In the spring of 2016, highly acclaimed chef Traci Des Jardins showed up at the test kitchen of *Food & Wine* magazine to cook some burgers. She prepped the fare in typical fashion: lightly seasoned, seared until medium-rare with just a touch of pink in the middle, and placed between two buns. The only surprise? These burgers weren't made from animals—they were made from what Impossible Foods calls "meat from plants." These plant-based burgers are made with coconut oil to simulate the mouthfeel of beef fat, and wheat and potato proteins to encourage the slight external char burger lovers are familiar with. But what truly sets these burgers apart is the inclusion of one ingredient no other plant-based food has been able to replicate: heme. Heme is a component of hemoglobin, the red pigment in blood that gives animal-based burgers their color and distinctive flavor. Scientists at Impossible Foods are able to extract a plant-based version of heme from yeast that exactly mimics this difficult-to-capture taste. As a result, these burgers truly look like meat, bleed like meat, and taste like meat. They even have 19 grams of protein in an 85-gram burger, which is more than 25 percent more protein than a comparably sized beef burger.

Equally remarkable, Impossible Foods reports that its plant-based meat uses 95 percent less land and 74 percent less water, emits 87 percent less greenhouse gases than conventionally sourced animal meat, and is 100 percent free of hormones, antibiotics, and artificial ingredients. The company, based in Northern California, was founded by celebrity chef and author Tal Ronnen, former Stanford biochemistry professor Patrick Brown, and cheese maker Monte Casino. The group recently raised more than $100 million from investors—including Google Ventures, now called GV—to "transform the global food system by inventing a better way to make the meats and cheese we love, without using animals."

Another major entrant in this arena is Beyond Meat, a company based in the Los Angeles area that has already brought a number of products to market, including the Beast Burger, Beyond Chicken Strips, and the blockbuster Beyond Burger. Made from non-GMO soy and pea protein, Beyond Meat's motto is: "We're bypassing the animal and sourcing meat's core parts from the plant kingdom and making a new form of meat." Beyond Meat's products have successfully passed many taste tests—including a tasting on the *Today Show*, in which the program's anchors could not differentiate between Beyond Meat's products and actual beef and chicken. Bill Gates even tried the company's Beyond Chicken Strips and couldn't tell they were made from plants, not animals. Gates said, "What I was experiencing was more than a clever meat substitute. It was a taste of the future of food."

Beyond Meat was founded in 2009 by then forty-four-year-old Ethan Brown. Ethan, towering over me at six feet five inches, has a deep, bravado voice, kind blue eyes, and a youthful face dotted with freckles. He is a compelling speaker, but he gives the impression of an introvert who found his public voice for the sake of his company and everything it stands for.

Growing up, Ethan's college-professor father bought a farm in the westernmost part of Maryland and started a Holstein dairy business. But Ethan wasn't interested in traditional animal farming—after graduating from Columbia Business School, he entered the clean energy field. As time went by, he discovered that thoughts of his father's farm would prompt the question: Do we really need animals to create meat?

To find an answer, he started working with two University of Missouri professors who had developed a system for making plant-based proteins with the texture of meat. "Others might say, why don't you make something better than meat, something that doesn't look like meat. But billions of people like meat just as it is now. So we intend to make something that will satisfy those people." In many ways, though, Beyond Meat's products are far superior to their animal-based counterparts. Solely from a nutritional perspective, the Beyond Burger contains more iron and protein than a beef burger, with none of the cholesterol, hormones, or antibiotics—and only a fraction of the saturated fat.

Ethan believes that companies like his will eventually be able to supply the world's appetite for meat with better replacements. "Sometime in the future the majority of people will no longer eat animal-slaughtered meat. It's a critical step if we are to have a planet that resembles the one we inhabit today."

If plant-based meats follow the same path as plant-based milks, that will mean about a billion fewer animals slaughtered each year. Impossible Foods and Beyond Meat are only two players in this burgeoning market, which in 2015 represented just 0.25 percent of the national expenditure of meat ($500 million vs. $200 billion). But whereas conventionally farmed meat sales are stagnating in America, plant-based meat sales are growing rapidly. Plant-based meats are projected to take up a full third of the protein market by 2050, signaling that this industry is on the cusp of a major market revolution. A sign of this upheaval that I find particularly encouraging is that in 2016 Tyson Foods made a large investment in Beyond Meat, showing that even a multinational animal-food conglomerate understands that investing in plant-based protein is a smart business move.

THE SECOND DOMESTICATION

Fifty years hence, we shall escape the absurdity of growing a whole chicken in order to eat the breast or wing by growing these parts separately under a suitable medium.

—British prime minister Winston Churchill, 1931

In August 2013, an English chef named Richard McGeown cooked a hamburger. An Austrian food researcher named Hanni Rutzler then took a bite of it. She liked it. An American food writer named Josh Schonwald also took a bite. He also liked it.

Things were not actually quite as simple as that—for this was not your average $3.50 burger. It actually cost about $350,000, and it did not come from a slaughtered cow. It came from muscle stem cells grown outside of an animal. The man behind the burger was Dr. Mark Post, a professor at Maastricht University in the Netherlands. It took him three months to make the burger, which was financed by Google cofounder Sergey Brin.

A burger that costs more than most people's homes is not commercially viable. Yet. But the leading experts in this groundbreaking field of cellular agriculture, including Dr. Post, believe that this technology will be cost-competitive in a matter of years and will eventually become more affordable than even the cheapest of conventionally produced meats. In fact, Post was quoted in 2016 as saying that he thought he could produce a kilogram of this meat for $80, or a little over $11 per burger. As Bruce Friedrich is fond of saying, the first iPhone cost $2.6 billion in research and development costs, but today the phones sell for a tiny fraction of that.

This begs the question, what exactly is this technology that is commonly referred to as "clean meat"? Simply, rather than raising live animals for their muscle tissue, clean meat is produced by taking a small sample of animal cells and growing them in cell culture, eliminating the need for slaughter and factory farming. These cells are placed inside bioreactors that resemble the fermenters (which are also bioreactors, of course) used in beer breweries, where they are given a mixture of nutrients to grow into a full-fledged hamburger, chicken tender, or meatball. The result is meat that is clean: It contains no antibiotics, growth hormones, *E. coli*, salmonella, or waste contamination—all of which come standard in conventional meat production. The term "clean meat" is also a nod to "clean energy," since producing meat in bioreactors will require far fewer resources and cause far less pollution, including climate change–inducing greenhouse gases, than producing conventional animal agriculture.

A number of companies are salivating at the chance to commercialize this potentially world-changing food technology. One of the most promising of these clean-meat start-ups is Memphis Meats, which launched in 2015 and early the next year debuted the world's first meatball grown outside of an animal. *Fortune* magazine called this development "The Hottest Tech in Silicon Valley." Keep in mind that the magazine didn't say the hottest "food" tech: Clean meat is generating more excitement than any other transformative technology coming out of Silicon Valley today. Memphis Meats plans to bring its clean meat to market by 2021 and is rapidly reducing the cost of production to make these products widely accessible.

Memphis Meats got its start at IndieBio. Short for Independent Biology, IndieBio is a cutting-edge accelerator devoted to funding and building biotech start-ups that seek to solve humanity's most pressing problems. Twice a year, IndieBio selects a dozen fledgling entrepreneurs and provides them with lab space, seed money, and business support for four months. Start-ups that go through IndieBio seek to address issues ranging from curing cancer to accelerating cell therapies, from creating natural alternatives to plastic foams to solving the vast challenges facing our food system.

The men who founded Memphis Meats in 2015 have very different, but complementary, backgrounds: Uma Valeti is a cardiologist, Nicholas Genovese is a stem cell biologist, and Will Clem is a tissue engineer from Memphis whose family owns forty-three barbecue meat restaurants in Tennessee. Will isn't as involved in the company's operations, but his restaurants inspired Memphis Meats' name.

For months, Uma and Nicholas worked in the IndieBio shared lab space tucked away in the basement of an unassuming former furniture building off a back street in downtown San Francisco.

Uma, Memphis Meats' chief executive officer, had been working as a cardiologist before a nagging question caused him to make a pivot in his career path: What if the skills he learned growing heart muscle as a medical doctor could be used to grow food that's better for us and for the planet? Uma was saving lives every day in the hospital, but he realized that reinventing animal agriculture would impact billions of people and animals globally, while potentially saving the world from a climate-induced disaster.

Uma considers this trend as "the second domestication" in human evolution, the first being the use of livestock nearly 10,000 years ago. This second domestication, he says, represents the ethical and scientific evolution of humankind toward a food process that is both humane and far more sustainable. Says Uma: "Many are calling us clean meat, because our products are expected to be better for us, the animals, and the environment. We expect our products to require up to 90 percent less natural resources, such as land and water, and to produce up to 90 percent less greenhouse gas emissions compared to conventional meat production."

Nicholas, Memphis Meats' chief science officer, is a stem cell biologist by training and currently works mainly on farming the cells used for production of Memphis Meats. He focuses on finding the best-quality cells and pioneering cultivation techniques to turn them into the highest-quality muscle and eventually meat.

Nicholas grew up in Michigan, where he raised chickens and turkeys as a teenager and often won prizes for raising the largest bird at various shows. His passion for making meat originates from these early days, but he eventually came to believe that by growing meat directly from the building blocks of life, the cells, he could bypass both the cruelty and the unclean practices of the poultry industry.

Bruce Friedrich was alerted to Memphis Meats by Ryan Bethencourt, one of the people who runs IndieBio and who is on The Good Food Institute's advisory board. Bruce immediately saw the potential. Soon GFI's first project was born: helping launch Memphis Meats.

I stepped in to work with Uma on marketing and communications. The first thing I noticed about Uma was his genuine, kind personality punctuated by his infectious smile and frequent laughter. Tall and athletic, Uma sports short black hair, thin wire-framed glasses, and a classic button-up dress shirt, suit jacket, and jeans.

Uma and Nicholas were preparing to make their debut on the world stage. But first, they needed a product, a proof of concept. And so along came the world's first clean meatball—made with real bovine cells, grown outside a cow, without slaughter.

I volunteered to help oversee the company's video and film shoot. To do this, we rented a beautiful chef's kitchen on the second floor of a hundred-year-old building on Columbus Avenue in downtown San Francisco.

On a chilly morning in January 2016, we were ready. Uma,

Nicholas, and I met up at IndieBio and headed to the kitchen. When we arrived, our film crew was waiting, along with celebrated chef David Anderson. Years earlier, David worked with Ethan Brown and the team at Beyond Meat to develop some of their initial signature products.

Uma carried with him a white Styrofoam cooler, inside of which was a small dish with clean meat that was about to be cooked into the world's first meatball of its kind. We had arranged for a model to be present to taste the meatball on camera and to pose for photos to be distributed to media around the globe.

Then, at the last minute, my assistant, Disney, spoke up. "Bad news," she said. "I just received a call. The model is sick. She can't make the shoot."

"Not good," I said. "We need to find someone fast."

Disney started making phone calls and soon located a possible substitute—a friend of a friend. But we had no idea what might happen next. Would the mystery stand-in like the taste of the $1,200 historic meatball? What would she say on camera when she tasted it? Would she make a face? Would she even eat it?

Dave proceeded to cook the meatball, adding seasonings and fat, while Uma and Nick watched nervously over his shoulder. Soon the meatball began to sizzle and cook. Once browned, Dave plated it on a bed of waiting pasta, adding olives, fresh tomato sauce, salt, and pepper and topping it off with cilantro. Just as he was finished plating, the mystery taster arrived. Uma pulled her aside to explain the situation. The model seemed a bit overwhelmed.

Then, the moment of truth: Dave placed the meatball and pasta in front of her. Cameras rolled. The model picked up her fork, broke off a piece of the first clean meatball, and ate it.

"It tastes like meat," she said, smiling.

"It's good!" she then added, before asking, "Can I have some more?" She dug in for a second bite.

We were ecstatic!

After the camera and lights were turned off, I pulled Uma aside. "Can I have a small taste, too?"

"Sure, but just a small bite. We have to save the rest for potential investors," Uma responded.

It had been sixteen years, or half of my life, since I'd eaten meat from an animal. But now, ready to try clean meat, I grabbed a fork, cut off a small piece of the meatball, and put it in my mouth. The taste, texture, mouthfeel, and sensation were all there. It was the future of meat.

A year later, Uma and his team made history once again, this time by producing the first-ever clean chicken strip. The *Wall Street Journal* broke the story, declaring, "A Bay Area food-technology startup says it has created the world's first chicken strips grown from self-reproducing cells without so much as ruffling a feather." The strip was a hit. The *Journal* added, "Some who sampled the strip—breaded, deep-fried and spongier than a whole chicken breast—said it nearly nailed the flavor of the traditional variety. Their verdict: They would eat it again."

With this new product Memphis Meats is hoping to revolutionize the global chicken market—which currently slaughters more than sixty billion birds annually.

Growing Leather

Meat isn't the only animal product being created in labs. Brooklyn-based Modern Meadow, founded in 2011 by Andras Forgacs, is entering the $63 billion leather-product market. The leather "growing" process is similar to the one used to make clean meat: Cells are sourced from animals, grown in sheets, and then developed into layers that can be designed to emulate leather products. The resulting material is cheaper and more durable than leather. And, of course, the process is environmentally friendly, energy efficient, and saves our land and water resources. Forgacs estimates a 2018 arrival date for his products. He also predicts that Modern Meadow could herald in a new kind of biotech sector—one that is focused on consumer products such as food and clothing rather than medical applications.

ANIMAL-FREE
ANIMAL PRODUCTS

A few years ago, Alexander Lorestani was a graduate student in molecular biology at Princeton University, dreaming of becoming an infectious disease specialist and running a hospital where no one ever picked up an infection. Alex was also keenly aware of the fact that the overuse of antibiotics in factory farming was making the antibiotics used to fight infectious diseases in humans ineffective at a rapid pace. As he began to learn more and more about the relationship between animal agriculture and public health, Alex made the decision to move from academic research to food production, still with an eye on making the maximum impact on global public health. Alex and his business partner, Nick Ouzounov, formed Geltor, a company that produces gelatin without animal ingredients. Conventional gelatin is derived from animal by-products including skin, tendons, and bones. Alex was convinced that Geltor could find a way to bypass this gruesome process—and even improve the end product. To achieve this, Alex and Nick discovered a way to program yeast to produce collagen (the main component of gelatin) from the DNA strands of any animal. This means that Geltor can not only create gelatin without involving animals, it can also create gelatin that is specially designed for a specific function, unlike the inconsistent results of traditional gelatin production.

The duo chose gelatin in part because, Alex says, "I am completely obsessed with gelatin." No wonder: Gelatin is currently a $2 billion to $3 billion industry. Although it's most often used as an ingredient in foods, gelatin is also used in pharmaceuticals, cosmetics, photography, and other industries. Alex expects Geltor's product to be ready to sell to any of these industries by 2018.

What Geltor is doing to redefine gelatin, another San Francisco start-up is doing for milk. Perfect Day Foods is a bold new company that uses fermentation to create a product that is biologically identical to cow's milk. By growing and extracting milk proteins from a specially programmed yeast, Perfect Day is able to produce animal-free milk that contains the same proteins, fats, vitamins, and minerals as regular milk but has neither cholesterol nor lactose (a common allergen). It is also immune to bacterial growth, so pasteurization and refrigeration aren't needed. Perfect Day plans to eventually use its animal-free dairy milk as a base to replicate other dairy products, such as cream, cheese, and yogurt. "We're basically using biotechnology to make milk without pasteurization and without the risk of contaminants like pesticides, hormones, or bacteria that can spoil the milk quickly," cofounder and CEO Ryan Pandya says.

Bay Area–based Clara Foods is another company that's redefining food production by taking animals out of the equation. Using the same methods described above, Clara is producing egg whites without the chickens. These whites will have all the protein of normal egg whites with virtually no fat or cholesterol, and they can be used as a clean, humane, and sustainable stand-in for the animal-based egg products that are currently used in so many foods. Clara's clean protein is even poised to usurp the role of other ingredients such as whey in popular protein snacks and drinks because of its uniquely high-protein, low-fat composition. The company, founded in 2014 by Harvard grad Arturo Elizondo, expects to be on the market by 2019 with its products, which not only replace egg whites but are bioidentical to them.

A HUMANE ECONOMY

I believe we can solve the problems outlined in this book provided we turn to innovation; that is, to a plant-based diet supplemented by clean and plant-based proteins.

Moral arguments are persuasive and crucial, but offering people something better than what they currently enjoy is imperative in our path to success. To that end, plant-based meats are being developed that are not only delicious and affordable but also free of meat's fat and pathogens. Similarly, clean meat, although technically still an animal product, is also a solution for our reliance on unsustainable and inhumane systems for producing food, and it could have a broad impact on public health by eliminating both food-borne illnesses and the need for antibiotic use in the food system.

In other words, the future of food rests on mainstreaming animal products that are derived either from plants or from animal cells grown in a culture, and which, in taste, texture, and nutrition, are identical to—if not better than—the meat that comes from slaughtered animals. I believe that once introduced to the public, these new, sustainable, healthy foods will take off quickly, as prominent chefs will line up to endorse them for their appetizing flavors; trusted doctors, vouching for their safety, will recommend them for their patients' health; and influential food bloggers will applaud them for their convenience and tastiness.

Prices for these products will decrease as demand increases to the point where they will cost even less than their animal-bases counterparts. And, they won't carry the hidden costs lurking behind today's meat, such as taxpayer subsidies and the astronomical health care costs associated with all the diseases created by a diet high in traditional animal proteins. Our economy will shift as our diets change, with workers who were once employed by the meat sector finding new, violence-free jobs producing clean, plant-based meats.

Critical to the success of these products will be the fact that they are created in an open, transparent system. As the stories of our undercover investigators graphically illustrate, today's factory farming industries work hard to keep people from seeing what goes on inside their facilities, proving what musician Paul McCartney once said: "If slaughterhouses had glass walls, everyone would be a vegetarian." The companies developing these new clean foods, however, are already eager to give tours of their operations: There will be nothing to hide and everything to share in this new, humane economy. Transparency will be a key component of our nation's food system, and ethical food choices will become the default choice instead of the difficult one.

13.

The Power of One

How wonderful it is that nobody need wait a single
moment before starting to improve the world.

—Holocaust victim and writer Anne Frank

believe in the power of transformation. Each of us holds the power to write a new chapter in the story of our lives, one in which we live fully in line with our values, choosing kindness over cruelty at every turn. We can do this through our food choices and through social activism.

START WITH YOURSELF—MAKE THE SWITCH TO VEGAN

Despite what some people imagine, becoming a vegan doesn't take much effort—millions of people make the switch every year, and the numbers are increasing rapidly. Granted, one of the biggest hurdles people face when leaning in toward a vegan diet is that they simply don't know how to begin or what to eat. I'm here to offer you a primer.

KNOW YOUR OPTIONS

You can switch slowly, all at once, or somewhere in between.

Start Part-Time

Once you've decided to go vegan, you don't have to stop eating all animal products immediately. Consider making a gradual move in that direction. In so doing, you'll have plenty of time to stock up your pantry with plant-based staples and discover new alternatives to your favorite animal-based foods. For many, Meatless Mondays has become a standard practice, and once you're comfortable with one vegan day, perhaps you'll decide to add Animal-Free Tuesday and All-Plants Friday as well. Or you might consider giving yourself a daily animal-free eating window, when you eat vegan fare from the time you wake up until, say, your last meal of the day.

Eliminate the Most Suffering First

If the cruelty of the factory farm system is uppermost in your mind, consider formulating a diet based upon reducing the number of individual lives affected by your choices. More than 95 percent of the animals consumed for food in America are chickens (including their eggs) and fish. Therefore, you can reduce the most suffering by eliminating them from your diet first, and then reducing and finally removing all other animals (and their milk).

Go "Cold-Tofurky"

If you hang around the vegan community long enough, you'll eventually hear the term "cold-Tofurky." Tofurky is the brand name of a popular vegan substitute for turkey. Thus, around Thanksgiving in the United States, many people will say, "Happy Tofurky Day!"

So consider going cold-Tofurky! Decide right here and now to stop eating animals and begin your plant-based journey.

However you decide to make the switch, remember that no one is perfect. If you find that you have accidentally eaten something containing meat or dairy, or if you gave in to a craving for an ice-cream cone, don't get glum. Just realign your actions with your values at your next meal. Many people take up to a year (or more) to fully transition to a plant-based diet. The important part is not the occasional lapse—it's the end result that counts. Remember: Don't let perfect be the enemy of progress.

YOUR NEW FOOD PLATE

How will you fill up your new and improved vegan plate? Eat all five of these food groups every day:

- *Whole grains* are loaded with vitamins, fiber, and protein.
- *Beans and lentils* are filled with protein and iron.
- *Vegetables* are nature's healthiest foods, overflowing with macronutrients, micronutrients, phytonutrients, and fiber.
- *Fruits* hydrate your body and supply it with fiber, potassium, and antioxidants.
- *Seeds and nuts* are protein- and iron-packed powerhouses.

Plants: The Perfect Protein

One of the most common questions vegans get when they stop eating animal foods is: What will you do about protein?

Don't worry for a second. There are plant foods that pack a powerhouse of protein. Twenty-five percent of the calories in your average vegetable comes from protein—and many of the leafy green vegetables contain up to 50 percent protein. The average grain is composed of about 12 percent protein, and even most fruits contain around 5 percent protein.

Another nagging question you may hear: Even if plants do have protein, isn't it "incomplete"?

Nope. The notion that plants contain incomplete proteins was first proposed by Frances Moore Lappé in her best-selling 1971 book, *Diet for a Small Planet*. She was wrong, and a decade later she admitted her mistake. But somehow people paid more attention to her error than to her retraction. According to the Academy of Nutrition and Dietetics, "Research indicates that an assortment of plant foods eaten over the course of a day can provide all the essential amino acids."

By the way, protein deficiency is so ridiculously rare in America that I have never run into a single person who knows the medical name for this ailment. (It's "kwashiorkor," a word we had to borrow from another language!) But almost everyone has heard of heart disease, which kills more people than anything else and is very often caused by diets heavy in meat and other animal products.

To Your Health

On the evening of May 21, 1997, with his family by his side, my grandfather, aged seventy-one, died of heart disease. The path to his demise was a common one: food. Grandpa loved his rich, fatty foods, such as pizza smothered with extra cheese and ham. Sadly, my grandpa's story is all too common in America. Heart disease has become our country's leading killer, accounting for one out of every four deaths. The biggest tragedy of all? Heart disease isn't inevitable.

When I think about my grandpa, I can't help but wonder: *What if he had known that heart disease was preventable?* Nowadays there are studies published seemingly every week showing how animal-based foods can make us ill and how plant-based foods can make us healthy. But the truth is, the science has been saying this for quite some time now.

Among the first to uncover the link between a plant-based diet and heart health was a forty-one-year-old American engineer named Nathan Pritikin, who, in the 1950s, was diagnosed with coronary heart disease. His doctors told him there was nothing he could do but take lots of naps, avoid stairs, and spend as much time with his family as possible while preparing to die. But Pritikin decided to take matters into his own hands, and, after meticulously studying the subject of heart disease, he realized that a diet of fruits and vegetables rather than meat, dairy, and eggs was the answer. He reversed his heart condition,

(continued)

wrote the influential best-selling book *The Pritikin Diet*, lived a full life, and helped countless people reverse their heart disease. A multitude of books containing conclusive studies have since corroborated Pritikin's work.

Plants can work their curative magic with other diseases as well, such as type 2 diabetes, which afflicts twenty million Americans, and many forms of cancer, which the American Society of Clinical Oncology estimates will surpass heart disease as our leading killer by 2030. Studies have also shown that Alzheimer's disease, which leads to eighty-six thousand deaths every year, can also be prevented or treated with a plant-based diet.

The good news in my family is that my dad, who had a cholesterol level like his father—278—went vegan in 2001, four years after Grandpa died. Dad's doctor was skeptical. But within three months Dad had lost twenty pounds and his cholesterol plummeted to 188. In addition to a healthy heart, the move to a plant-based diet has provided my dad with something even greater: peace of mind.

Eat the Rainbow

The most important component of any diet, plant-based or otherwise, is to consume a wide range of fruits and vegetables. One way to make sure you are getting the most well-balanced plate of food is to eat produce from every part of the color spectrum.

Those wonderful hues in fruits and vegetables reflect the nutrients inside them. For example, the lycopene that makes tomatoes and watermelons red may also guard against certain kinds of cancers. The beta-carotene that makes carrots and sweet potatoes orange converts to vitamin A in your body, helping to maintain your vision and support your immune system. The resveratrol and anthocyanidins in purple grapes and blueberries may help ward off cancer. The lutein in greens such as spinach and kale supports eye and lung health.

So head for the produce aisle and pick out ruby red, deep green, and spectacular yellow veggies that will make your plate look like a painter's palette. Then discover new ways to prepare and dress them up with healthful herbs, spices, dressings, and sauces, and you'll never get bored at mealtime.

Fruit is nature's original fast food, and a great way to take in all the colorful phytonutrients. I recommend starting your day with a fruit smoothie, as I do. And why not venture out of your comfort zone and consider trying fruits (and vegetables) you don't normally eat? There are so many—dozens of different berries; stone fruits, such as yellow and white nectarines, plums, apriums, apricots, and pluots; fresh figs; and tropical fruits, such as mangoes, cherimoyas, sapotes, passion fruits, and papayas. By expanding your options, you may find you start reaching for fruit instead of pastries or chocolate to satisfy your sweet cravings!

Supplement Sensibly

While a plant-based diet is the healthiest choice for animals, the planet, and yourself, a few key nutrients are essential to include in any diet. Make sure you are getting the appropriate amount of vitamin B_{12}. Even meat eaters are at risk of deficiency and should supplement their diets with B_{12}. A B_{12} deficiency can cause serious harm, so you'll want to either take a supplement or feast on foods fortified with this important vitamin, such as nutritional yeast and plant-based milks.

Just as critical as B_{12} is vitamin D—researchers estimate that up to 50 percent of the American population is deficient in this essential vitamin. Vitamin D is essential for bone growth, cell growth, fighting inflammation, and many other functions. Look for plant-based milks, cereals, protein bars, and meal-replacement bars fortified with vitamin D. And go outdoors—the easiest way to get your daily dose of vitamin D is through healthy exposure to sunlight (but not too much sunlight, of course).

FIND YOUR VOICE

Becoming a vegan is one of the best ways you can reduce cruelty to animals. But perhaps you'd like to do more. Maybe you'd like to help inspire others to join you in compassionate eating. The more people who join the cause, the better lives animals will have. Following are some examples of individuals who were once steeped in meat but who became plant-based activists, all finding unique platforms to spread the word for their newfound beliefs.

THE FORMER MEAT KING

Brian Swette is the president of California-based Sweet Earth Natural Foods. The company, launched in 2011, creates all-natural plant-based delights, including veggie burgers, burritos, and even "Benevolent

Bacon," made of buckwheat, red beans, vital wheat gluten, and thirteen spices.

What is particularly interesting about Brian's company is his personal story. Brian is the former executive chairman of Burger King. Yes, *that* Burger King. Before that, Brian was the executive vice president and chief marketing officer for PepsiCo. During his seventeen-year tenure, he was responsible for the worldwide advertising, promotion, and product innovation efforts of all Pepsi brands. "I was kind of on the dark side of food," Brian recalls.

Brian's transformation started several years ago, after his daughter became a vegetarian and his wife, Kelly, became interested in how nutrition affects health. As Brian learned more about diet, food, and sustainability, he had his aha moment.

"Knowing that health is one of the biggest challenges that faces the country, I had this epiphany," Brian said. "We could make a difference if we actually made a vegetarian food company."

Brian's new venture isn't just helping improve people's health, it's saving animals' lives. In just the first two years of operation, Sweet Earth has produced 425,000 pounds of plant-based proteins, which is the equivalent of the meat of more than fifty thousand chickens!

THE MAD COWBOY

Howard Lyman, almost eighty years old, has short gray hair, wire-framed glasses, and a tall, sturdy build that hints at his younger years as a three-hundred-pound football player. Back in April 1996, Howard was a guest on *The Oprah Winfrey Show*. The topic: Dangerous

Food. Howard became the first person to speak publicly about bovine spongiform encephalopathy (more commonly known as mad cow disease) and the threat it posed to the public. He explained how the carcasses of cows, which could be infected with the disease, were being ground up and fed back to living cows, who were then slaughtered for beef, which was then sold to consumers.

Oprah was appalled. "That just stopped me cold from eating another burger," she declared.

The Texas Cattleman's Association wasn't pleased with the publicity. The cattle producers, claiming the remarks sent cattle prices tumbling, sued both Oprah and Howard under a 1995 Texas law that held people liable if they made false and disparaging statements about perishable food products. Oprah and Howard spent the next six years in and out of court defending themselves.

In the end, they won the lawsuits—because what Howard had said on Oprah's show about mad cow disease was true. Howard should know, as he's a fourth-generation farmer, cattle rancher, and feedlot operator. His parents operated the largest dairy farm in Montana, where he was raised.

One day, Howard was diagnosed with a cancerous tumor on his spine. His doctor suspected that the harsh chemicals and pesticides used daily on his own farm could be a culprit in causing his illness. Faced with the prospect of paralysis, Howard vowed that if he beat the cancer, he'd return to nonchemical means of farming. But the prognosis wasn't good. The doctor told Howard he had less than one chance in a million to ever walk again. After a twelve-hour operation to remove the tumor, Howard not only survived but thrived.

Howard, now tumor-free, transformed his land into an organic farm and reconnected with nature. But the journey wasn't over. Howard was still consuming animal products. His cholesterol level, at over 300 mg/dL, was dangerously high. Howard was worried: He had watched six of his ten closest friends die from heart attacks or cancer. He knew he needed to change, and he did. Howard went vegan, and his health improved immediately. His cholesterol dropped to 135, he lost 130 pounds, and he began feeling great—physically and mentally. Today, Howard is an outspoken advocate for veganism, animal rights, and environmental protection.

THE RACE-CAR DRIVER

Forty-three-year old Leilani Münter's motto is "Never underestimate a vegan hippie chick with a race car."

Minnesota native Leilani grew up in a family that had horses who were boarded at a nearby farm, allowing Leilani to interact with cows and pigs and chickens whenever she visited. Leilani soon learned that there was no difference between farm animals and horses in terms of their intelligence, emotions, and capacity for love. Leilani became a vegetarian while still a young girl.

Leilani always loved fast cars, and in 2000 her life took an abrupt turn when she decided to try driving a race car. She was the only woman in her racing school class of forty students. Her male classmates heckled her, insisting that a racetrack was no place for a woman, but Leilani silenced them by becoming the fastest driver on the track. A career was born. Within a year, she scored her first sponsorship—and went fully vegan as well. By 2007, *Sports Illustrated* had named her one of the top ten female race-car drivers in the world.

As one of the few female drivers in a sport dominated by men, Leilani has found a unique platform. She is breaking down barriers and misconceptions not only about women but also about vegans. By bringing vegan food to the track, Leilani has inspired many of the guys on her race team to use plant-based meat substitutes. And through her frequent speaking engagements, she's managed to reach millions of others as well.

Leilani's advice: "One of the most important things any of us can do is to speak up! Whatever your talent is, you have the ability to use your voice in your field to speak to your community." For example, in 2017, she began driving the first ever vegan-themed race car to hit the track on the high banks of Daytona, or any track for that matter. The green and blue car declared VEGAN POWERED in big letters on the side.

PUT YOUR MONEY
WHERE YOUR HEART IS

"Besides going vegan, how can I help transform the world into a kinder place for animals?" This is one of the most frequent questions I hear—from young and old, from longtime vegans and from those who still eat meat, from people who have just gotten their first glimpse of a factory farm and from those who have been aware of their cruelty for decades.

My first, foremost, and final answer is: donate!

Organizations like Mercy For Animals operate almost entirely on financial support from individuals, so the number of animals we can protect depends directly on the generosity of our donors.

At this point people's eyes usually glaze over as they try to move past my obvious response. "Yes, of course," they say, "I will donate. But what else can I do to make a difference?" Question posed, they wait with bated breath, hoping I'll let them in on the hidden secret of how a regular person with a job, a family, and personal obligations can still play a big role in helping spare farm animals from misery.

I'll tell you that secret now, although the answer is not very mysterious. Donate even more! Putting a check in the mail or filling in your credit-card number on an online donation form may sound mundane. But donating as much as you can to the top farm animal protection groups is your best opportunity to make a difference.

Think of it this way: Money is power. It's energy. Used effectively, money has the ability to save and transform lives. The animals, and the effective organizations that fight to protect them, always need it. Money to wage campaigns. Money to pressure corporations to change. Money to prosecute abusers, to carry out investigations, to change laws, and to educate people.

When you think about giving money to any cause, it's important to consider how you can make the greatest impact. Does this sound obvious? The reality is that most people don't follow that basic principle.

Years of research show that people would rather make a donation to save the life of an identifiable victim than unnamed members of a large group. In one landmark study, researchers at Carnegie Mellon University found that most people would rather make a donation to save one malnourished seven-year-old girl in Mali than contribute to generalized food assistance for millions of famine victims in Africa.

All of them need help, yet clearly the money would be better spent on the latter cause.

The same is true when it comes to protecting animals: Our charitable dollars are best spent where they can help the greatest number. There are currently more than thirty thousand tax-exempt organizations in the United States focused on animal-protection issues. Most of them—local shelters, breed-specific rescue groups, and the like—are focused on pets. However, of all the money donated annually to charities in America, just 3 percent goes to organizations that protect animals of any kind (or the environment). And of this small percentage of donations to animal charities, fewer than 0.25 percent of these groups—one-quarter of 1 percent—work primarily on behalf of farm animals. Yet these creatures are in greater need of our help: For every dog or cat euthanized in an American shelter, more than *three thousand* farm animals are slaughtered.

Here's another reason to donate: It not only improves the well-being of animals but also your own. Donating money to animal welfare groups and other important causes isn't an act of sacrifice. It's an act of fulfillment. I've spoken with countless donors who say that giving brings them deep and profound joy.

Ari Nessel is one such example.

Ari is a successful real estate entrepreneur who has embodied kindness to animals since childhood—even going out of his way to relocate spiders and other insects who made their way into his bedroom. But like most Americans, Ari grew up eating meat.

Then one day in 1986 Ari was walking down a busy street when he was handed a booklet about factory farming by a volunteer working

with an animal-protection organization. After seeing the horrific images of suffering animals, Ari decided right then and there to become
a vegetarian.

Fifteen years later, Ari was watching television when a thirty-
second commercial for MFA appeared, featuring somber, slow-
motion images of animals confined in tiny stalls on factory farms. The
ad concluded with, "Please choose compassion. Choose vegetarian."
Struck by the ad's power, Ari wanted to help it get more airtime. So
he pledged to match all donations made over the next month, up to
$3,000, so the commercials could continue to air. The money poured
in quickly.

Ari chose to focus on farmed-animal protection because he wanted
to reduce the most suffering and harm. He even contemplated leaving his business to become a full-time animal advocate, but before
making the leap from millionaire entrepreneur to grassroots activist,
Ari consulted with the leaders of national animal-protection organizations on the type of role he could play. Their advice? Don't do it.
Keep making lots of money and donate as much of it as possible.

Ari learned that the main challenge facing the animal-protection
movement wasn't the number of intelligent people who wanted to
turn their passion into full-time careers but rather the protection
organizations' limited financial resources. So Ari chose to remain
in business and to give generously instead. His motto became "Earn
to give."

Ari can't estimate how much he's donated. "Ballpark, seven or
eight million dollars over the years," he says. But giving makes Ari so
happy that, in 2012, he founded The Pollination Project, which gives

away $1,000 each and every day to individuals and organizations whose projects help animals and the environment.

By staying in business full-time, Ari is able to keep effective organizations afloat. This is a necessary and strategic form of activism.

Ari says he's never been happier.

Scientific research backs up this concept of happiness through giving. A study by researchers at Oxford University found that donating money elevates mood, leading to feelings of happiness. This same group of researchers conducted studies in nearly 140 countries, asking half of the participants to buy a goody bag for themselves and the other half for a sick child in the hospital. The study found that those who donated their goody bag had happier moods than those who kept them.

It gets better. The results of a recent study by researchers in the department of psychology at the University of British Columbia suggest that spending money on others can also improve your health. Researchers gave 128 adults ages sixty-five to eighty-five $40 a week for three weeks. Half the participants were instructed to spend the money on themselves, and half were told to spend it on others. The researchers measured the participants' blood pressure before, during, and after the payments. Among participants who had previously been diagnosed with high blood pressure, the study concluded, "Spending money on others significantly reduced their blood pressure over the course of the study." The magnitude of these effects was comparable to the benefits of taking antihypertensive medications and exercising.

Giving to important causes isn't only the right thing to do; it also increases happiness and improves our health. It doesn't get much better than that.

Giving Well

How do you know where your money will do the most good? Few donors have time to do all the digging to find out how well different organizations allocate their dona- tions. Now you don't have to. Instead, turn to Animal Char- ity Evaluators (ACE), a watchdog organization dedicated to evaluating charities so donors don't have to. ACE examines the thousands of animal charities, evaluating the impact they have on saving animals and on reducing suffering. ACE also looks at how much each dollar accomplishes (there is a vast difference among organizations) and then recom- mends its picks for Top Charities. I am proud to say that for four years running, MFA has been selected as one of just three organizations in this category.

MEANING: EVEN BETTER THAN HAPPINESS

Clearly, donating has multiple benefits. And here's one more! It's a path to a meaningful life. What's the difference between happiness and meaning? Being happy is all about personally feeling good. Meaning is derived from contributing to society in a larger way.

Think about it: America has an entire economy devoted to happi- ness. Books are written every month on the topic. There are happi- ness training camps, workshops, and life coaches. Pharmaceutical companies earn billions by manufacturing and marketing pills aimed at easing depression and increasing contentment.

And yet it turns out feeling good may not be enough to help us thrive. A recent study published in the *Proceedings of the National Academy of Sciences* examined this distinction at the genetic level. Researchers asked eighty people to score their level of happiness. Then they asked the same group to score how meaningful their lives were. The researchers next studied the genes of these eighty subjects and discovered that people who are happy but have little to no sense of meaning in their lives have the same gene-expression patterns as people who are responding to or enduring chronic adversity. In other words, the bodies of people who said "I'm happy but have no meaning in my life" were found to have chronic inflammation, a stress-related condition that affects how our genes operate and is associated with major illnesses, including various cancers and heart disease. The genes of people who said they had meaning in their lives (many of whom also self-scored high on happiness) showed a different pattern. These individuals were found to have healthy immune-system function.

I can't think of anything more meaningful than easing the suffering and increasing the happiness of our fellow creatures. Protecting animals has certainly brought profound meaning to my life.

E-ACTIVISM

Of course, if you've already given money, and still want to do something more—or if you simply have no money to spare—there are indeed other ways you can help out. One of the best is to become an e-activist.

Computer technology has created a new world. Two decades ago, change took time. Information spread slowly, because the world moved at a different pace. Today, a simple tweet can ignite a revolution overnight.

Take the simple act of signing a petition. Not too long ago, you had to physically sign a piece of paper in ink. Similarly, if you wanted to share a video, you had to hand someone a DVD or VHS tape and hope that they would put it in their player, watch it, and then pass it on or screen it for a larger group.

Nowadays, millions can lend their names to online petitions within hours or watch videos within minutes, all with just a few keystrokes. And they can do it from the comfort of their homes.

The power of social media in e-activism has been game-changing. In November 2016, at the World Meat Congress in Uruguay, Ted Bilyea, a meat industry consultant, bluntly stated, "Social media is seen as the industry's worst nightmare." And Mike Reidy, the senior vice president of mozzarella cheese giant Leprino Foods, the target of a graphic 2014 undercover investigation by MFA that exposed criminal animal cruelty, stated:

> One of the things that we learned in this incident was that there are new rules to the game, and that is that social media [has] completely changed the speed with which this information transfers. . . . The virtual response to this incident was stunning. I don't know how else to describe it. The information was placed on all their Facebook pages, there was a petition that our president had by 6 a.m. in the morning—6,000 signatures. By 24 hours later it was 18,000, and ultimately

over 200,000 were delivered to our corporate office. And the consumer-facing brands are saying, "What are you gonna do about this?"

Ultimately, Leprino, whose "consumer-facing brand" clients include Pizza Hut and Dominos, took decisive action by adopting a sweeping animal-welfare policy that aims to improve the lives of millions of cows. Real-world change, driven by e-activism.

Bruce Feinberg, the global animal health and welfare officer for McDonald's, also acknowledged the power of social media when explaining why consumer interest in animal welfare has significantly ramped up in the last five to eight years: "I attribute a lot of [this concern] to social media, the ability of the average consumer to reach out and self-educate.... Consumers have a different set of expectations, and they're communicating those expectations to companies like McDonald's in ways that they've never done before."

So where can you get started and what can you do, aside from posting updates about hard-hitting campaigns or breaking investigations?

You can start by following Mercy For Animals and other wonderful individuals and organizations working to protect animals, including The Humane League, Animal Equality, and The Good Food Institute. All of us have Twitter accounts, Facebook pages, and other social media channels.

Each social platform has a slightly different feel and audience. On MFA's Pinterest page, for example, you'll find an endless supply of glossy photos and a ton of veggie recipes. At Tumblr, our animal-welfare offerings include a mixed bag of GIFs, photos, and even blog posts. Our Instagram account is driven by photos and endless hashtags. Take some time and discover which platform feels right for you and start to participate: comment, "like," share, post, repost, tweet, and retweet!

Remember, social media is about being social. Keep in mind that your posts have the power to open the eyes of people in your social circles to new information. So the simple act of sharing can have a real impact. At MFA, we receive tens of thousands of comments each year from people across the world who've read our posts and have decided to go vegetarian or vegan.

Some quick tips on being an effective e-activist:

1. Keep posts short and to the point.
2. Remember to use hashtags, particularly on Twitter and Instagram.
3. Try to be the first one to post a story.
4. Sign petitions and share them on your social media networks.
5. On Facebook, try to share video content. It tends to be the most widely shared and thereby leads to the most engagement.
6. Don't be afraid to respond in the comments section. As long as the conversation is respectful, speak up and start or continue a dialogue.

GET POLITICAL

The treatment of farm animals is as much a political issue as racial and gender equality, LGBTQ rights, and the environment. The issue has far-reaching implications that affect our society, our health, and our planet. Unfortunately, the topic has not yet made its way into the mainstream political debate. Yet the vast majority of Americans polled say they believe all animals, including farm animals raised and killed for food, should be treated humanely and spared unnecessary pain and suffering.

Farmed-animal laws do exist on the federal, state, and local level—although shamefully inadequate, currently. Federal laws, enacted by Congress and the president, affect all fifty states. Each state can also enact state-specific farmed-animal laws through a vote in the state legislature and presentation to the governor. And on a local level, municipal ordinances can be enacted by a city or town council. Each of us has an important voice in moving animal-friendly laws forward at all three levels of government.

That voice is in our vote. If we are united in our advocacy for farm animals, we have immense power: power to elect lawmakers who will represent our core value of compassion; power to remove from office the elected officials who bow to corruption; power to influence which laws they enact; and, ultimately, the power to ensure that farm animals get the legal protections they deserve.

Over the years the agricultural industry has spent billions of dollars on high-powered lobbyists and campaign contributions to state and federal politicians, skewing the rules around farm animals in its favor and defeating many bills that would have improved conditions for these creatures. It has also used its political clout to obtain exemptions from a vast number of state and federal laws governing labor practices, environmental reporting, and animal cruelty, and to enact ag-gag laws to prevent the sharing of material gathered in undercover investigations.

One of the main reasons for the agricultural industry's historical success in shaping politics in its own favor is that it stands united. Animal advocates must learn from this powerful industry and do the same. Acting together, we have immense power.

The first step in this strength-building process is for each of us to become politically active. Compassionate citizens have many options. For example, citizen-led ballot measures can be a remarkably effective way of creating better laws for farm animals. Unlike traditional legislation, ballot measures are passed or rejected by voters themselves. Proposition 2, the 2008 California ballot measure that is still in effect, banned the extreme confinement of egg-laying hens, pregnant pigs, and baby calves within the state. The mere threat of a successful citizen-led ballot measure can spur reluctant government officials into action, as occurred in Ohio in 2010.

While ballot measures are not an easy undertaking, often requiring the gathering of hundreds of thousands of signatures, and millions of dollars, they are a shining example of how people can work together to make meaningful changes in the law and have a significant impact on the political process. There are a number of other ways to effect legislation as well. One proven method is to reach out to legislators. Call, e-mail, or write them letters about laws you support. Share information about animal-related laws on social media. These same tactics can be used to help defeat legislation. An outpouring of citizen opposition, hundreds of thousands of calls and e-mails to state legislators, citizens writing letters to editors of local newspapers, demonstrations at state capitols, and a frenzy of social media activity all have led to the defeat of dozens of anti-animal bills.

Perhaps the most crucial political role you can play, though, is to help elect the best candidates to office. Urge candidates to take a position on farm animals and ask them to commit to their stance. Far too often, politicians pay lip service to these issues or decline to commit to a firm position in order to escape future accountability. But no one has to settle for political gamesmanship. Ask politicians to elaborate on their positions at town hall meetings, by e-mailing or writing their offices, or by posing questions in local papers or on social media, inviting them to respond.

I believe animal welfare is as important a political issue as health care, education, marriage equality, and other major issues. But it is not recognized as such in our current political system. Candidates for office are unlikely to willingly address these issues without prompting. Force them to do so!

Demand Change

If you want to call, write, or e-mail your political representative, here are the five most important issues for which you can lobby:

1. **Putting an end to intensive confinement.** Hundreds of millions of farm animals around the United States—

including hens who lay eggs, pregnant pigs, and baby calves—lead lives of extreme misery in cages so small that they cannot stretch their limbs, move, or turn around. Although a few states—as well as hundreds of major grocers, restaurants, and food service providers—have banned intensive-confinement systems, their use is still widespread. We need better laws (either federal or on a state-by-state basis) to ban these cruel production systems.

2. **Eliminating common farming exemptions.** Although animal cruelty is now criminalized in all fifty states, those laws are primarily designed to protect companion animals rather than farm animals. The vast majority of states still exempt common or standard industry practices—such as thumping, tail docking, castration, and debeaking without painkillers—from the scope of their animal-cruelty laws. We need laws to ban these practices in every state.

3. **Including birds in the Humane Methods of Slaughter Act.** The HMSA requires that animals (specifically adult cattle, calves, horses, mules, sheep, and swine) in federally regulated slaughterhouses be rendered insensible to pain before they are slaughtered. The biggest deficiency in this law is that it is currently interpreted to exclude poultry (chickens, turkeys, and ducks). A congressional amendment to the HMSA, or an action by the USDA, to include poultry within the act is a necessary step to improve the welfare of billions of animals each year in this country.

(continued)

4. **Making farmed-animal cruelty a felony in all fifty states.** Currently, all fifty states make cruelty to animals a crime, one that is punishable as a felony in certain situations. Unfortunately, many of those situations are limited to cruelty to companion animals. As a result, individuals who beat, kick, stab, and torture farm animals are often let off with a mere slap on the wrist, and jail time is seldom imposed. Farm animal cruelty should be made a felony nationwide.

5. **Ending subsidies that support the meat, egg, and dairy industries.** The federal government gives tens of billions of taxpayer subsidies annually to the meat, egg, and dairy industries. Originally introduced to keep small farmers from going out of business, over the years the vast majority of the subsidy programs line the pockets of some of America's biggest corporations. Lawmakers in ag-heavy states have vehemently opposed any efforts to end these subsidies. As a taxpayer, you have a right to object to your money being used to support animal abuse and exploitation, environmental degradation, and a growing public health crisis. Let your representatives know!

ANIMAL PROTECTION: AN OPPORTUNITY FOR ALL

Looking back at the sweep of history, it's clear how much society has advanced in just the last few centuries. Only in the eighteenth century did truly democratic governments begin to appear. Not until midway through the nineteenth century was slavery officially abolished in America. Similarly, only in the last hundred years did we see the banning of child labor, the criminalization of child abuse, suffrage for women, and a growing trend toward equal rights for minorities. When I was born, same-sex marriage was illegal. Today, it is the law of the land.

Each generation must pause, evaluate where our society stands, and then ask, "How can we make this world better?"

I believe that one of the primary ways we can improve the world is to fight for animal rights. Animals protest against oppression—they kick and scream, they struggle and fight to escape violence inside slaughterhouses and factory farms. They want to live. But animals cannot speak up on their own behalf. They can't call for boycotts, organize protests or marches, sign petitions, or lobby Congress. They silently rely on us to do that on their behalf.

Progress happens because we make it happen. It happens when we provide the support, make the phone calls, and attend the rallies that push society to a more compassionate place. It happens when we speak up for animals in often difficult situations.

Martin Luther King Jr. once said, "Human progress is neither automatic nor inevitable. . . . Every step toward the goal of justice requires sacrifice, suffering, and struggle; the tireless exertions and passionate concern of dedicated individuals."

The social justice achievements our country has witnessed are emblematic of the indisputable fact that mountains do not move on their own. Together, through actions large and small, we can shift the very foundation of our society's relationships with nonhuman animals.

We can write kindness and compassion into the history books of tomorrow.

Animal liberation can and should be our future. As an article in the *Economist* concluded, "Historically, man has expanded the reach of his ethical calculations, as ignorance and want have receded, first beyond family and tribe, later beyond religion, race, and nation. To bring other species more fully into the range of these decisions may seem unthinkable to moderate opinion now. One day, decades or centuries hence, it may seem no more than 'civilized' behavior requires."

Let us be the ones who bring about this next great ethical advance. We should revel in the opportunity to be part of something so profound and so fundamentally good. To do so would yield as meaningful and joyous a life as I can possibly imagine, for everyone, everywhere.

ACKNOWLEDGMENTS

First, I must thank my family: my mother, Joyce; my father, Mark; my sister, Lana; and my grandma, Donna. You've always supported and believed in me, even when others wouldn't. You've shown me love and understanding in ways few could imagine. I also want to thank my best friend, David Gangel, for everything he is. Thank you all for supporting my journey. I love you.

I also want to thank all the animals throughout my life who have not only brought me companionship, but also taught me valuable lessons about love, loyalty, friendship, and life. You opened my eyes to the reality that we are all connected. All similar. All seeking the same basic things. You opened my heart to others and myself in ways that made me a more empathetic and compassionate person. You'll never be forgotten.

The animal protection movement is a family, one that I'm honored to be a part of. I'm grateful to work alongside so many brilliant individuals and organizations. I want to thank The Humane League, Animal Equality, Vegan Outreach, Farm Animal Rights Movement, Compassion in World Farming, The Good Food Institute, Animals Australia, and The Humane Society of the United States. Their incredible, dedicated, kind, and strategic staff and volunteers have dedicated their lives to help animals. You are changing the world. It's an honor to work alongside you. Specifically, thank you to Paul Shapiro, Josh Balk, Kristie Middleton, Matt Prescott, Bruce Friedrich, David Coman-Hidy, Alex Hershaft, Leah Garces, Jack Norris, and Matt Ball.

Thank you to the wonderful animal sanctuaries that provide a safe haven for the lucky few animals who are fortunate enough to escape factory farms. Your work not only saves lives but inspires others to act. Thank you to the founders, staff, and volunteers of these special places, including Karen Davis at United Poultry Concerns, Kim Sturla at Animal Place, Jenny Brown and Doug Abel from Woodstock Animal Sanctuary, Gene Bauer at Farm Sanctuary, Ellie Lak and Jay Weiner at The Gentle Barn, and Mindy Mallet at Sunrise Sanctuary.

A special thank-you to Jeffrey Moussaieff Masson, Danielle Konya, Ari Nessel, Molly Fearing, Amy Makenzie, Uma Valeti, Sylvia Elzafon, Travis Chantar, Andrea Grimes, Leilani Münter, Cheri Shankar, Moby, Bob Barker, Russell Simmons, Tony Kanal, Diane Warren, Sarah Smith, Debbie Miller, Phil Letten, Bill Long, Linda Orenchuck, Dawn Moncrief, Andy Nahas, Jim Greenbaum, Jeff Thomas, Kathy Head and Linda Delma, Max Stone and Deb Hayes Stone, Suzy and Jack Welch, Laurie McGrath, Peggy Kaplan, Michael Webermann, Steve Kaufman, Elisa Wolfe, Michael Schwarz, Dr. Michael Greger and Andrea Cimino, Candice Bergen, Joaquin Phoenix, Girish and Shikha Bhakoo, Khaled bin Alwaleed, and Alinta Hawkins.

I want to thank the many advocates and organizations who came before me, whose blood, sweat, and tears have paved the way. You sparked a movement and got things moving at a time when our activism was considered by many to be an outlandish notion.

I want to thank the entire team at Mercy For Animals—to all of our past and present volunteers and staff around the globe. This incredible journey is your journey as well. It hasn't been forged alone. The progress we have made has been together. You give me hope every day and I couldn't be more proud of you. Above all, I specifically want to thank Matt Rice, Vandhana Bala, Nick Cooney, Ari Solomon, Derek Coons, Jake Morton, Disney Bolin, and Alice Coleman.

I also give my deepest, most sincere appreciation to all of the individuals who have made donations, large and small, over the years to fund Mercy For Animals' work. Without you, none of this would be possible. You give generously, selflessly, and with such great love. Because of you, the world is changing. We are winning and lives are being spared. I appreciate you standing by our side and believing in me and our team. You are the reason for our progress and success. Thank you.

From the bottom of my heart, I must thank our undercover investigators. Pete, Cody, Liz, Ryan, Andy, Jess, Maria, TJ, and the many, many others whose stories are not covered in this book. You are my heroes. You have sacrificed so much for the animals, the movement, and the organization. While you operate in the shadows, without recognition, please know that you are valued and seen. Your struggle is honored. You bring light to dark places.

Thank you to my coauthor, Gene Stone, as well as Nicholas Bromley and Miranda Spencer. I also want to acknowledge Peter McGuigan, my agent at Foundry, as well as the incredible team at Avery, including

Megan Newman, Brianna Flaherty, Lindsay Gordon, Farin Schlussel, and Casey Maloney.

Finally, I want to thank you, the reader, for picking up this book. I hope it moved and inspired you. I also hope it inspires you to live compassionately.

NOTES

Down on the Farm

7 The price of corn dropped by nearly 80 percent: Maureen Ogle, *In Meat We Trust: An Unexpected History of Carnivore America* (Boston: Houghton Mifflin Harcourt, 2013), 93–94.

19 "The human gastrointestinal tract features the anatomical modifications": Milton R. Mills, MD, "The Comparative Anatomy of Eating," *VegSource*, November 21, 2009. Retrieved from http://www.vegsource.com /news/2009/11/the-comparative-anatomy-of-eating.html.

Still in the Jungle

86 Just nineteen states and Washington, DC: David Wolfson, *Beyond the Law: Agribusiness and the Systemic Abuse of Animals* (New York: Farm Sanctuary, 1996).

"That Place Is Hell"

93 A government report noted: United States Government Accountability Office, *Workplace Safety and Health: Safety in the Meat and Poultry Industry, While Improving, Could Be Further Strengthened*, Report to the Ranking Minority

Member, Committee on Health, Education, Labor, and Pensions, US Senate, January 2005. Retrieved from http://www.gao.gov/new.items /d0596.pdf.

Three Hundred Every Second

108 Georgia poultry producers were shipping 1.6 million chickens by 1939: Ogle, *In Meat We Trust*, 108.

109 According to an analysis in the scientific journal *PLoS ONE*: Toby G. Knowles, Steve C. Kestin, Susan M. Haslam, et al., "Leg Disorders in Broiler Chickens: Prevalence, Risk Factors and Prevention," *PLoS ONE* 3, no. 2 (2008): e1545.

110 hens observing confrontations among other hens: Cecile Borkhataria, "Never Underestimate a Chicken: Researchers Find Birds Have Distinct Personalities, Can Count and Even Show Machiavellian-like Tendencies," *Daily Mail*, January 3, 2017. Retrieved from http://www.dailymail.co.uk/sciencetech /article-4085004/Chickens-intelligent-empathy-distinct-personalities.html.

111 researchers at Vanderbilt University found: Vanderbilt University, "Bird Brain? Ounce for Ounce Birds Have Significantly More Neurons in Their Brains Than Mammals or Primates," *ScienceDaily*, June 13, 2016. Retrieved from www.sciencedaily.com/releases/2016/06/160613153411.htm.

111 A study in the journal *Animal Cognition* found: Springer, "Think Chicken: Think Intelligent, Caring and Complex: Review Looks at Studies on Chicken Intelligence, Social Development and Emotions." *ScienceDaily*, January 3, 2017. Retrieved from www.sciencedaily.com/releases/2017/01/170103091955 .htm (accessed February 28, 2017).

116 a Reno, Nevada, woman died from a superbug infection: Helen Branswell, "A Superbug Resistant to Every Available Antibiotic in the U.S. Kills Nevada Woman," *PBS Newshour*, January 13, 2017. Retrieved from http://www.pbs .org/newshour/rundown/superbug-resistant-every-available-antibiotic-u-s -kills-nevada-woman/

Behind the Carton

149 removing hens from cages increases their welfare: R. M. De Mol, W. G. P. Schouten, E. Evers, H. Drost, H. W. J. Houwers, and A. C. Smits, "A Computer

Model for Welfare Assessment of Poultry Production Systems for Laying Hens," *NJAS–Wageningen Journal of Life Sciences* 54, no. 2 (2006): 157–68.

No. 2640

161 "Forget the pig is an animal—treat him just like a machine in a factory": Matthew Prescott, "Your Pig Almost Certainly Came from a Factory Farm, No Matter What Anyone Tells You," *Washington Post*, July 15, 2014. Retrieved from https://www.washingtonpost.com/posteverything/wp/2014/07/15/your -pig-almost-certainly-came-from-a-factory-farm-no-matter-what-anyone- tells-you/?utm_term=.08b57788931b.

161 In 1950, about two million individual farms were raising pigs: Ogle, *In Meat We Trust*, 152.

162 between 1997 and 2012 the number of pigs on factory farms: Food & Water Watch, *Factory Farm Nation: 2015 Edition*, May 27, 2015. Retrieved from http://www.factoryfarmmap.org/wp-content/uploads/2015/ 05/FoodandWaterWatchFactoryFarmFinalReportNationMay 2015.pdf.

162 pigs are one of the few species: D. Broom, H. Sena, and K. L. Moynihan, "Pigs Learn What a Mirror Image Represents and Use It to Obtain Information," *Animal Behaviour* 78, no. 5 (2009): 1037–41.

162 pigs can even empathize with other pigs: Felicity Muth, "Can Pigs Empathize?" *Scientific American*, January 13, 2015. Retrieved from https:// blogs.scientificamerican.com/not-bad-science/can-pigs-empathize/.

171 Elsie Herring, a senior citizen who lives near the lagoon: Sara Peach, "What to Do About Pig Poop? North Carolina Fights a Rising Tide," *National Geographic*, October 30, 2014. Retrieved from http://news.nationalgeographic .com/news/2014/10/141028-hog-farms-waste-pollution-methane-north -carolina-environment/.

"You'll Learn to Hate Them"

184 One study revealed that calves who stay with their mothers longer: F. C. Flower and D. M. Weary, "Effects of Early Separation on the Dairy Cow and Calf: 2. Separation at 1 Day and 2 Weeks After Birth," *Applied Animal Behaviour Science* 70, no. 4 (2001): 275–84.

184 Another study found that calves who are separated from their mothers: University of Veterinary Medicine, Vienna, "Early Separation of Cow and Calf Has Long-Term Effects on Social Behavior," *ScienceDaily*, April 28, 2015. Retrieved from http://www.sciencedaily.com/releases/2015/04 /150428081801.htm.

185 Holly later wrote: Megan Cross, "Mother Cow Proves Animals Love, Think & Act," *Global Animal*, April 13, 2012. Retrieved from http://www.globalanimal .org/2012/04/13/cow-proves-animals-love-think-and-act/.

186 young female cows, known as heifers, demonstrate behavioral signs of excitement: Jonathan Balcombe, "It's Time (magazine) to Respect Cows," *Psychology Today*, August 18, 2010. Retrieved from https://www .psychologytoday.com/blog/the-inner-lives-animals/201008/it-s-time -magazine-respect-cows.

186 cows used for dairy who are given unique names: C. Bertenshaw and P. Rowlinson, "Exploring Stock Managers' Perceptions of the Human–Animal Relationship on Dairy Farms and an Association with Milk Production," *Anthrozoös* 22, no. 1 (2009): 59–69.

186 a study out of Northampton University: "Heifer So Lonely: How Cows Have Best Friends and Get Stressed When They Are Separated," *Daily Mail*, July 5, 2011. Retrieved from http://www.dailymail.co.uk/sciencetech/article-2011124 /Cows-best-friends-stressed-separated.html.

Gagged

230 One state senator compared Pete and other investigators: Dan Flynn, "Federal Judge in Boise Strikes Down Idaho's New 'Ag-Gag' Law," *Food Safety News*, August 4, 2015. Retrieved from http://www.foodsafetynews.com/2015/08 /federal-judge-in-boise-strikes-down-idahos-new-ag-gag-law/# .WI4ZR7GZNSw.

231 US District Judge B. Lynn Winmill wrote: Eugene Volokh, "Thoughts on the Court Decision Striking Down Idaho's 'Ag-Gag' Law," *Washington Post*, August 6, 2015. Retrieved from https://www.washingtonpost.com/news /volokh-conspiracy/wp/2015/08/06/thoughts-on-the-court-decision-striking -down-idahos-ag-gag-law/?utm_term=.7cddd1950736.

The Future of Food

261 **A Bay Area food-technology startup:** Jacob Bunge, "Startup Serves Up Chicken Produced From Cells in Lab," *Wall Street Journal*, March 15, 2017. Retrieved from https://www.wsj.com/articles/startup-to-serve-up-chicken -strips-cultivated-from-cells-in-lab-1489570202

The Power of One

281 **In one landmark study, researchers at Carnegie Mellon University:** Caroline Preston, "New Research Sheds Light on What Works in Charitable Appeal," *Chronicle of Philanthropy*, July 17, 2007. Retrieved from https://www .philanthropy.com/article/New-Research-Sheds-Light-on/163459.

284 **donating money elevates mood:** Fiona Macrae, "Helping Others DOES Make Us Happier: Doing Good Deeds 'Has an Effect Like Paracetamol' on Improving Mood," *Daily Mail*, October 4, 2016. Retrieved from http://www .dailymail.co.uk/news/article-3822502/Helping-DOES-make-happier-Doing -good-deeds-effect-like-paracetamol-improving-mood.html.

284 **"Spending money on others significantly reduced their blood pressure":** Ashley Whillans, "Want to Do Something Good for Your Health? Try Being Generous," *Washington Post*, January 1, 2016. Retrieved from https://www .washingtonpost.com/posteverything/wp/2016/01/01/want-to-do-something -good-for-your-health-try-being-generous/?utm_term=.1a4424a39ddc.

286 **In other words, the bodies of people who said "I'm happy but have no meaning in my life":** Emily Esfahani Smith, "Meaning Is Healthier Than Happiness," *Atlantic*, August 1, 2013. Retrieved from https://www.theatlantic.com/health /archive/2013/08/meaning-is-healthier-than-happiness/278250/.

287 **Ted Bilyea, a meat industry consultant, bluntly stated:** Oscar Rousseau, "Social Media Erodes Consumer Trust in Meat," *Global Meat News*, November 15, 2016. Retrieved from http://www.globalmeatnews.com/Industry-Markets /Social-media-erodes-consumer-trust-in-meat.

INDEX